D0449631

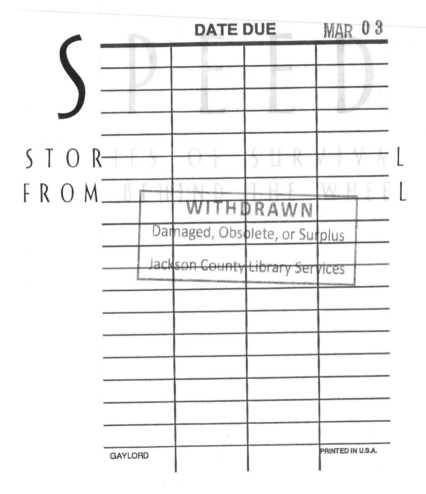

SPEED

DATE DUE   MAR 03

STORIES OF SURVIVAL
FROM BEHIND THE WHEEL

GAYLORD   PRINTED IN U.S.A.

SPEED

STORIES OF SURVIVAL
FROM BEHIND THE WHEEL

EDITED BY NATE HARDCASTLE

SERIES EDITOR CLINT WILLIS

Thunder's Mouth Press
New York

SPEED: STORIES OF SURVIVAL FROM BEHIND THE WHEEL

Compilation copyright © 2002 by Clint Willis
Introductions copyright © 2002 by Nate Hardcastle

Adrenaline® and the Adrenaline® logo are trademarks of
Avalon Publishing Group Incorporated, New York, NY.

An Adrenaline Book®

Published by
Thunder's Mouth Press
An Imprint of Avalon Publishing Group Incorporated
161 William Street, 16th floor
New York, NY 10038

Book design: Sue Canavan

frontispiece photo: © George D. Lepp/Corbis

Library of Congress Cataloging-in-Publication Data

Speed: stories of survival from behind the wheel / edited by Nate Hardcastle.
    p. cm
    ISBN 1-56025-391-6 (trade paper)
    1. Automobile racing—Anecdotes. 2. Automobile racing—Fiction. 3.
Adventure stories. I. Hardcastle, Nate.

GV1029 .S717 2002
796.72–dc21   2002018001

Printed in the United States of America
Distributed by Publishers Group West

For Elisabeth Thomas, for her support

Also for Lance Gray, a good driver, and Bo Webster, a good passenger

c o n t e n t s

photographs

introduction

"Speed provides the one genuinely modern pleasure."
—*Aldous Huxley*

One recent fall evening I found myself drinking with friends in front of a huge bonfire in the middle of a field in mid-coast Maine. We had driven to the spot in three pickups, up a long, gradual, grassy hillside, through a copse of young trees on the edge of some woods, and finally out into the field.

When the time came to leave, my friend Lance and I jumped in his truck. We shot off and were first to reach the woods, where Lance surprised me by accelerating. He sped through the woods on a path barely wider than the truck, the slender aspens and oaks blurry in the headlights with speed and drunkenness and jostling from the path's ruts. Scared but ecstatic, seatbelt-less, I arched my back into the seat and pressed my feet hard against the floor and Lance and I hooted and cackled as he tore through 90-degree turns, missing the trees by inches. We burst out onto the top of the hill and Lance punched it; the truck careened down the hill, bouncing so much I thought it would roll.

I rarely have felt so good. I can't pretend speeding through the woods drunk wasn't stupid and criminal, but it felt great.

• • •

Paris newspaper Le Matin in 1907 issued a challenge that set off the first Peking-to-Paris rally: "What needs to be proved today is that as long as a man has a car, he can do anything and go anywhere." That sense of the car's promise and power hasn't changed during the past 95 years; similar sentiments echo through every car and truck and SUV ad.

This illusion—that cars make us omnipotent—is powerful because it sometimes feels so true: Speed in particular can feel like freedom, which is one reason that racers and other fast drivers become addicted to it. Few speed junkies acknowledge how dangerous their addiction can be—and in fact that ability to ignore or disregard danger is part of what makes a great racer. Author and former race-car driver Dan Gerber describes the state of mind as "a kind of Zen by default, in which survival depends upon nonattachment and single-mindedness."

Racing journalist Denis Jenkinson navigated for auto-racing legend Stirling Moss during Moss' record-shattering 1955 run in Italy's *Mille Miglia* (thousand miles). The pair averaged 98 miles per hour over the course of the race, much of which ran through tiny village streets. Jenkinson shortly afterward wrote an article for *Motorsport* describing the experience. He was amazed by Moss' tranquility, as in this episode:

> In one village, less than 50 miles from the finish, we had an enormous slide on some melted tar and for a moment I thought we would hit a concrete wall, but with that absurdly calm manner of his, Moss tweaked the wheel this way and that, and caught the car just in time, and with his foot hard down we went on our way as if nothing had happened.

Veteran racing journalist Ed Hinton spent a lot of time with Dale Earnhardt, the driver known as "The Intimidator." This anecdote about riding down the highway in the Earnhardt family station wagon comes from a column Hinton wrote for the *Orlando Morning Sentinel:*

• • •

Raining so hard you can't see Interstate 40 . . . Maybe 50 yards ahead, out of nowhere in the fog and rain, both lanes of traffic are stopped dead still.

Nowhere to go, I mean nowhere for a mortal man to steer that station wagon safely . . .

The left forefinger flicks toward the right. Now we are on the center white line of the highway, maybe 60 mph, headed right up the bumpers of both lanes of traffic—now we've slipped between both lanes of traffic. There's a gap— flick left. Another gap—flick right . . . flick left again, flick right, and just as suddenly we have come to a stop, safely, in the right lane of traffic . . . He turns and glances at me and winces mightily for a moment—to let me know he knows just how close to disaster all of us just came.

But even the greatest drivers aren't always that lucky. Earnhardt going into the 2001 Daytona 500 was the greatest active NASCAR driver. He died on the final lap of that race when he lost control of his car.

Speed robs us of control, so that mistakes or surprises become potential calamities: We underestimate a curve or bump; a dog or deer runs into the road; a piece of a car fails. The night before my high-school graduation, my best friend and I were flying down a favorite stretch of country road, on our way to see a girl, when a snapped accelerator cable at the end of a straightaway sent us hurtling through an S-curve. We didn't hit anything, and five minutes later a man stopped and mended the broken cable with a twist-tie. (I sometimes wonder if he was a ghost, like Big Joe in Tommy Faile's song "Big Joe and Phantom 309.") Even now I wonder what would have happened to us if a car had been coming the other way.

The thing is, driving fast can kill or cripple you, your friends, your family and people you've never met. Police reported more than six million car crashes in this country in 2000; those crack-ups caused almost 42,000 deaths and three million injuries. With numbers like that, it's not surprising that we all know of people who have died in cars.

Driving's dangers are amplified and celebrated in rallies and on the racing circuits, where two-ton cars hit speeds greater than 200 miles per hour. Deaths are almost commonplace—Earnhardt, Adam Petty, Kenny Irwin and truck racer Tony Roper died during the 2000 and 2001 seasons, all within a 12-month span. This is not new: Racing journalist Robert Daley in 1961 wrote a column in *Esquire* lamenting the motor-racing industry's lack of response to the deaths of its racers. "If you go to the races, and care about the drivers, you will suffer twenty times a season," he wrote. "Every time a car doesn't come around on schedule you will wonder if its driver is dead." He quoted star driver Dan Gurney: "'That's the essence of this, isn't it, to drive as fast as you can without getting killed?'"

It's impossible to untangle speed's attendant euphoria and exhilaration from its risk. That's because speed's risk reminds us that we are playing for high stakes, that we aren't always in control, that however free or powerful we may feel at moments, we are all subject to the same ultimate rules. At the same time, speed offers one way to tamper with those rules. We don't always get away with it, but it feels good when we do.

—Nate Hardcastle

from A Little Bit Sideways
by Scott Huler

Journalist Scott Huler (born 1959) got his first dose of NASCAR in 1993, when he was assigned to cover Charlotte race week for the Raleigh News & Observer. "I was there about 15 minutes before I went completely native and never wanted to come home," he wrote later. Huler in 1997 shadowed driver Kenny Wallace's Square D team at Martinsville, Virginia. His book about the experience provides a rare view of life as a NASCAR crew member.

The pageantry at the beginning of the race is mostly over. Brief driver introductions started around 10:30, and the drivers are in their cars. Newt and Frank stand at the car with Kenny, helping him inside, helping latch the driver's window net, and saying a few words before the race starts. In the pit, Vic Kangas and Eddie Jarvis take seats atop the war wagon. They'll be keeping lap times and keeping an eye on the scoring computer. The third seat is for Newt. Andy Thurman does knee bends and stretches; other crew members smoke cigarettes or watch the ESPN prerace show on the TV set in the war wagon. "This track is part pavement, part concrete, and all wall," Dr. Jerry Punch says into the camera. Kenny, sitting in his car, looks up into the grandstand. "Looks like a lot of people got off work today," he says. The stands look at least 90 percent full.

The national anthem plays. Each team lines up along the front of its pit, hats off, at attention, during the song. In the Square D pit, that means about a dozen of us, wearing blue shirts with that big yellow D in a square logo. There's an invocation by a preacher, and then, at last, the command from the flag stand: "Gentlemen, start your engines!"

"Engine's on," Kenny says over the headset, thumbing a button on his steering wheel to talk.

"Ten-four, Herman," Newt says. Kenny is nicknamed Herman by some, a name he was given in school after the rambunctious cartoon character Herman the German. Newt and Frank unplug the generator, bang the car once in salute, and head back toward the pit. Forty-two other teams do exactly the same.

The pace car gets ready to pull the field around the track a couple of times, giving the cars a chance to heat up their engines and their tires. "We're rolling," Kenny says. The pace car pulls the field past the pits so the drivers can set their pit road speed. With no speedometers, the drivers just find their rpms in a certain gear when the pace car is driving them at the required pit road speed. Kenny says, "4,600, second gear," over the headset. Newt says, "Ten-four," and writes the number down on a piece of paper. Every time Kenny comes in for a stop, he'll remind him of the pit road speed to keep him from speeding and getting penalized by NASCAR. At Martinsville, that translates to 35 miles per hour. Newt paces nervously during the pace laps; the rest of the team lines the pit wall, waving to Kenny on his first time by, or just holding up an arm in salute. I do as I have been trained, rocking my sign up and down as he paces by so he can see where the pit is on pit road. "Where are you guys?" he asks, going by—then, "OK, got it." Newt pulls me aside briefly to remind me that in certain race situations he'll tell me to stop Kenny short, a few feet in front of his mark.

"It makes it easier for him to get in the pit that way?" I ask.

"It makes it easier for him to get *out*," Newt says, and climbs atop the war wagon for the start of the race.

For all the madness of the start of a Winston Cup race in the grandstand and on TV, down in the pits the start feels almost subdued. Instead of the building excitement and increasing roar, what you hear in the pits, with your two-way radio headset on, is just the crew chief talking to the driver. With 43 cars lined up a few feet apart, if some-body gets out of line at the start, or starts too slowly or too quickly, the ensuing wreck could gather up dozens of cars. So each driver, instead of watching for the green flag himself, keeps his eye on the car in front of him and listens to his crew chief. Everyone else in every crew keeps quiet and watches the front stretch in front of them, the only part of the track they can see clearly.

"OK, pace car's in, buddy," Newt says. "Here we go. OK, wait . . . wait . . . wait . . . green-green-green!" The moment the man in the flag stand above the start-finish line drops that green flag, 43 crew chiefs tell 43 drivers to mash that accelerator. Forty-three pedals go down, and the race has begun.

In the pits, crew members see only the flash of the cars as they zip by on the front stretch. Very little of the rest of the track is visible from where they do their jobs. So they cluster around the TV sets on every war wagon (look down the row of war wagons along pit road and you see a neat line of little dish antennas mounted on each one, pointing the same direction like a row of sunflowers), or they keep an eye on the computer monitor showing the NASCAR scoring program, which collates the work done by the scorers in the scoring tower and picks up signals generated by transponders in each car as they go over a wire loop in the track. The system, a simple grid that looks pretty much like an Excel spreadsheet, shows each car, how many seconds it is behind the leader, and what lap it's on. It can take the program a moment to unscramble the order during pit stops or after a wreck, but it does the trick.

The cars circle the track a few times, working quickly up to their top speed: 120 miles per hour or so on the straightaways, down to 75 or 80 in the turns. The engines, tuned for this track to provide maximum acceleration and deceleration rather than power over a sustained run, grind up and down with each straightaway and turn, an alternating buzz and whine that sounds almost more like motorbikes than cars. Key at Martinsville are brakes; slowing from 120 miles per hour into a turn twice in a lap is more than 1,000 brake applications, as Two-Can told Kenny. "You gonna set those brakes for me today?" he asked, reminding Kenny to feather the brakes during the pace laps to heat them up and get the pads seated.

"Ten-four," Kenny replied. Kenny grew up around short-track racing. His father was a track champion at St. Louis-area racetracks, and Kenny, like his brother Rusty, has always done his best driving on short tracks.

The beginning of the race passes fairly smoothly. Ward Burton, in the number 22 car, starts on the pole and holds the lead for the first few laps, loses it to Mark Martin in the number 6, then regains it. Through the first 50 laps the cars remain bunched up, an almost stately procession around the track, as drivers feel out the track surface and find out how their cars, set up for a track covered with rubber from days of practice, handle on a track that's "green," cleared of rubber buildup by the rain. Kenny holds his spot in sixth, fighting off Rusty, who started seventh. Rusty gets by him, and he's beginning to have trouble with Jeff Gordon, who's crept up from eleventh.

Then there's trouble in Turn 3. Car 97, seemingly untouched, breaks loose and spins.

Almost simultaneously, every hand in the pits goes up above a head and makes a spinning motion. In the grandstand, the crowd looks like the people at the beginning of a Superman show: "Look! Over there!" Everyone stands, every finger pointed the same way.

The crews of every car respond in exactly the same way. First they crane their necks to see if they can see the spot on the track—they can't. Then they scramble. The cars will be in for pit stops as soon as the 97 car is cleared from the entrance to pit road. A NASCAR official stands with a red flag at the entrance to pit road while the cars slowly circle the track another couple of times, and then he clears out of the way.

The crew has made the pit ready for the stop: Don has hoisted one of the full cans of gas and balanced it on his shoulder. Right-side tires are balanced on the wall; left-side tires are waiting next, with guys prepared to put them on the wall when the others are gone. Danielle and any friends or corporate types have backed away, watching from behind the extra wheels. It's time for action, and they don't want to be in the way.

Filbert, from his spotter's position on the racetrack roof, tells Kenny there's no wreckage on the track to watch for, then tells him when pit road is open. Newt says "Next time in."

Then Kenny pulls onto pit road—"4,600, Herman," Filbert reminds him. Newt says, "Here he comes guys, here he comes—five . . . four . . . three . . . two. . . . Here he is."

And the pit explodes into action.

Say it once and get it over with: The over-the-wall gang.

The guys going over the wall to do pit stops in Winston Cup racing have to do more in less time than just about any athletes in any sport. Sprinters running 100 meters only have to run; hockey players skate full tilt for 45 seconds or so, but they're not carrying 50-pound tires, and avoiding a body check isn't the same thing as keeping an eye over your shoulder so you're not run over by the 3,500-pound race car behind you. Plus, even the hardest hitter on the ice, field, or court isn't liable to explode into a ball of flame if you mistime your play.

Think, for comparison, of the field goal unit on an NFL team—only say they have to start from the sideline, run to the middle of the field, set up and execute a successful field goal, and get back to the sidelines. All in 20 seconds, and there's no such thing as a time out.

The guys jumping over the wall to gas up and change the tires of the Square D number 81 Filmar Racing Ford are not what you'd call a team of craggy veterans. Frank Good has been with the team for two years, and he's about the veteran of the gang. In an arena where a tenth of a second can mean the difference between winning a race and coming in fifth, where teamwork and cooperation and practice mean thousands of dollars per tenth of a second—this team has been assembled from rookies and free agents. Still, that's who they are. That's having a small sponsor in a big-sponsor sport. That's being a single-car team in a multiple-car world. They're willing to take their chances.

Frank is the rear tire carrier: He carries the rear tires over the wall and hands them to Andy Thurman, who uses an air wrench to remove five lug nuts in just over a second, making the second most familiar sound in racing: that staccato Vrr!-Vrr!-Vrr!-Vrr!-Vrr! that is just the definition of "sounds fast." He'll let the nuts scatter. Fresh lugs, cleaned and buffed that morning, have been lightly weather-stripped on the new tire. He throws the air drill onto the ground, but not before slamming the switch on the top of it to reverse the rotation, so when he picks it back up it will be ready to tighten the new lugs. He yanks the tire off, flings it aside to his left—the jack man, after all, is to his right and won't do his job well if he has to dodge the wheels—and grabs the wheel Frank has carried over with him. The same procedure is going on with the front tire, where Rich Vargo hands a tire to Ricky Turner. Ricky, by the way, just joined the team today. He takes the place of a personal friend of Newt Moore's, who stepped in last week when two crew members quit unexpectedly.

If everything's going as planned, the jack man—in this case Duze—has done his job. He's vaulted the wall a half-second before Kenny came to a stop, carrying the jack and cutting to his right around the front of the car as it smoked to a stop. The jack weighs about 35 pounds, and many people say that the jack man leaping the wall with the jack looks like a running back cutting through a hole in the line. But Duze looks much more like a soldier rescuing a baby from sniper fire, cradling that thing, his back hunched over it almost protectively, ducking around the car and sliding the jack under a post identified by the paint scheme of the car and an extra arrow made of duct tape and magic marker. He's lifted the handle and jumped down on it, and he's lifted it again and gone another half pump with it, and the right side of the car's in the air. In the car, Kenny's got the clutch compressed and his foot on the brake, so the wheels don't spin while Andy is ripping the tire off and replacing it.

Frank has taken the second-and-a-half while he was standing around with nothing to do and lined up the holes in the tire with the lugs—the lugs were highlighted on the hub by magic marker, to make that easier. So the tire he hands to Andy is ready to be slammed onto the hub, lug nuts waiting on the wheel.

If one of the nuts flies off the lug as Andy's jamming the wheel on,

Andy just reaches to his left and grabs one from a stiff wire loop clipped to Frank's belt—three nuts hang there as extras, ready to slip off the loop. Andy spins all five nuts onto the tire and leaps up, flinging the drill's air hose wide as he does so; if it gets caught on anything—the corner of the car, a tire, another crew member—the pit stop could be disastrously slowed, and if the hose ends up under Kenny's wheels and he drives over it on his way out of the pit, he'll be assessed a penalty.

As soon as the front and rear right side wheels are on the hubs and a couple of nuts are tightened, Duze twists the handle of the jack, drops the car, and races around to the left side of the car, finding space between the car and the pit wall to pump the jack a couple of times, while Andy and Ricky, having whacked their drills to reverse the rotation once again, have removed the lugs on the left side. Frank and Rich, after first rolling the discarded right-side tires toward the pit wall to keep them off pit road, have taken the new left-side tires off the pit wall, where they were placed as soon as the pit stop started, and handed them to the changers. Frank and Rich fit them onto the hubs with Andy and Ricky, who then spin on the five nuts.

Behind the rear wheel changers, meanwhile, Don has been filling the car with gas. He stepped over the wall with that 100-pound tank of gas balanced on his shoulder the second the car pulled in, and he jammed the nozzle into the car's gas tank, which has a spring-loaded receptacle. Stan Blaylock, at the same time, has placed the catch can (it looks a little like a sprinkling can for your house plants) into the over-flow hose that vents air from the fuel cell. Like shotgunning a beer, the gas pours directly into the tank (like the tank, the gas can is vented at the top), forcing air out the rear through the vent hose.

When Don's first can of gas empties—after say, eight seconds or so—he hands it to Stan and turns to the wall, where someone else—usually big Steve Baker—hands him the second can. As soon as that's done, Stan tosses the empty back over the wall and Steve catches it. Stan and Don both lean into the car as close as they can, to stay out of the way of the rear tire changers, who are running around them to the right side of the car and back.

As soon as the tank is full and gas, instead of air, starts splashing into the catch can, Stan begins waving his arm so that Duze can see him—his signal that the car is refueled, so as soon as the wheels are changed he can drop the car.

The moment the final lug nut is tightened on the left side of the car, Duze twists the jack handle to release the pressure and drops the car. Kenny's signal to move is the car dropping, and he spins his wheels and is gone.

It takes a thousand words to describe it—gas cans and tires flung through the air, lug nuts spraying the ground like machine-gun fire, the car screeching to a halt and then roaring off—and it all happens in less than 20 seconds. When it's right it's ballet, it's a peak experience, it's scoring a goal and hitting a home run and running a sweep all at once. It's winning.

It's almost impossible to describe what it feels like. Stan Blaylock, who holds the catch can during the pit stops and flies Filbert's plane the rest of the time, explains. A pit stop doesn't feel fast, he says. In fact, quite the opposite. "When it's a good stop, it feels like slow motion." Hyperaware, Stan sees the tire changers and jack man running around the car as slow and smooth as an NFL Films highlight, and he can move out of anybody's way at any time. The flow feels almost magical, smooth and silent instead of machinegun fast and jackhammer loud. "It's when things are going wrong that it feels fast." There are so many ways for it to suddenly feel fast, like so much is happening while that race car is sitting in one place. Lug nuts fall to the ground. Tires go flat. Jacks fail to rise, or drop too soon. Tires bounce away. Lug nuts are not put on correctly and wheels fall off. That happened to the Square D team once last year. It happened once to Dale Earnhardt and cost him a Winston Cup championship. At Martinsville, the cars are going 120 miles per hour on the straightaways. A car is about 200 inches long, so call it 16 feet. Driving 120 miles per hour means a car goes about 180 feet per second, about 11 car lengths. Brace it all out, and that means that under green flag conditions, every 10th of a second in the pits costs a racer one car's worth of position on the track. Come in in fifth place and have somebody drop a lug nut and take less then half a second extra to replace it and you could go out in tenth. So, Blaylock says, you definitely don't want to get that flickery, Keystone Kops feeling during a pit stop. It means things are going wrong, and the result can be dire.

But that's the worst case. "Otherwise it doesn't feel fast until the car's pulling away," Blaylock says. "When you back away from the car again, everything catches up to full speed."

The first stop at Martinsville, on lap 57, goes without a hitch. I keep my cool, wave the sign, and lower it perfectly—it hits the ground right on the duct tape stripe and at that exact moment the nose of the race car bumps it. The tires, left and right side, go on without a hitch. The jack works. I use the brush on the grille without beheading Duze or the tire changers. The gas goes in, and the car goes out in a shade less than 19 seconds, 18.8, which is a strong stop even for a team that has worked together for months, much less a bunch assembled race morning.

"Great stop guys, great stop," Newt says from the roof of the war wagon. Crew members slap each other on the back, pull headsets off to shout "Great job!" into each other's ears over the roar of the engines.

But just for a moment. Then there's too much to do. Eddie stands the finished tires up and measures them with a pyrometer and a durometer, checking temperature and wear, which will give clues to the car's handling and help him prepare the next set for the driver. He scrawls temperatures in yellow directly on the tires: "200—220—215" across one tire, showing the range of temperatures the rubber has reached.

Other guys are getting the next set of tires prepared, leaning them against the wall. Newt is talking over the headset to Kenny about the car. "I need a little more bite in the right front," Kenny says, and Eddie gets to work, scrambling his sets of tires before Kenny's finished his statement.

"I'm OK right now," Kenny goes on, "but I could use a little more bite, right where I get from the asphalt to the concrete" at the end of the turns.

"Ten-four," Newt says. "Everybody's probably having the same trouble you are. But don't worry, we're gonna take care of you."

Don finishes his gas calculations and shows the book to Newt, showing him how many laps Kenny can go before he'll run out of gas. Newt nods. Filbert chimes in from the roof: "Newt, you need to ask about the 44 car. He came out after us." Newt says 10-4 and asks a NASCAR official, who straightens things out; passing under caution is not allowed, and cars commonly have to shift positions after coming out of the pits under caution, depending on the judgment of the officials watching them leave pit road.

Within minutes the pit area is cleaned up. The old tires are out of the way; the next set is on the wall and ready for the next stop. Don has prepared the extra gas cans and sent them off in a cart to be refilled. Finally each team sends someone over the wall to sweep the pit itself, keeping lug nuts and other junk from getting in the way of the next stop.

And then it's back to Gatorade, cigarettes, and waiting in the hot sun to the roar of the engines.

Kenny stays in the top ten, floating around sixth and seventh position, for another hundred laps. Two cautions come and go, but the leaders don't pit, so Kenny doesn't. "Stay out there, Herman," Filbert says. "Just keep driving." He's holding tight, and at about lap 100 he pulls into fifth place for a while. The race is a fifth over, and Kenny is racing with the leaders. The mood doesn't so much tense in the Filmar Racing pit as deepen. This is what it's all about. This is why they're here. Eddie's working like crazy on his tire sets, fine-tuning to find any edge. It's possible, once a pit stop or two have gone by, to begin thinking of strategy—when to pit under the green flag if there isn't a caution. Try to gain track position by changing only two tires instead of four, saving five or six seconds? Then again, try that and after about 30 laps the cars with four new tires will be passing you, racers say, like you're tied to a stump.

All stuff to think about, and nobody's relaxing. Kenny goes hard toward the bottom of the track to fight off his brother Rusty on lap 131, and when he shows up next time around on the front stretch he's got a tire doughnut—a black circle where the tire rubbed against Kenny's car—from Rusty on his door. The team cheers him on.

Then, on lap 141, the number 7 car tries a little too hard to get around the 90. Both cars spin, collecting the 46, and it's time for another round of pit stops under the caution flag. Again Newt counts Kenny in, again the team attacks the car, again everything goes fine—until Duze drops the car for Kenny to take off. Which Kenny does, only to discover down pit road that he has a flat left rear tire.

"Coming back around!" Newt calls. "Cut left rear! Two tires! Two tires!"

The team, about to begin reorganizing the pit, is instantly scrambling again. Kenny roars in, they change the two tires on the left side, and he roars back out again. He's lost track position, dropping all the way back to 33rd place. But because the pit was under caution, he's remained on the lead lap.

The mood in the Filmar Racing pit is somber, but not dead. "Just our luck," Duze says, walking around the pit, shaking his head. "Just our motherfucking luck!" It was almost worse, Duze says. He was fixing the jack when Newt said Kenny was coming back in. "That fucker had air in it," he says. "I ran behind the pit box to fix the jack, and then he had a flat, so I grabbed that other jack I never use, so that was like a happy clusterfuck." Crew members cast back to the race two weeks before, at Richmond. Running OK but losing position, the team gambled on a strategy called short-stopping, in which instead of waiting for the leaders to pit, a car pits 20 or 30 laps early, losing track position and probably getting lapped in the short run but coming out with fresh tires that can help the car regain the lost position and more. Then, if it can hold out until the next round of pits, whether under caution or under green, the car can retain the 5 or 10 positions it gained by taking the chance. So Newt pulled Kenny in, costing valuable track position—and before he was even back on the track, a spin brought out the caution flag, putting Kenny not only on tires no fresher than his competitors' but a lap down at the back of the field as well.

And now this flat. They think back to the blown engines, the untimely wrecks, the missed race in California. It begins to seem like the bad luck they've been wrestling all year long won't let up.

They look down, but they don't quit. Today Kenny's car is still hooked up well. It's running as well as his car has run all season, and nobody's giving up on this race. Eddie especially focuses in on his tires. He starts separating sets of tires. He's got a plan.

At lap 185, a NASCAR official walks by and nods at Newt, making a little circular motion with his hand. This happens at about the middle of most Cup races. From now on, an eighth man will be allowed over the wall, but only to clean the driver's windshield, now getting covered with grit and tire goo. As the race wears on into the hypnotic middle laps, Kenny is still running well, picking off a driver or two every few laps. Still, the leader is running better, and Kenny's in danger of going a lap down, killing any chances for a strong finish. "That's the leader, half a straightaway behind you," Filbert tells Kenny on lap 199. During the middle of the race, a mesmerizing peace descends on pit road—the rhythmic, overwhelming roar of the engines douses any other sound; the sun pounds down, reflected with the sound into the infield from the track and the stands. The heat, light, and sound form a kind of sensory womb, and people in the pits enter an almost dreamlike state: there's only the race, only the noise. Everything else kind of disappears. It's not a powerful awareness, it's just the opposite—almost a sort of floating unconsciousness of everything beyond the race, and even of the race. It's just happening, and it's not so much that they're aware of the race as they just are the race. A few puffy clouds dot the sky, and when one covers the sun, for example, everyone in the pit instinctively flinches, glancing up. It's almost like they are awakened from a nap.

Eddie climbs up to the war wagon and Newt leans over, looking at tiny 3x5 cards on which Eddie has scrawled information. Newt nods. Something will have to give if Kenny is to fight off the leader and remain on the lead lap.

Then finally there's a spin on lap 204. "Two tires! Right side only!" Newt yells, and with precision Kenny comes in, gets his change, and goes out. The two-tire stop helps. Kenny is 13th after the stop. "God damn, it's about time!" Kenny yells into the radio. The team exchanges high fives, and Kenny starts complaining about the feel of this set of tires. Newt remains calm: "Give those right sides time to build up pressure." He's also watching the track: "That outside groove is the way to go now, Herman." Another spin on lap 237, but Newt shakes his head. "We're staying out," he says. "Track position is too important."

On lap 264 another spin brings Kenny in; coming out of that he's back to 20th position, but he's picking off cars one by one. He's lost position, but his car's running right. Newt and Filbert start coaching in earnest now. "Good job, buddy," Newt tells Kenny, urging him not to waste the tires rushing by lapped cars. "Save your stuff until you get ready to race 'em." Then, "Good lap, buddy, keep it up, Herman. Good and smooth. Way to roll through there. Looking good."

By the time another caution comes out on lap 321, the number 81 car has fought back to 15th place. Newt and Eddie call for another two-tire stop, and on his way out of the pit Kenny almost runs over a tire that has strayed from the pit of the number 10 car, one slot ahead of him. "Those sumbitches think we're rookies," Kenny says. "Tell 'em if they do that one more time. . . . We'll get 'em."

Newt is about to calm him down when Kenny starts giving him updates on the car: "It's loose—it's baaaad loose!" "Ten-four, buddy," Newt says. "We're working on it right now." Eddie scrambles to set up a set of four tires for the next pit stop, which comes under caution on lap 370. The car is in and out for a four-tire stop in 18.35.

"Great job, fellas, great job!" Newt shouts from the war wagon. And it's starting to feel like maybe something has shifted for the guys in blue and yellow. Kenny's 13th, with about 130 laps to go.

"OK buddy, good and smooth," Newt says. "Take care of your equipment"—code for either "don't waste a lot of effort racing with guys who are a lap down" or "we're working our asses off down here: Stay out of any wrecks and finish the damn race."

But taking care of equipment gets harder to do as the race nears its end. "Tell Ward to give me a break!" Kenny yells at one point, when he's having trouble passing Ward Burton's 22 car, which started on the pole. "Nudge him a little bit," Filbert suggests. Kenny moves up to 11th, and every car on the track has at least a couple of those tire doughnuts by the time the 400-lap mark comes and goes. Kenny's in 11th, racing the number 75 in tenth and the number 28 in ninth. When Kenny nears the 75, Newt yells, "The 75 car is for position." Kenny tries to get a nose underneath him in Turn 1, and he can't quite get there. Finally he opts for the outside, and he passes him a lap later. The crew, standing on the pit wall, cheers and applauds. "Good job! Good job!" Newt yells. Two-Can uses a stopwatch to take lap times, for his own benefit. Rich, his gloves off, sits on the pit wall, sweating.

But Kenny's tires have been on for 100 miles, and if he weren't concentrating so hard on racing, he'd be doing as Don said and screaming like a dog. Filbert, on the roof, sees other cars losing their handling as their tires give out: "Go after the number 10, he's backing up to you," he says. "And the 6, he's backing up to you." But Kenny's losing his tires as well, and he's running out of luck catching anybody. Something will have to give.

Finally, on lap 450, there's another wreck—the 21 cuts a tire and slams head-on into the wall, collecting the 31 when it bounces off. It's time for the final pit stop of the race; risking all, Eddie and Newt decide on another two-tire change. By the end of the remaining laps the unchanged left-side tires will be shot and Kenny will be running on much less car than the other top-10 cars. He'll have to work like hell to protect his spot, but that's the only way they can gain track position. The wreck that brought out the caution is in Turn 4, and by the time it's cleaned up and pit road is opened, it's lap 460.

"All right, boys, let's get ready," Eddie says, staticky over the headsets. "This is the race right here."

Newt looks down at me and nods toward the sign. "Stop him short," he says. The first five cars—the 2, 99, 24, 3, and 94—slide in, and their pits scramble. Four tires for everyone.

Then here comes Kenny. Newt counts him in. "OK, he's off the track . . . he's on pit road . . . here he comes . . . three, . . . two, . . . one, . . . OK, here!" He stops two feet before the mark, exactly where Newt wants him.

The car explodes in, and for the last time, with everything on the line, the scramble is on. Duze is across the pit before the car's even stopped—grit and tire fragments still fill the air like dust in a windstorm, and he squints and frowns as he rushes into the breach. Rich and Frank have the tires in place and ready to go by the time the jack lifts the car to its full height, and with lug nuts splattering the asphalt Ricky and Andy pull the tires off. Frank and Rich hand over the replacements.

No failures among the lugs, and Andy and Ricky step away from the car. Newt has wiped the window, Don has jammed in a single can of fuel, plenty for the final 40 laps. He's tossed the fuel canister back over the wall, and he and Stan, waving his hand to show he's done, back away too.

Then the jack drops, the wheels spin, and Kenny roars out of the pit, speeding out just ahead of the 33 car behind him and in plenty of time to establish a position on pit road before the 10 car ahead of him is even dropped. In fact, he pulls out so close to the 94, which pitted way back in Turn 4, that both cars grind by the 22, even though it has the lead pit and is on the ground by the time they come up on him.

Changing only two tires works. After the pack prowls around the track and picks up the cars that pitted on the backstretch, Kenny's number 81 car shakes out in seventh place. "Good job, guys, great job!" Newt squawks over the headset. "Great job!" He stalks around the pit, slapping hands and backs, exchanging a long nod with Eddie. Then he climbs back onto the war wagon.

"OK, K. W., you're in seventh position," he says to Kenny. "It looks like one more time around [before the green flag drops for the restart], so get ready to rock and roll. Concentrate like you've never concentrated before." There are 34 laps to go, and on the restart they're driving to win the race.

There's one last piece of drama in the pit, though. Ken Schrader, in the number 33 car, had the pit right behind Kenny's. When he raced out himself seconds after Kenny, he cut through the Square D pit. He ran over the hose of the rear air wrench, and the wrench caught in his wheel well, stretching and stretching the cord.

"Look out! Look out!" guys yelled in the pit as the hose stretched tighter, but nobody could hear. The guy in most danger, though, was already on the ground. The hose caught Stan Blaylock by the legs as Schrader took off, and flipped him onto his back. When the hose finally gave out and snapped back, the gun stayed stuck in Schrader's car for half a lap. Nobody was hit. Duze walks around shaking his head.

"An official wanted to know where the fucking gun was," he yells into the roar. "It got *misplaced*! Motherfucking Schrader tried *stealing* it. It's on the fucking backstretch!"

As they approach the green flag for the final laps of the race, Kenny clicks on for a second: "OK," he says, "it's gonna be a barn burner." Kenny's brother Rusty, leading the race in the number 2 car, jumps the green flag on the restart, almost passing the pace car. NASCAR officials put out the black flag for him, requiring him to drive onto pit road for a stop-and-go penalty. He does; an official in his pit, hands out, guides him to a stop; as soon as the car ceases to move, he waves it on by like a bullfighter. Furious, Rusty roars back out and finishes 15th, the last car on the lead lap.

Up front there's a little more bumping and banging between Jeff Burton's 99 and Bobby Hamilton's 43, but Burton wins comfortably, with Hamilton fading to third behind Dale Earnhardt. Kenny closes up on the bumpers of Jeff Gordon and Bill Elliot, but he spends more time fighting Ward Burton off his own sixth position. "Cover the bottom, Kenny, cover the bottom!" Eddie yells over the radio at one point as Burton gets the nose of his number 22 underneath Kenny's left rear quarter panel in Turn 1. Kenny covers the bottom, and he crosses the finish line in sixth place.

"Beautiful job, guys—you did a hell of a job!" he yells over the radio as he finishes, and Eddie and Newt do the same: "Way to go in the pits today, guys; Awesome job today. Awesome!"

Newt, walking from crew member to crew member, nodding his head, pointing, and slapping shoulders, seems not just excited by the strong finish but, for a moment, actually relieved. "I told you guys you could do it! Sixth-place finish; 500 laps, lead lap! Let's get this stuff loaded and get out of here." Dave Ensign walks over to lend a hand pulling the carts and equipment back to the hauler. "Hey, there's big D!" Newt says. "How you doing, buddy? How's everything?"

The transition after the race occurs so quickly that it jars everyone but the crews themselves.

For more than three-and-a-half hours, the speedway has roared and boomed with noise so loud that as far away as the highest seats in the stands, to make yourself heard to the person right next to you, you have to pull aside some kind of ear covering and scream as loud as you can. The air has been filled with the climbing and descending of 43 engines humming up to 9,000 rpms and grinding back down again, twice a lap, for 500 laps; sand, tire fragments, and decomposing asphalt grit have filled the air like stinging hail. Then once the cars on the lead lap have finished, suddenly the noise abates. Car after car cuts its engine, quickly enough that the first sound you hear if you remove your headset to give your aching ears a rest is the crowd still cheering for the finish. But then that subsides too, as everywhere in the infield teams pull headsets off and start taking things apart and putting them away.

In Sunday's rain, groups of crew members huddling under the eaves of the infield concession stand looked like parrots weathering a rainforest storm. Now, hustling together in groups, responding to commands only they can hear, or doing jobs they don't need to be told to do, they look like tiny schools of tropical fish, changing direction all at once or suddenly swarming to a cart, to a toolbox, to a car.

In the Square D pit, talking almost stops. Jacks are taken apart and stored; air wrenches come off their hoses and go into a drawer, the hoses are coiled into their spot in the war wagon. The TV is off, the dish slid into its panel. Computers are unplugged.

As every team scrambles to clean their area and head for home, the doors to the grandstand are opened, and fans pour into the infield, taking an already crowded garage area and pressing it further. The crew members barely notice; they push carts, stacks of tires, cans of nitrogen and gasoline where they need to go. The fans seem to get out of the way.

At the Square D hauler, the car rolls to a stop behind the lift gate. It's covered with tire fragments and doughnuts from Martinsville's tight turns. Kenny pulls himself out the window to congratulations and slaps on the back from Newt, Eddie, and the other crew members as they come back and forth from the pit. Eddie Jarvis, the driver of Kenny's motor home, is waiting for him with a cup of water with ice and a towel. Kenny, his face flushed, hair mussed from his helmet, drinks the water, smiling, leaning on the car. He talks about trying to run down Gordon, the series points leader and star, late in the race. "I had my nose right up under his ass," he says, but he never quite got by. "I was going to go outside like I done on the 75 car, but I never got time." Then, of course, his tires wore and his handling went away, and just holding off Burton was as much as he could do. It's pointed out to him that he finished higher than every one of the five cars that started in front of him, and he pops his head back, pleased. "Hey, let me think about that. Every car—I like that! That's good!" That he finished behind five cars that started behind him, including the 43 car, which started 22nd? That's just racing. The point is a top-10 finish. Newt pulls Kenny away, disappearing with him into the hauler office for a few minutes of debriefing.

For everyone else, it's endgame here. The lift gate of the truck, stuck out as a canopy all weekend, is lowered. The crew pushes the car onto the gate, throws aluminum chocks under the wheels, and then hits the button to lift it up to the top of the hauler. Leaning on the car as it goes up, they can feel that the hood, the tires, and the rims are all still hot. The car gets pushed into the space atop the hauler in seconds, and it's strapped in behind the backup car. Down comes the lift gate, and the load-out continues: the war wagon, the tool chest, the crash cart, the generators, the coolers, the chairs, the gas grill. Everything that has made the Martinsville infield a home to the crew for the last three days is loaded into the hauler, filling the tiny hallway with equipment.

Don comes up smiling with the gas cans, emptied at the collecting station. He saw a NASCAR official and asked for the air gun that Ken Schrader ran over. "He said, 'You don't get it back.' I said, 'You don't understand, it wasn't our fault!' He said, 'OK, we'll see that you get it back.' " Don shakes his head and gets to work, pushing carts into position to be loaded on the hauler.

Before 45 minutes have passed, the only thing that says "Square D" in the infield is the hauler, and that's started and rumbling and ready to go. The side door is open, and one last cooler sits on the ground in a growing puddle of water. The postrace beers, and everyone has one. "Got any beer left?" someone asks, walking in from a last check of the pit area. "The round cooler," Dave Ensign says. "You know I always take care of my boys."

The team stands around, down to T-shirts and pants, wearing Square D hats and sunglasses. Newt's hat, instead of the plain blue with the logo on it, has a lightning bolt pattern, and for the moment it looks like he wears it not just proudly but happily. He sucks down a beer and looks around the asphalt infield, suddenly seeming bare as the haulers pull out, turning onto the track in Turn 1, circling once, and heading out the crossover gate in Turn 4. Seven haulers are enough to completely fill the backstretch.

The Filmar Racing team was wise. They parked the white van they drove up in from Charlotte in a parking area outside the track. They walk out to it and head home, fighting traffic. It's not as comfortable or as fast as Filbert's 10-seat plane, where they play poker and listen to Two-Can tell stories, but they're on their way home.

When they get back to the team headquarters outside Charlotte, most of the guys go their separate ways; the truck can be unloaded in the morning. Newt and Eddie get in a car and follow Two-Can, who's got them all tickets for that night's Charlotte Panthers game. It turns out that they lose Two-Can on the highway (you should never have to try to drive behind a race team member immediately after a Winston Cup race) and never find him at the game. So they go home and go to bed. Just as well; the Panthers lose.

Frank Good has a last errand to run. He has to get an engine hoist, load the extra engine into the back of a pickup, and drive around to return it to the Robert Yates engine shop. That's how it is when you rent your engines.

He says he gets home before 9.

• • •

The speedway doesn't exactly clear out at 4 p.m. either. For one thing, the fans let in from the grandstand are crawling over the garage area. They're looking for souvenirs: a tire valve cover, a piece of sheet metal loosed by a wreck, anything that was used during the race. People grab lengths of hose out of the junk piles left by the haulers and in the garage. They root for clipped wires and frayed belts in the trash. They look, especially, for lug nuts. Lug nuts used in a Winston Cup race are the foul balls into the stands of Winston Cup racing. A lug nut is the best souvenir you can bring home from a race. Lug nuts from the car of your favorite driver—the number 24 of Jeff Gordon, the 6 of Mark Martin, the 88 of Dale Jarrett, the 3 of Earnhardt—from a race he won are more like the ball from a game-winning homer your favorite player hit in an extra-inning game.

"Rusty's my man," says a man rooting through the wash of clipped nylon cable zips and crushed Gatorade cups and auto parts boxes covered with oil and rear end fluid and film boxes and food bags and concession stand litter that has built up around every one of the trash barrels and cardboard trash boxes everywhere on the infield. Ile's not too happy about the black flag that cost Rusty the race, but he knows that Rusty likes to jump the green flag on restarts, and once in a while he gets caught. Rusty only finished 15th, but he led the race, and in fact led the most laps, at one point keeping his car digging into the corners in first place for 150 laps in a row. If it's going to be a lug nut, it's going to have to be Rusty's, and he walks slowly along pit road, trying to determine which pit was Rusty's. "But don't think I don't root for his brothers, man." That would be Kenny and his brother Mike, who in the Saturday race at Martinsville (sort of the weekend's undercard), raced the number 52 Chevy truck to 22nd place in the NASCAR Craftsman Truck Series race.

In a crowd of fans, kept away by the omnipresent Winston Cup flag tape wound around trash barrels, several cars are receiving postrace inspections: The number 99 Ford that won, the number 3 Chevy that came in second, and the 43 Pontiac that came in third. NASCAR inspects the winner every race, and usually the top finisher of every make. The cars receive an inspection as detailed as the one every car got several times before the race.

Along the front of pit road, a hauler with a Racers, Inc. logo prowls along slowly, with three guys loading in the piles of used tires the pit crews left out front. Racers, Inc. is one of two companies that, by contract, recycle the tires. They pick up the used tires after the race, remove them from the rims, take the rims to the Goodyear race shop for the next race, and dispose of the tires. Some, of course, end up in the hands of fans, where they become planters, mirror frames, coffee table bases.

Those grasping hands can be a frustration to the guys trying to finish their jobs and go home. Anyhow, so says Vince, a radio frequency camera technician who works for Broadcast Sports Technologies, which supplies remote cameras to the network televising the race, in this case ESPN. He shakes his head as he winds cable around his arm, wrist to elbow, to spool it. "Digging through the fucking trash," he says of the fans. When the cable is spooled, he cinches it with nylon strips and tosses it into his golf cart. "That's the worst part about it. The people come out here picking up lug nuts, tire caps, going through the garbage."

His friend, Lorne, is a pointer. He's one of the guys who follow around the camera guys wearing a backpack with a transmitter in it and holding a metal rod taped to a broomstick with a tiny dish broadcast antenna with a foam soccer ball on the end of the center spike. He gets paid $75 a day to be a pointer at Martinsville. He points that spike at a collecting antenna on top of the home stretch grandstand. No benefits, no nothing. Just this year pointers started getting their hotel rooms paid for; people like Vince demanded they get at least that.

"We said, we need these guys," Vince says.

Vince's job is to sit in his little golf cart, parked behind a junction box that connects about a dozen pit areas. He controls video feeds from the overhead pit cameras from cooperative crews as well as feeds from a couple of remote cameras used by the pit reporters. Not every team allows their overhead camera to provide a live feed. The number

3 team of Dale Earnhardt always says no, "and no tobacco teams," he says, showing the uneasiness beginning to develop between NASCAR, its broadcast partners, and the tobacco sponsorship that has made it what it is.

They arrived in Martinsville on Wednesday two days before the haulers and the Winston Cup teams. They arrived this morning at 6:30, same time as the Winston Cup teams. They'll be going home around 9 tonight, around five hours after the Winston Cup teams.

And not only do they have to spend hours after the race retrieving shotgun microphones and ripping up cables duct-taped onto the ground; not only do they have to get covered with tire goo and brake dust and asphalt fragments all day while they do their jobs; not only do guys like Lome get paid barely enough to make air fare to their next assignment, whether it's another Cup race or an Indy car race or a basketball game, but they have to put up with "these fucking race fans," Lome says, who get stuff on them and trip over their cables and engage them in endless discussions of why ESPN doesn't show their favorite driver more often and ask if they can look through the cameras and want to take pieces of the cable for souvenirs.

Then Lorne smiles a wan smile as he washes his hands with the ice from a soft drink cup: " 'Course, I used to be one of them race fans I'm cussing."

By 4:30 or so, even the fans clambering around pit road are straggling toward the crossovers back to the grandstands and parking areas. The lines of cars are moving now, and the camps are being struck. As the cars filled with tired race fans wearily grind up the just-not-quite-too-slippery grass slopes, if you look out over the camping or parking areas, you don't necessarily think "Woodstock," but you don't think anything too far from it. It's been a long, wet, hot, and satisfying four days for these folks.

But it's over now. The sun is setting in a blue sky whitening toward the horizons. No stars are visible yet, but just a hint of peach, of pink, is starting to seep into the light above the shadows of the pines. It's time to go home.

• • •

The last image of Martinsville Speedway in the rearview mirror, as the sun sets among the Piedmont hills, is that tiny road leading out of the speedway, with the cars rolling out and kicking up just a little cloud of that famous red dust. Traffic this late isn't bad on Route 220, heading south, down a big hill and then back up again, following the hills southwest into North Carolina. Toward Charlotte.

And you'd never believe it in the rapidly suburbanizing South, where cul-de-sacs are replacing tobacco fields and choking the land like kudzu, but rolling through the countryside from Martinsville back to Charlotte, you drive two-lanes through some rural stretches where you still don't see too many lights. In fact, if you take North Carolina Route 87 all the way over to U.S. 29—if, on the map, you stay on a gray line for a while instead of getting right on a double red line—you can stop at a yield sign at the top of a hill, in the middle of the night, where a gravel road angles in from the forest and through some cleared pasture to meet Route 87. And you can pull your car over onto the wide part of the gravel road so you're not in the middle of the road in case another car comes by, even though you know one won't. And you can turn off the lights of your car, but not the engine, because if it doesn't start up again there's nobody around.

And you can stand outside and look up at the stars. There isn't a streetlight within miles, you can see millions. And it's still a day or so before the new moon begins rising, so even Venus and Mars, on a line slightly sloping downward in the clear sky of the west, barely draw your eye. And then you can notice.

Your car is still running. It's a motor, and it's running, cycling over and over, thousands of times a minute, working. Driving.

You like the sound.

from Indy—The World's Fastest
Carnival Ride
by Dan Gerber

Dan Gerber (born 1940) is a former professional race-car driver as well as a poet, journalist, short-story writer and novelist. Here he meditates on the meaning of the Indianapolis 500.

In the early fifties it was a movie starring Clark Gable, titled *To Please a Lady*, with actual race footage and the faces of real drivers like Mauri Rose and Wilbur Shaw and huge ferocious cars resembling U-boats on wheels. The tires were absurdly narrow and grooved with tread only on the right half of the running surface. The movie was my first glimpse of a world that had previously enthralled me purely with sound. I was ten years old and had already decided that to become a racing driver and to drive at Indianapolis was the only thing worth growing up for. Each Memorial Day was spent with engine sounds and the voice of Sid Collins. It didn't matter much what he said; it was just the sound of his voice, the switching to his reporters around the track, the roar of the cars in the background, and the litany of what were, for me, almost holy names: Troy Ruttman, Tony Bettenhausen, Jimmy Bryan, Sam Hanks, Johnnie Parsons, Pat O'Conner, and, most holy of all, Billy Vukovich. It meant school was getting out and I could get sunburned and go fishing and spend three months on

Lake Michigan trying to let the magic names fade into some kind of perspective. Whenever I wasn't in a bathing suit, I wore slightly grimy white duck trousers and a grease-smudged white T-shirt, because that's what "Vuky" had been wearing in the one photo I'd seen of him, sitting on a workbench, barefooted, his knees pulled up to his chest, exhausted and dejected after leading the 1952 race for 191 laps until a fifty-cent steering part let go and put him into the northeast wall. "The tough little driver from Fresno," the papers called him, using his standard quote, "Just don't get in my way."

Then Vuky won in 1953 and again in '54. It was the way it had to be. Speeds had climbed past the 140-mph barrier and everybody wondered if they hadn't reached the limit. "We're going too fast out there," Vuky said. "Well, Vuky," the interviewer reflected, "you're the only one who can slow it down." But he didn't slow it down. He qualified for the 1955 race at 141.071 mph, led the race for fifty-six laps, then crashed and was killed attempting to avoid a pileup on the back straight. I saw the newsreel and the photograph of the now-primitive-looking Hopkins Special lying upside down, the hand of my boyhood hero protruding from the cockpit as if waving good-bye. I remember feeling somehow responsible for Vuky's death. It was the first time I hadn't listened to the race. My father had taken me fishing in Ontario, and on Memorial Day we were flying down from Saddle Lake in a floatplane when the bush pilot tuned in the race on his radio and told us that Vukovich had been killed. I asked him to turn it off. I didn't want to hear the cars or Sid Collins and the magic names if Vuky wasn't among them anymore.

Another year went by and my aversion to racing cooled. But it would never be quite the same without Vuky. My interest turned to road racing and more exotic, if somehow less personally awesome names, like Juan Fangio, Stirling Moss, Phil Hill, and the Marquis de Portago. It was more intricate and interesting racing, and I learned to pronounce Le Mans like the French, and Sebring and the Mille Miglia and Nurburgring. Yet as much as I pontificated that it was dumb to turn left all the time, Indy and Sid Collins and Tony Hulman orating "Gentlemen, start your engines," was still where the magic was.

The day I got my driver's license, I borrowed, without permission, a 1955 Thunderbird and pushed the speedometer needle up over 100 to see what it felt like to be Vuky; speed is always in the present tense. I raced motorcycles and an assortment of cars and pickup trucks on Michigan back roads, and two weeks after my twenty-first birthday, drove my first real race on a dirt track in an Austin Healey, and won. A boyhood friend who, with skepticism and boredom, had endured years of my racing dreams, now regarded me with a certain reverence and said, "Well, Vuky, you really did it." It was a far-fetched comparison, but at that moment I was God's gift to racing, and Indianapolis seemed only a short step away.

I never drove at Indianapolis, never even came close. I raced sports cars for five years, with moderate success, then stuffed one into the end of the pit wall at Riverside, broke every bone in my body, and quit. For seven years I stayed away from racing, not wishing to taunt myself with failed aspirations. Then, two years ago, at the invitation of Bob Jones, a friend who covers racing for *Sports Illustrated*, I went to Indianapolis to watch qualifying and the race. Somehow I always knew that sooner or later I'd have to confront this track, if not as a driver then at least as a spectator.

It wasn't quite the way it had been in *To Please a Lady*. The bricks had been covered with asphalt, the great wooden pagoda replaced by a glass and steel tower, and most of the names had changed. There was a Bettenhausen, a Parsons, and a Vukovich; and though they were a new generation of drivers, the sons of the men I had idolized, the names retained their fascination. There were newer names that had acquired their own aura—Foyt, Ruby, Unser, and Andretti—and several, like Donahue and Revson, I'd competed with on road courses ten years earlier. I remember being a little awed by the realization that those men I'd learned to race with, and sometimes beaten, were driving and even winning at Indianapolis. Of course, they weren't the same men, and neither was I. But Indianapolis was the same track (at least it was in the same place), and coming to it finally was like visiting a historic battleground, with one important exception. Another battle would soon be fought here, and another and another. New monuments would be built over the old. Racing drivers must perforce live totally in the present and pay no more than a token deference to last year's winner or last year's dead.

That was in 1973, and it proved a bad year to reacquaint myself with racing. During the final practice session before qualifying began, I had just come through the Sixteenth Street tunnel on my way to the pits when I heard a loud *wuump* and turned to see Art Pollard's car, both right wheels broken off on impact with the wall, sliding sideways through the short chute. About one hundred feet in front of me, the axle stubs dug into the infield grass and the car began flipping. Upside down, it skidded back onto the track, flipped right side up and came to rest in the middle of turn two. Pollard sat motionless amid the alcohol flames, visible only as heat vapor rising from the car, and at that moment a strange thing happened. Looking back on it, it seems improbable, but I could have sworn I heard the crowd in the bleachers on the far side of the track, in unison, scream "Save him!"

It was a full thirty seconds before the crash truck arrived, put out the flames, and extracted Pollard from the car. The two disembodied wheels rolled together in formation and came to rest in the infield as neatly as if they'd been stacked there for future use. Several hours later, in an interval between qualification attempts, they announced that Pollard was dead. A fat woman in the bleachers behind the pits broke into tears. There was an official minute of silence, then qualifying resumed. The announcer announced a new one-lap record. The fat lady was cheering.

Two weeks later I came back, waited through the tension of two days of race-delaying rain and two aborted starts, one of them catastrophic, and went home. I watched the carnage on television, Salt Walther's legs protruding from the wreckage of his burning, spinning car, Swede Savage's fatal crash in turn four, and the STP crewman hit and killed by an emergency truck speeding to the rescue. It seemed a more macabre spectacle couldn't have been planned. Indy had lived up to its reputation, and anyone who'd paid his five dollars hoping he might see blood got his money's worth.

The rules were changed in the interests of safety. The fuel capacity of the car was halved, to diminish fire hazard. The size of the airfoils was cut, and pop-off valves installed on the turbochargers to limit boost, all in hopes of slowing the cars down. The track facility was improved, spectator barriers strengthened, the pit entrance widened, and the inside wall in turn four, the one that had killed Savage, was eliminated. The 1974 race was one of the safest in the Speedway's history, no fatalities and no serious injuries. *Maybe I would go back to Indianapolis*, I thought. After all, it's the possibility of an accident that is racing's fascination, the risk, without which racing would be sterile and pointless; but it was the almost historical certainty that sometime during the month of May someone would be killed there that had tended to make Indy seem more like a Roman circus than a twentieth-century sporting event.

May 2, 1975. The day before the track opens and I've got nothing to do but pick up my credentials and have a look around. It's quiet—almost eerie—like visiting an amusement park closed for the winter. Nothing seems to be moving, and the only sound is the grandstand-muffled traffic passing on Sixteenth Street. Two men are painting new Coca-Cola and Sprite billboards on the scoring tower at the north end of the infield. In Gasoline Alley a dilapidated golf cart sits outside locked garage doors near the pit entrance, Jim Hurtubise—#56—Miller High Life, in oxidized red letters. It has two flat tires and looks as if it hasn't been touched since last May. Strange to think of this huge arena empty all but one month a year. The seasons change, the pits, the track, and the grandstands covered with snow, but in everyone's mind—save a few maintenance men and administrators—this place has no existence apart from the month of May. And to those for whom racing is a way of life, it *is* the month of May. I stand in the middle of the front straight, where, tomorrow, highly specialized machines will be traveling at over 220 miles an hour. Heat waves rise from the track and the huge tier of grandstands above turn four. Now there's one sound, a regularly sequenced rachidic burst. I walk back into Gasoline Alley and around the rows of ancient wooden garages till I find its source, a mechanic with bulletproof thick bifocals, an oil-soaked cowboy hat, and a patch on the back of his shirt that says: *Smokey's—Best Damn Garage in Town.* He's sitting on what looks like a railway baggage cart, polishing the ports of an intake manifold with an air-powered buffer, the first indication that someone's got in mind to go racing here.

To kill time, I take the fifty-cent track tour in a Chevrolet minibus. Once around the Speedway while the driver, with marginal accuracy, relays the speed the racers will be traveling, swings the van high on the nine-degree banking to show us how close the cars come to the wall, and points out the prices of various grandstand and tower terrace seats and the locations of the most recent notable crashes: "Salt Walther ended up here, and he'll be racing again this year. Swede Savage hit the wall right there where there used to be a wall, and the part of the car with him in it ended up way down here." I find myself silently augmenting his list with the names of heroes and friends: Pollard in the south chute, Pat O'Connor in turn two, Vukovich on the back straight, Jim Malloy in turn three, Eddie Sachs and Dave MacDonald coming out of turn four—their names now eclipsed by Swede Savage's.

At first reflection, this catalog of crash locations—both the minibus driver's and my own—seems a morbid preoccupation with tragedy, but these are places of history (like the location of Pickett's charge at Gettysburg or the box at Ford's Theater in Washington), important to us for the violently abbreviated lives with which we have identified our own. What seems morbid to me is the propensity of most racing people and sports journalists to pretend those deaths never occurred. I remember that I was fishing in Key West with Bob Jones when we heard the news that Peter Revson had been killed while practicing for the South African Grand Prix. I had known Revson and raced against him back in the early sixties. Jones had done a personality piece on Revson for *Sports Illustrated* and spent many evenings with him in the course of five years covering major races. The news came over the radio, and for what seemed like almost an hour, neither of us had anything to say. Finally, when so much time had elapsed that it seemed to come almost out of context, Jones said, "You realize that for the next six months now, nobody will mention his name."

"Yeah," I reflected, "and when they do it'll be as if he had lived twenty years ago."

It is easy to understand this sense of detachment among the drivers. If they were to ponder too deeply the dangers to themselves or the deaths of their competitors, their imaginations would take control and make it impossible for them to continue. Physical courage relies, to a great extent, on the ability to suspend the imagination, and sometimes this kind of control is transmitted to the outsider as callousness. I was standing a few feet away when Johnny Rutherford was interviewed shortly after the death of his close friend Art Pollard. "It's too bad that you can't turn back the clock," he said matter-of-factly. "Art was doing what he loved to do, and there's a risk we all take." His statement seemed to echo Faulkner's that "The irrevocability of action is tragic." A few minutes later, Rutherford went back out on the track, qualified for the pole, and set a new one-lap record of 199.071 mph, a heroic effort that would have been impossible for any man whose mind hadn't been totally on his business.

The tour bus pauses in front of the pits and the driver explains how the names of the drivers qualifying for the race will be painted: "Right between them various red marks you see along that wall there." The teenage girl sitting next to me spots a driver with long frizzy hair and a flowered Hawaiian shirt. "There's Rick Muther. Hey, Rick! Rick, can I have your autograph?" Muther is talking with another girl and seems not to hear the request.

Saturday, May 3. The track is supposed to officially open for practice, but the sky is overcast and threatens rain. Nobody expects any really hot laps the first day out, and with qualifications still a week away, most of the top drivers haven't shown up. There are several rookies (highly experienced racers, but new to Indianapolis) who must learn the track and turn twenty observed laps within each of several speed brackets to pass their driver's test, and a few veterans, anxious to get back in the groove and check out their cars. The only real question on anyone's mind is who will be the first driver on the track. Being first out has no effect on qualifying or on the race, but, like everything else here, it is part of a tradition. It's supposed to be a coup. It generates a good deal of publicity, and publicity is what attracts sponsors and sells their products. It's why Gatorade and Surefine Foods and Jorgensen Steel invest up to three hundred thousand dollars to run this race, the hope that their sponsorship will generate millions of dollars worth of publicity, maybe even get a picture of their car, their billboard on wheels, on the cover of a national magazine, the kind of advertising money alone can't buy.

Dick Simon, a forty-one-year-old retired insurance executive from Salt Lake City, wheels his car to the end of the pit lane, ready to go. Then a few drops of rain fall and his crew covers the car with a plastic sheet. A band of Scottish pipers march onto the track, and the absurdly elaborate pageantry of May in Indianapolis has begun. Every flower show, car wash, and tea party will append the label "500 Festival." Today's official events include a radio-controlled model-car race, a bridge tournament, a Dress Up Like Mom parade, a Look Like Your Favorite Television Personality contest, a bubble-gum blowing contest, and the mayor's breakfast, at which 1,665 paying guests will hear Jimmy "The Greek" Snyder pick A. J. Foyt as the race winner, meet the 500 Festival Queen, and then adjourn to the track for opening ceremonies, where each of those attending the breakfast will be permitted to make one lap of the track in their Corvette or Cadillac.

The thirty-three official Buick pace cars stream by, bearing celebrities. I'm leaning on the pit fence, eavesdropping on two Speedway guards, sad-faced old men with the perennial look of small boys who got what they wanted for Christmas and then discovered it didn't make any difference. "Who was that boy got his head cut off down in Dayton? Shit, that 'as a good track till they ruined it with blacktop. You could come outta turn one, aim'er at the grandstand, pour the coals to it and slide 'er all the way round. I remember when Mel Kenyon slid . . ." The Speedway, Indiana, High School Band plays "The Eyes of Texas" for Johnny Rutherford, last year's winner. A few more drops of rain. The Festival Queen accepts her crown and steps up to the microphone: "I wanna reckanize the twenty-eight princesses behind me." Now it's pouring. The band marches off, the crowd scatters for cover, and Dick Simon's car sits abandoned, fogging its plastic shroud in the pit lane. The rain pools up all afternoon, discouraging everyone but the golfers on the Speedway golf course, their official black and white umbrellas dotting the fairways.

The bar at the Speedway Motel has the atmosphere of a neighborhood tavern. Everybody knows everybody, and if you don't know everybody, everybody knows you don't. But the waitress will flirt with you all the same, and you're invited to listen in on any stories you like. It's fairly quiet this evening and as I sip my gin and tonic I remember sitting there the evening after Art Pollard's crash, overhearing a large man with ruptured capillaries tell how once in Korea he'd put a forty-five to the head of his "moose," when he'd come back to his "hooch," and found her "shackin' up with a nigger supply sergeant."

"Whad you do?" his companion asked.

"I shot 'er head off."

"Really?"

"Yeah, but I missed and shot off her foot instead." The scalp beneath his silver flattop flared with laughter and, still laughing, he turned toward me. "Say, you don't know what happened to that fella crashed in turn one, do ya?"

"He's dead." I didn't want to discuss Pollard in this context, but it was the only straight answer to his question.

"Aw, shit, I'm sorry," he said, as if apologizing to me.

"You really shot her in the foot, huh?" His companion was intrigued.

"Naw, I never hit her at all. I just shot the bed full of holes." He leaned toward the bar and covered his face with his hand. "Aw, Jesus," he said and began weeping. Something bumped my leg, and I noticed seat belts dangling from each of the bar stools.

It was getting dark and the rain still hadn't let up. A man well decorated with official badges and patches introduced himself. "Everybody knows everybody here."

"So I noticed."

"These paintings, see these paintings on the walls?" He swept his hand in a slow circle indicating a half dozen pictures by Leroy Neiman, impressions of the 1963 race. "They're valued at more than a million dollars, and they don't even have a guard here to watch 'em. Like I said, everybody knows everybody here, and they're good people." I raised my glass and we drank to the good people. "I'm the weighmaster here."

"Pardon me?"

"I'm the weighmaster. I weigh the cars. My company's got twenty-five thousand invested in the scales, and we can't afford to have anything go wrong." I raised my glass again and we drank to his scales.

The next morning a rookie named Billy Scott beats Dick Simon to the track. Scott passes his driver's test with no problems. "A cakewalk," he says to me as he steps out of his car. But Jigger Sirois, who in six years at the Speedway has yet to make the race, is having trouble again. He takes four or five laps to warm his engine, then stands on it coming past the pits. I am standing next to a track photographer when we hear the engine noise fade in the first turn, the horrible scrubbing of tires, an instant of silence, and the dull, grinding thud of rubber, steel, and fiberglass embracing concrete. "Oh, goddam Jigger"—the photographer slaps his thigh—"he done it again." Now the track is officially open. A middle-aged lady with ultramarine blue wings painted on her eyelids walks by. The wing tips extend to her temples. No cars are moving now, and she's leaning on the pit fence, casting a spell on the empty grandstands across the track. The infield bleachers are three-quarters full of spectators, yawning and turning pink. They respond like a chorus each time they hear the putter of a wheel horse or the pit-gate guard blow his whistle, stretching their spines to see whose car is being pushed into the pits, then collapsing again in the shade of their newspapers, swatting flies and occasionally each other. The guards drag off a streaker.

With the exception of the two qualifying weekends and the race itself, it'll go on this way most of the month. Already there is gossip about cheating, and Foyt, as everyone's nemesis, is the center of attention. George Bignotti, who for years had been Foyt's crew chief, has publicly accused Foyt of carrying more fuel than the rules allow. Foyt won the California 500 in a walkaway, and Bignotti has suggested he did it carrying an extra five gallons of methanol in the canister of his fire extinguisher. The controversy rages all month, and though the concerns are genuine, I sense a certain patina of showmanship.

When and if he finally gets around to it, no one, even those with the most peripheral interest in racing, seriously entertains the possibility that anyone could go faster than A. J. The hitchhikers I picked up last night had no doubt about it.

"We come up here with a couple a cunts, but they dropped us," said one. He was wearing the first honest-to-God duck's-ass hairdo I'd seen since 1961. "'Course we was drunk, I'll give 'em that. But you can bet your ass I'll be straddling my B.M.W. the next time I hit this town" He leaned forward from the backseat and tapped me on the shoulder. "Say, you an Elk?"

"No."

"You ain't even from around here, is you?" The one beside me had tattoos on his arms.

"No."

"Well, if you was, you'd be an Elk too. We're from Greencastle. Ever hear of it?"

"Something about Dillinger. He robbed a bank there, didn't he?"

"He sure did." The tattooed one seemed to point to it as a matter of civic pride. "Everybody knows that, I guess."

The D.A. laid his arm across my shoulder and pointed to an overpass about a mile ahead. "You can just drop us off on my bridge up there."

"Your bridge?" I was being set up.

"I laid every inch of concrete in that sucker and sloped the banks with a dozer. I was the first one to drive across it, too."

In the rearview mirror, I could see I was being regarded with suspicion, a foreigner, not even an Elk. "What're you doin' here anyway?"

"I'm here for the race."

"Well, I don't give much of a shit about that, but I know Foyt's got a few more miles in his pocket. You wait an' see."

"Can I quote you?"

"Hell, I said it, didn't I?"

On the first day of qualifying, Foyt pulls in after one lap at 189.195. It is the fastest lap turned in during the first half hour of qualifications, but not close to the 192-plus laps he's been turning in practice. He rants around the pits, ostentatiously complaining about his tires, then storms off to his garage and locks the doors. The story goes around that he was so pissed off he took a screwdriver and punctured all four tires on his car. "That'd be a good trick," he says later, "I'd like to see somebody try it." There is also some speculation that the tire tantrum is a ploy to get his car back into the garage so he can tamper with the turbocharger pop-off valve installed by the United States Auto Club (USAC) and illegally increase its pressure.

Late in the afternoon when the track is cooler and three other cars have qualified at over 190, A. J. tries again. The first time he goes by, everyone knows that, if he survives, the pole position will be his. I watch him power through turn two, using every inch of the track. I can feel everyone around me holding their breath, with A. J.'s engine screaming at full power as he slides up to the back straight wall till there isn't an inch of daylight between his right rear tire and the unimpressionable concrete. I can feel his engine vibrate all the way down the back straight and into turn three. No one is really surprised when they announce his first lap speed of 195.313 mph, and we know we were watching something so frivolously momentous, so ethereally and courageously executed and yet so seemingly pointless: A man, unquestionably the best in the world at what he does, transcending even his own abilities, extending himself to the mercy of intricately overstressed steel and rubber and any stray speck of dirt on the track, to go nowhere faster than anyone else possibly could. For three minutes and five and a half seconds all the allegations of cheating seem pointless. A. J. Foyt owns the track and no one will dispute it. "I thrilled the hell outta myself three or four times out there," he says, just to let everyone know it hasn't been quite as easy or predetermined as it looks.

Apart from Foyt's run, the greatest spectator interest on the front straight is generated by a rabbit. Qualifying is stopped and several spectators chase the rabbit up and down the track in front of the pits, the crowd cheering, as in the lion feeding scenes from *Quo Vadis*. The rabbit has strayed into a jungle without cover, nothing but asphalt, concrete walls, and four pairs of Adidas track shoes pursuing him. Five minutes later he is strung from the infield fence, dead from an apparent heart attack.

In the bleachers behind the pit fence, I notice a cheering section of thirty or forty men in orange T-shirts. I'm attracted by the wry, subtle wit of the posters they've hung from the railing in front of their seats: *Fire Up Go Nuts, Super Tits, Take I-69 to the 500, Give Harlen the Fengler,* and *I'll Bet My Ass on Loydd's Rubys*. One sign, *Sandy Lovelace* (with a phone number), they disclaim but admit they've rented the space to a new girl in town and that they've "all been behind her 1,000 percent." Their P.R. man insists I have a Coors with him before he'll answer any questions. It's a hot day and I hadn't realized how thirsty I was. "You're okay," he tells me. "We like the way you drink your beer."

The Classics were founded by "fifteen men of like vision" in 1963 and have had the same block of seats each year since. They even have a special Speedway guard assigned to protect and contain them. "For years it was Pops Middleton, but when he died we acquired ole Larry here." The P.R. man puts his arm around the porcine and obviously pleased track attendant, who beams deferentially from under his pith helmet. "We got our own hospitality suite at the Mayfair Motel and our own clubhouse here under the stands. That's where we have our Rookie of the Year Contest."

Their number has grown from the original fifteen to thirty-five, and each year any member may sponsor a rookie, who becomes a probationary member until he distinguishes himself with a bold and forthright act such as mooning the sheriff, entering the topless go-go contest at Mother Tucker's, or jumping onto the stage at the Red Carpet Lounge and stealing the entertainer's hat, as one desperate rookie did last night. "Oh, we got lawyers, accountants, factory workers, salesmen, bartenders, a heterogeneous mixing of fine fellows. We come from all over the country, Washington, Oregon, Davenport, Tallahassee."

I ask him about their uniform beer hats and sunglasses. "Oh, we all wear these so our families won't recognize us when they see us on TV."

I finish my beer and I thank the P.R. man for his time. "All part of the service," he says. "Here, have one of these." He hands me a cigar with a printed wrapper: *The Qualls are the Balls.* "We give one of these to each of the drivers. It's good for three miles an hour."

Their slogan is less facetious than perhaps even The Classics realize. Jerry Grant is running Indy for the ninth time, and it never gets any easier, he tells me. I remember when we were racing together in the United States Road Racing Championship series in 1965, and Jerry had just run at Indy for the first time. "It's not really much different from road racing," he told me, "just more specialized, and all the turns go to the left." But he doesn't see it that way anymore. He's large for a racing driver, six-three and over two hundred pounds. It's ninety-three degrees, with matching humidity. The perspiration beads up on his forehead as he leans against the tool bench, sipping a Fresca. "It's gotten so fast and so technically intricate here." His dark brown eyes fix on mine with a kind of intensity that seems at odds with the casual attitude of his body. They never seem to blink. "You remember when we were racing, how if the car wasn't handling quite right, you could drive it a different way, throw it into the corner a little differently, and make up for the way the chassis was? Well, you can't do that here any-more. This race isn't really much different from any other race I run, but qualifying here is the greatest pressure I'm put under all year. Every-thing depends on those four laps, so much money and prestige and sponsorship. You just drive it the only way you can and hope every-thing's working for you, the car, the tires, the track, the air, cause if it isn't, there isn't much you can do about it."

In 1972, Grant qualified on the pole for the California 500 and was the first USAC driver to run an official qualification lap at over 200 mph, but today everything *isn't* working for him, and he qualifies fourteenth. Johnny Rutherford, who holds the one-lap record at Indianapolis and won the pole position in 1973, makes the definitive statement on those four crucial laps after qualifying a disappointing seven mph off the pace: "Some days you eat the bear and some days the bear eats you."

It's a fairly reliable axiom that the best drivers will be offered the best cars, and rookies, unless they're already established superstars, consider themselves fortunate to have any kind of a ride for Indy. Usually they have to struggle with fairly antique and uncompetitive equipment. Billy Scott, the rookie for whom the driver's test at 170 mph had been "a cakewalk," finds that trying to push the same car just twelve mph a lap faster to make the race is a nightmare. And inferior equipment isn't his only handicap. The intimidation of Indianapolis itself, the most important and tradition-bound race in the world, takes time and many laps of practice to overcome. "It's the biggest race in the world," Scott says. He leans close to be sure I can hear him over the din of the bar. "I saw those huge grandstands full of people watching me, and it suddenly hit me where I was. A couple of times it happened during practice. I'd start down the front straight and hear myself thinking, *Gee, I'm at Indy, I'm really at Indy.* Then I'd catch myself and say, *Cut that shit out and drive.* Finally I took an 869-foot spin coming out of turn three and ended up on the grass inside turn four. The car was okay, and so was I, but that really got my attention, like a dog shittin' a loggin' chain."

Scott fails to make competitive speed on two qualifying attempts and is waved off by his crew. The car owner decides to try another driver and puts Graham McRae, an Indy veteran, in the car. But McRae's times are no better than Scott's. "I was pushing that car as fast as it was ever gonna go on this track," Scott explains, "but the old man wouldn't believe it." On his last attempt, Scott overcooks it coming out of turn four. The rear end comes loose, and he makes a spectacular spin down the front straight, shedding fiberglass and suspension parts like a dog shaking water. "Too bad he didn't stuff it beyond fixin," another driver quips. "Now some other poor son of a bitch'll have to struggle with it next year."

I tell Billy Scott about my friend Dave MacDonald, who was killed eleven years ago, coming out of turn four in an unstable car; tell him how Jimmy Clark has followed MacDonald in practice; and told him he should refuse to drive it in the race. "But I couldn't do that." Scott seems shocked by the suggestion. "I mean, if I stepped out of a ride, I'd never get another one. I'd be all washed up."

"The thrill isn't there anymore." Andy Granatelli, who with his legendary Novis and his turbine car that died four laps short of winning the 1967 race has been responsible for more innovation and spectator interest than any other man in the Speedway's sixty-year history, looks tired and almost on the verge of tears as he talks about his twenty-nine-year lover's quarrel with Indianapolis. "Driving down here each year, I used to get so excited I'd start edging down on the accelerator, going faster and faster, till by the time I got to Lafayette I was driving flat out."

"But there's been too much tragedy," he explains. "That and USAC's continual legislation against innovation. It all comes down to the rules." He gets up and goes to the refrigerator for a can of diet pop. He's lost fifty pounds and waddles less conspicuously than he used to in those STP commercials. "Want one?" I accept. He pops the top, hands the can to me, and sits back down at the end of the couch. "If they went to stock blocks, stock oil, stock gasoline, and street available tires, you'd have a better race, and you'd have something about the cars the spectators could identify with."

"What about the changes they've made," I ask, "like wing restrictions and fuel limitations?"

"That's a start." He pauses for a swig of diet pop. "But they didn't go far enough. Look . . ." He moves up on the edge of the couch and makes an expansive sweep with his hands. "You've got a governing board made up of twenty-one car owners, drivers, and mechanics, all legislating their own interests. I mean, you ever see a committee of twenty-one that ever got anything done? No. What racing needs is a czar. Limit the fuel to two hundred gallons. You'd slow the cars down to one-seventy, and you'd have a better race. The spectators wouldn't know the difference. They can't tell if a car's going two hundred or one-fifty. You ever notice during qualifying, how they never cheer for the fastest cars till after they hear the time announced? They can't even see the drivers anymore, can't see their style or the way they drive, can't even see the numbers from the pits anymore."

"They killed my driver and my mechanic." There's a kind of forlorn intensity in his expression which, though he doesn't say it, pleads *Don't you understand?* Two years ago, the last year Granatelli entered the 500, Swede Savage, driving one of his cars, was leading the race after fifty-seven laps when he lost it coming out of turn four, crashed brutally into the inside retaining wall, and suffered burns from which he was to die a month later. A Speedway crash truck, rushing the wrong way up the pit lane, struck one of Granatelli's crewmen from behind and killed him instantly. Those in the pits, already horrified by the explosion and almost total disintegration of Savage's car, saw the mechanic's body tossed like a rag doll sixty feet in the air.

"Swede had just come out of the pits." Granatelli pauses and draws his hand across his forehead. "He'd taken on eighty gallons of fuel, and it was a completely different handling car than he'd been driving a lap earlier."

To understand why Savage lost control in that particular corner, it's necessary to speculate on what he must have been thinking just before it happened.

Bobby Unser, who had previously been Savage's teammate, had insulted him in print, had told the media that Savage couldn't drive, that he wouldn't even include him on a list of the hundred top drivers. Jerry Grant, who, like Unser, had been driving a white Olsonite Eagle, explained it to me: "The track was oily, really slippery in the groove, and Swedie was running high, making time by staying above the groove where the track was dry. I think what happened was that he saw a white car in his mirrors, and thought Unser was closing on him. I guess he didn't realize it was me and that Bobby was a lap down at that point. Anyway, he must have been thinking about what Bobby had said about him, 'cause he dove down into the groove to close the door on me. The car was heavy with full fuel tanks, and he was just going too fast to hold traction when he came down into the oil slick. It just must have been brain fade. For a second there his mind must have been somewhere else."

The race was stopped for an hour and fifteen minutes after the crash, restarted, and then called because of rain after 332 miles. Granatelli's other car, driven by Gordon Johncock, was declared the winner, but it was a sad victory for Andy.

The diet pop can is empty now, and he sets it on the table at the end of the couch. "Last year when we were coming in over the airport, my wife looked down from the plane and saw the Speedway. 'The thrill is gone, Andy'—that's what she said." He looks down at the floor and taps his chest. "It just isn't here anymore."

Dan Gurney is balancing on a small bicycle in the Jorgensen Steel garage in Gasoline Alley. I'm leaning against a workbench, and he seems to have me pinned in the corner with the flashing wheels of his unruly mount. He pulls up into an occasional wheelie, and I notice, with some relief, that the frame brace bar is thickly padded. "We can't forget we're in show business." His blue All-American Eagle rests unattended in the adjacent stall, race-ready and immaculate. "We're competing for the entertainment dollar with football, baseball, hockey, whatever's going on at the same time, and those other things are more solidly entrenched and better organized than we are. I think that's the most important thing about this sport to keep in mind, even more important than the rules."

Like Andy Granatelli, Gurney feels the rules, as they now stand, are stifling championship car racing. "I'd like to see us get more in line with the rest of the world, go with the Grand Prix formula and get a full international sanction so we could attract foreign drivers again." I recall Granatelli's complaint that Indy has become too homogeneous, that there are basically only two kinds of cars here anymore, the McLarens and Gurney's Eagles; and no more Jim Clarks, Graham Hills or Alberto Ascaris. "If we had foreign drivers here again," Gurney continues, "they'd have to build a third tier on the grandstands." He also wants to eliminate rules that favor turbochargers. "Turbocharged engines cut down the noise and the diversity of sounds, and frankly, that's a big part of the spectator appeal."

I remind him that the Indianapolis 500 is already far and away the largest spectator event in the world.

"I know that," he smiles earnestly, "but that doesn't mean it couldn't be bigger." A man from ABC interrupts to tell Gurney they'd like to film an interview for *Wide World of Sports.* Dan politely explains that he's busy right now, and that he'll get to it as soon as he's free. I feel slightly impertinent, holding up ABC, like the flea with an erection who floats down the river, hollering for the drawbridge to be raised, but Gurney takes one thing at a time. While they are talking I notice three Indiana State troopers with nightsticks, Sam Browne belts, and mirror-finished sunglasses in the bright alley beyond the garage door. I don't like to reinforce stereotypes, but they look polished, impersonal, and just plain mean, like licensed bullies. Their presence is an integral part of the atmosphere of this race, as is that of the rioters, sadists, muggers, streakers, fornicators, motorcycle gangs, Frisbee players, and drunks who occupy the infield like thirty armed tribes. The faint odor of tear gas is almost as common on race day as beer, popcorn, and hot rubber. The man from ABC will wait outside with his crew.

"Where was I?" Dan smiles in apology for the interruption. "Okay, another thing about turbochargers is that they make the race so technologically intricate that it works against younger, less experienced drivers, so that you've got the same crop of forty-year-olds out there leading the race every year. We don't have a farm system like they do for Formula I racing, so there isn't a big crop of young fast drivers coming up all the time, pushing the older guys the way it is in Europe."

Dan's wife, Evi, walks into the garage and talks to Pete Biro, Gurney's P.R. man. The attention of the pit gawkers shifts from Dan and the car to a truly beautiful woman.

"What makes this race unique is tradition and the ripples that it causes all around the world. But what I don't like about it, and I guess it's a part of the tradition, is the amount of time we have to spend here. It's like a whole month in a police state." I smile and notice the troopers are talking to Bobby Unser, who last week was made a special sheriff's deputy, had a police radio installed in his car, and, thirty minutes later, drove across town at unrecorded speeds to be the first on the scene to arrest three teenagers suspected of smoking marijuana behind an all-night market. "Maybe it's necessary for it to be that way in order to put this race on the way it is," Gurney says as he scratches his head and smiles wryly, "but we're all anxious to get back to the United States when it's over."

It's the morning of carburetion tests, three days before the race and the last opportunity any of the drivers will have to practice. I'm walking along Sixteenth Street toward the main gate to pick up my race-day credentials. I'm on a hard-packed dirt path just outside the chain-link fence that defines the official boundaries of the Speedway. Beyond the fence is a grass slope, a service vehicle road, then a rise, crested by the concrete retaining wall of the short chute between turns one and two. Above the wall is a catch fence woven of heavy steel cables, but the wall itself is low enough so that I can catch a glimpse of the wing, the windshield, and the driver's helmet as he drifts to the wall, setting up for turn two.

It's a hot morning. There aren't many spectators at the track today, and the traffic on Sixteenth Street is relatively light. There's a deceptively relaxed atmosphere as this day begins. Qualifying is over, and the tension seems to have subsided. I hear the Doppler effect of an engine, wound tight and rising down the front straight. It's getting louder, then seems to fade momentarily behind the grandstands on turn one. Suddenly it rises again, then, *zap*, one startling reverberation off the wall, one strobelike flash of sunlight off orange and white, and it's past, powering into turn two, the pitch rising and fading down the back straight. My stomach tightens. The sheer speed has given me a light punch in the solar plexus and a prickly sensation all over my skin, and I realize how much of that sense of speed is lost on television, where telephoto lenses and elevated camera angles convey the impression of a relaxed, almost slow-motion kind of game.

Television has come a long way in transcribing sports action on a field, court, or track to a circumscribed image composed of dots and spaces on a screen, capable of a multitude of points of view, but again, only one at a time. After several years of experimentation, they've learned to photograph tennis matches so that you can actually see both the players and the ball. The same can be said of football. With slow-motion instant replays you can have a more detailed, though still particularized, look at every bone-jarring nuance in your living room, bedroom, or bar than any ticket-buying, pennant-waving, crowd-braving fan in the stadium. But they haven't quite pulled it off with motor racing. They've got it down to covering every turn, accident, and pit stop, interviewing drivers and crews and explaining the particular challenges and characteristics of each track. But the one thing they haven't yet been able to adequately capture is speed.

Anyone who has gotten out and gone to a race after watching them on television is astounded at how fast the cars zoom past. Maybe part of it's being there with the ear-splitting engine noise, the smell of rubber, oil, and asphalt, but when you get out from behind the telephoto lens and see how long those straights really are and how little time it takes a racing car to cover the seemingly immense distance from turn four to turn one, it causes a certain physical sensation in the scalp and at the base of the spine that television viewers never know. "My God, they're going fast." It's no longer the sort of leisurely motorized game you've watched between commercials. You feel the ground shudder under your feet, and it feels a little threatening.

But maybe the camera is better than the naked eye at projecting the driver's experience of speed. Of course there are vibrations, sounds, and G force sensations that the driver alone can experience, but when a man lives long enough at 200 mph, 200 mph becomes the norm, and he slows it down. Through his eyes, as long as he remains in control, things don't happen with the frightening rapidity with which we perceive them. For him, the track isn't a chaotic blur, but a calmly perceived series of sensations; now, now, now, and now. He fixes on nothing and is therefore not startled by the brevity of his relationship with any object in the field of his experience. It's a kind of Zen by default in which survival depends upon nonattachment and single-mindedness, a gestalt from which no element can be removed and examined.

Most of the drivers would like to get on with it. The field is set, but tradition dictates the weeklong waiting game between the end of qualifying and race day. Today's carburetion test is the only chance they'll have to get back on the track until they line up for the parade lap preceding the race. Today they are given three hours to get in a little more practice, make a last-minute check of carburetion and tires, experience how the car will handle on race day with a full fuel load, and one hour to practice pit stops.

Twenty years ago a forty-five second pit stop to refuel and change tires would have been considered highly efficient, but today it would be a disaster, costing the driver almost a lap and probably putting him out of contention. The Gatorade McLaren team pulls Johnny Rutherford's car back up the pit lane, then pushes it in to simulate a pit stop. Each member of the crew is waiting in his assigned position, tires, jacks, impact wrenches, refueling hoses ready. For Rutherford it means practice in stopping exactly on his marks. During the race he'll be coming down the pit lane at almost 100 mph and must sight his crew and bring the car to a stop precisely at the spot where each crew member can do his job without having to change position. Tyler Alexander, the crew chief, stands in the pit lane to mark the point where the nose of the car should come to rest. Rutherford stops exactly on the mark, and five men go to work. The refueling and vent nozzles are inserted, impact wrenches twist off the right-hand hub nuts. A jack instantly lifts the right side of the car, two wheels are removed and replaced with another set, the jack is removed, and the tires come back to the pavement. The impact wrenches blast again, the refueling nozzles are removed, the front-tire man jumps out of the way, whipping his airhose clear of the car. I duck to avoid a mechanic as he hurtles over the wall. Only five men are allowed in the pit during a stop, while a sixth man offers Rutherford a cup of water at the end of a rod extended from behind the pit wall. Rutherford never takes his eyes off Alexander. Three crew members fall in behind the car, Alexander waves him off, and the car is pushed back into the pit lane. Teddy Mayer clicks his digital stopwatch: 12.5 seconds from the instant the car stopped until the wheels are rolling again.

Normally, most of the pit stops will be for fuel only. The crew will check the right-side tires and be prepared to change them if necessary. In Jerry Grant's pit, they've made five practice stops with tire changes and simulated refueling, the same procedure again and again until it's become mechanical routine. A sixth time, Grant coasts to a stop, but now he pulls a surprise and points to the left front tire, a frantic series of stabs with his index finger. The front man scurries around to the other side of the car and undoes the nut while the jack man moves to jack up the left side. When the tire man has changed the tire and secured the nut, he scrambles back to the right side of the car and gives Grant the all-clear signal. When the practice stop is completed, Grant motions the front-tire man over to confer with him. They've handled the unexpected tire change flawlessly and without hesitation, but Grant figures it has taken the tire changer an extra second or two to get back to the right front corner of the car to give his all-clear signal. The tire man kneels by the cockpit while Grant tells him to give the signal from the left side of the car in case they have to change the left-front tire.

Adrenaline will be running freely when the actual pit stops are made, and the tension can be felt in this last bit of practice before race day. The driver will be sitting with the car in gear, the engine running and the clutch in, and it's crucial that he has only one crewman to look to for his signals, that there are no misunderstandings. I remember seeing films of Parnelli Jones rolling on the pavement in invisible alcohol flames after a botched pit stop. Thinking he'd been given the all clear, he'd pulled away from his pit with the fuel hose still connected, rupturing the tank, eliminating himself from the race, sustaining some painful burns, and causing a potentially dangerous situation in the entire pit and front straight grandstand area.

I look up and down the row of refueling tanks mounted on scaffolds above the pit wall and realize that on race day I'd rather be anywhere else on the track. One 240-gallon tank of highly combustible methanol fuel for each of the thirty-three cars, and it would take only one careless act, one car out of control in the pit lane, to cause a chain reaction that could endanger hundreds of lives. "I'm surprised something like that's never happened," one driver confides. "I feel a whole lot safer out on the track than I do during a pit stop. It's not just the time lost from the race; I'm really anxious to get away from all that fuel and confusion."

Tradition dominates every aspect of Indianapolis, and not only in a ceremonial sense. There is a pervading attitude among those in authority that there is a *right* way of doing things, and that way has acquired its mantle of rectitude by virtue of the fact that "it *is* the way we do it." Actually, it may be the only way they are able to run this race, dealing with a group of men as egocentric and opinionated as racing drivers. "I don't know" is a statement seldom heard. Whichever aspect of race procedure is in question, each of them will not only have an answer, he will have *the* answer, and a dictator behind the badge of a Chief Steward is required.

Refueling tanks and the penalty for jacking to get the last bit of fuel from them is the first order of business at the driver's and crew chiefs meeting following pit practice. It's a Turkish bath. The main concourse below the tower is packed with rows of folding chairs and sealed off to the public as well as to ventilation by Speedway guards. Spectators press their faces against the glass doors, blocking the reflections of the afternoon sunlight with their cupped hands. From inside the meeting room, they look like visitors to an aquarium. Tom Binford, the Chief Steward, calls the meeting to order. His situation is similar to that of the president of the United States at a news conference, both man on the spot and the ultimate authority.

With each car limited to 280 gallons for the race, fuel and its handling become a controversial issue. Even if a car could mechanically withstand being driven flat out for the entire five hundred miles, with a consumption rate of between 1.2 and 1.4 miles per gallon, it would eliminate itself by running out of fuel in the process. Most of the teams, particularly those of the front-runners, will be depending on a certain amount of the race being run under yellow-light conditions in order to be able to stretch their allotted fuel over the distance. Binford settles the refueling controversy as soon as the meeting has been called to order. Refueling tanks may be mounted at an incline of eleven degrees. Pit stewards will check the angle of incline, and any tanks exceeding this angle or any tanks jacked during the race will be cause for disqualification. This will be the most definite ruling made during the entire meeting. Almost all other aspects of race procedure seem to be open to a certain variance of interpretation, and Binford generally chooses to let the penalties for infractions remain vague.

An argument over the use of pacer lights for regulating speed in a yellow-light situation occupies almost half the meeting time. A. J. Foyt, Bobby Unser, and Mario Andretti argue that while the pacer lights were a good idea, they just don't seem to work. They would prefer the use of the pace car to control speed in an emergency situation even though it would allow the field to close its distance on the leaders.

"The pacer lights stay," Binford states flatly.

"Well, hell," Foyt is on his feet, "those lights screwed up the other day during practice. They got sequenced at over two hundred miles an hour, and I had to scurry the hell outta myself try'n to keep up with 'em." Everyone but Binford laughs.

Grant King, a car builder and crew chief, argues that since most of the drivers would prefer the pace car, why not reinstate it and forget the light system.

Binford says, "Because the regulations call for the pacer lights."

King replies, "But none of these rules are irrevocable."

Binford fires back, "I know that, but the Speedway management prefers the lights." End of controversy.

Bobby Unser is up again, contending that since name drivers like "me and Al and A. J. and Mario are better known and get watched closer than these other guys, we get unfairly penalized for yellow light infractions."

"I guess that's the price of fame." Binford seems unmoved.

Someone raises the question of onboard fuel capacity, covertly referring to the controversy stemming from George Bignotti's insinuations that Foyt had carried an extra five-gallon fuel tank somewhere in his car during the California 500. Binford appears to have been expecting this one and states that they have already made plans to inspect the fuel capacity of the first ten finishers.

Grant King wants to know what the penalty will be for having too many men over the wall during a pit stop. Binford takes a deep breath and wipes his forehead. "Any crew with more than five men over the wall will be penalized accordingly."

"Well I want to know exactly what that penalty's going to be," King insists, "because if it's only gonna be a fifty-dollar fine, I'm going to have fifteen men over that wall."

Binford assures him that it will be more than a fifty-dollar fine. He wipes his forehead again.

Jerry Grant sips his Fresca. James Garner whispers to Al Unser and Mario Andretti, and all three smile knowingly.

Foyt stands up again, his arms bulging from his short-sleeved sport shirt. He looks impatient and impressive. He always looks impatient and impressive, on or off the track. Several nights ago, I watched him make his entrance in the Speedway Motel dining room. He seated his wife and walked over to another table to talk with four men, aware that every eye was on him. It was almost as if a tiger had wandered into the room, and while nobody wanted to make a scene about it, nobody wanted to lose track of where he was. Foyt now asks Binford whether or not Goodyear technicians will be allowed over the wall to check tires during pit stops.

Binford replies, "No, not if they make the total more than five."

"Well hell, you talk about safety, those Goodyear people are a hell of a lot better judges of whether a tire needs changing than any of these mechanics."

Binford concedes the point. Tire technicians will be allowed. But that doesn't sit well with Billy Vukovich. "But what if I don't have any Goodyear men in my pit? Then it isn't fair."

"You start runnin' out there in front"—Foyt twists the knife—"and you'll have so many of 'em you'll be wantin' to trade 'em off." A wave of laughter spreads through the meeting and then dies away uncomfortably. Salt Walther asks what the penalty will be for improving your position prior to crossing the starting line. I can see the black glove of his left hand, the full use of which he lost in a crash at the start of the 1973 race, a crash initiated by a charging car that bumped him into the outside retaining wall. It's an important question, and a pointed one coming from Walther. Binford states that anyone flagrantly charging before the starting line will be penalized one lap. He goes on to urge everyone not to really start racing until they've come out of turn two and started down the back straight.

"Look," he pleads, "for most of us, our livelihoods and our careers are centered around this one race, and it'd be stupid and pointless to spoil it by getting overanxious at the start of it."

The meeting adjourns with Binford asking several of the name drivers to stay for a briefing of the rookies. At speeds well over 200 mph, the "old boy-new boy" system is a vital part of the Indy tradition. There's a big show coming up in three days, the biggest one in sports, and it has to be made absolutely clear to the rookies how they are expected to play their parts.

• • •

It's the evening before the race, and Speedway, Indiana, has become a refugee camp. Every field and vacant lot within miles is packed with trailers, tents, motor homes, sweating bodies, piles of empty beer cans, and backyard barbecues. Refugee camps are better organized. These are the Mongol hordes, the Huns awaiting race day to storm the gates of Rome. Campfires glow. I'm certain I can hear the throbbing of tribal drums, unintelligible chanting. Police sirens are as commonplace as the random explosions of cherry bombs. A prison bus with heavily wire-meshed windows speeds past in a clusteral escort of flashing lights. There will be a total eclipse of the moon tonight, and it seems to hype the lunacy. Except for a few nervous mechanics and staff personnel, the Speedway is empty and quiet. From a helicopter it would look like a black oval, a void in a galaxy of fire and chaos.

The motel room I'm sharing with Bob Jones faces Sixteenth Street and is less than one hundred feet from an entrance to the track. It's a convenient bivouac, but only a self-hypnotist could sleep here. During the evening several gaggles of girls from tent city have wandered in to use our bathroom. Invariably their introductory line is, "I know it's a terrible imposition, but this is an emergency."

This one sits down and has a cigarette while her companion uses the plumbing. I offer her a drink, and Jones interrogates her. She's from Indianapolis and claims she's twenty-one, though sixteen seems more likely. When she laughs, she snorts through her sinuses and she laughs at almost everything she says. "You guys got any spare change?" She laughs at this too.

"No, none that's spare."

"You're selfish."

Jones asks her if she left a dime in the bathroom. "Oh, that," she says. "But I left something else." She finds this funny too. Jones and I are infected by her laughter and laugh ourselves because there's nothing to laugh at.

"What do you think about the race?" It's a rhetorical question.

"What race?" she snorts again and we all laugh.

I nod over my shoulder in the direction of the Speedway. She covers her lips with her cupped hand and snorts a mouthful of vodka and tonic through her fingers. "I don't even know who's racing."

I ask her why she's here, and she says it's for the crowd in the camp across the street. "It's the most exciting thing that happens all year. Ya live in Indianapolis, this is like Christmas, it's what ya wait for." I was reminded of all the middle-aged, middle-class women I'd seen cruising the bar at the Holiday Inn, doctors' lawyers' and salesmen's wives, race groupies for whom the race means only a chance to meet a stranger, a mechanic, a tire buster, or a P.R. man, maybe from far-off exotic California. There were also 150,000 fans who would fill the infield, most of whom, by midafternoon, would have forgotten why they'd come there in the first place.

Now the other girl has finished in the bathroom. "Ya know, we don't have to go," the snort queen offers. "I mean we could stay here."

"You could, but you can't." I hear the crackle of radios from the police cruisers along the street and encourage them to go back to tent city.

Although the gates won't open until 5:00 A.M., the traffic starts stacking up shortly after midnight. I close the door, turn out the lights, and lie awake with the sirens, honking horns, and motorcycle engines, and the anticipation of the race. I wonder how well the drivers are sleeping, or if they are.

I realize I must have finally fallen asleep, because I'm awakened at 6:30 by an immense pounding on the door. I swing my feet to the floor and sit for a minute trying to remember where I am and to determine whether or not I'd been dreaming. I open the door on the long shadow of early morning light. The traffic is still solid and the police radios are still crackling unintelligible messages. I've almost forgotten why I opened the door when someone grabs my right hand. "Hi, I'm Dayton Spengler. It's a beautiful day, and it's time for you boys to get up and go to work." A puffy, almost featureless, florid face, little pig eyes squinting out from under the visor of a white yachting cap. "You boys do a good job now."

"Thank you." I turn and close the door. Jones is still snoring. *Maybe it's a special wake-up service the motel has for the race day,* I thought. I'd promised Heinz Kluetmeier that I'd cover turn two with one of his motor-drive Nikons, so it did make sense. I did have a job to do. I look at the camera on top of the dresser and feel a momentary apprehension that I've already missed something important. I have barely settled back onto the sheets when the pounding resumes.

"Hi!" My hand is being pumped again. "You remember me. I'm Dayton Spengler."

"Sure." It's true, I do remember him.

"Say, this lady's kinda sick and I wonder if she could use your room to lie down a little while." I peer around the doorjamb in the direction he indicates, to a blonde lady with a beehive hairdo who seems bored and impatient. She is pretending to be interested in the traffic on Sixteenth Street and refuses to acknowledge either Dayton or me.

"Well, gee." I stumble for a moment, trying to figure out what I'll do while she is using my room and how I'll explain it to Jones. After all, Jones doesn't even know Dayton Spengler. Then Jones himself helps me out.

"No." I look over my shoulder and see the whites of his eyes glowing through the dark cave of the room. They don't look the least bit sympathetic toward Dayton's cause.

"No," I say.

"Well, that's okay." My hand is being pumped again. "You boys have a good day."

I close the door and look at Jones. He is laughing. "That's Indy," he says. "There's your story."

At nine o'clock, two hours before race time, I head over to the track. I've been given a pass to shoot photographs from the balcony of the Penske suite overlooking turn two. It's a precarious, though very pleasant, setup. Drinks, snacks, and air conditioning will be available a few steps away, and the view of the short chute, turn two, and the back straight is excellent, though I'll be sitting less than twenty feet from the edge of the track at the point where the cars begin to exit the turn. I'd felt a little exposed there, watching qualifying, feeling the vibration and heat from the passing cars and gauging the strength of the cables reinforcing the wire fence that was all that separated me from the track. I remind myself now that it is only steel cables that hold up the Golden Gate Bridge, and that if they do fail, anything that happens will happen so fast that I won't have time to torment myself trying to escape.

On the telephone this morning my nine-year-old son asked me to get the autograph of the winner. "It's not likely I'll be able to get close to him after the race," I told him. "Why don't you just pick a driver whose autograph you'd like and I'll get that." There was a long silence at the other end of the line while he searched for a name, then a tentative "Is Bobby Unser there?" I pull a small photograph from the Jorgensen Eagle press kit, slip it between the pages of a program to keep it from getting bent, and set off for the pits with a pre-race mission.

A few steps from the door of my room I can feel the juices begin to ooze from my skin and I expect to deliquesce like a maple-sugar doll. In the pedestrian tunnel that crosses under the track I fall in with a half-dozen slightly flaccid, halter-topped high school girls. They have already begun to pink a bit on the back shoulders and somehow smell like school lunch boxes, the redolence of overripe bananas. I am now part of the great event, a drone filing into the hive, *the people, yes,* and so goddamn many of them, hippies, rednecks, straights, and greasers. We are passed by a seemingly endless line of Buick convertibles carrying celebrities and race queens. I don't recognize any of the celebrities, though we scatter before them like peasants before the coaches of the king. At least a dozen bands are playing, and the atmosphere is already so bizarre that I half expect to see a guillotine in the next parting of the crowd. I'm concentrating on my own pace, trying to maintain some identity, trying not to fall in step with the martial music of whichever band is dominating the moment. But the crowd is moving in time, and I must move with it or be trampled. The Golden Girl of the Purdue Band is attracting all the photographers, who a moment before had been three-deep around A. J. Foyt as he checked over his safety harness and every detail in the cockpit of his Gilmore

Coyote. Most of the drivers are staying in their garages, avoiding the crowds and the heat as long as they can. The pit lane looks like Fifth Avenue on Easter Sunday, two ill-defined columns of aimless strollers with pit badges in lieu of bonnets, there to see and to be seen.

The pit crowd is noticeably better groomed than those in the infield, crews in bright-colored uniforms; photographers in bush jackets under tiers of Nikons; and car owners, sponsors, and officials in seersucker suits. I feel a little underdressed in my Levi's and short-sleeved cotton shirt. I decide it's time to head across the infield toward the suites. I cut through Gasoline Alley and stop by Gurney's garage to get Bobby Unser's autograph. There doesn't seem to be a great deal of tension in the garage. It's an hour until race time and Unser is still dressed in blue cotton trousers and a short-sleeved shirt. He gladly signs my photograph and seems relaxed, as if there were nothing special he had to do. Then it occurs to me that there isn't anything special he has to do. If you are a professional racing driver, driving races is what you do, and he's done it almost every week for the last twenty-six years. Indianapolis may be the biggest race around, but still, a race is a race. I thank him for the autograph and remember not to wish him good luck. There are so many uncontrollable variables in racing that drivers tend to be superstitious, and being wished good luck is one curse they'd rather do without. I pass Jerry Grant's garage and think of stopping to wish him good luck without saying it, but the doors are closed and I figure he'd rather be alone. I remember that when I was driving I never really had anything to say to anyone before a race. Any conversation that occurred was like that at a Christian Science funeral, about anything but the business at hand.

A few Frisbees are being tossed on the infield golf course, a few couples are making love in the sand traps, and the sweet aroma of marijuana hangs in the breezeless air.

At the Penske suite, the chairman of the bank whose travelers' checks co-sponsor the Penske McLaren driven by Tom Sneva extends himself to make me feel welcome, points out the bar and buffet, tells me not to hesitate to ask for whatever I need. He even suggests that I might be able to bribe the maintenance man to show me how to get up on the roof. "Anything we can do for you, anything at all, just sing out and it'll be done." A hearty clap on the shoulder. His graciousness seems quite genuine, though I am beginning to realize that my motor-driven Nikon and *Sports Illustrated* nametag represent some fairly heavy credentials. I stake out a seat on the corner of the balcony where no one will be moving between my lens and the track, fix myself a tonic water, and check my focus and exposure. There are no rednecks or hippies here in the suites, a madras and La Coste crowd, collegians of the fifties with a few crow's-feet and gray hairs, not surprisingly, the kind of people one would associate with Roger Penske, precise and successful.

The pre-race ceremonies have begun, the celebrities have been driven around the track, Peter DePaolo, winner of the 1925 500, has taken a lap in the Miller that won the race in 1930, the Speedway has been presented with a plaque designating it as a national historic landmark, and the final lines of the invocation drift across the infield, ". . . with a hand over the heart, a prayer in the soul, and brains in the head." Now everything seems to accelerate, including four hundred thousand pulse rates. Jim Nabors mouths every word of "Back Home Again in Indiana," a thousand helium-filled balloons are released, and Tony Hulman takes the microphone. "Gentlemen, start your *in*juns." The parade and pace laps come off without incident. Some of the drivers wave or salute as they pass the suites of their sponsors. I am reminded of knights dipping their lances to the ladies whose favors they wore. The ritual hasn't changed, only become more commercial. I know the drivers are very calm now. For them the pre-race tension is over and they are locked into that impenetrable concentration that comes the moment they are strapped into the car. As they approach the starting line, everyone becomes very quiet, probably the one moment when not one of the nearly half-million people in this arena has anything to say. The engine noise accelerates, a series of bombs explode in the air, and a great cheer goes up from the crowd. The announcer's voice booms, "And the fifty-ninth Indianapolis 500-Mile Race is under way, the greatest spectacle in racing."

After the start and the excitement of the initial laps, the race, for most of the spectators, diminishes to a monotonous stream of almost indistinguishable cars and anonymous drivers flowing by at over 200 mph. I don't mean that it isn't still exciting. The noise itself is enough to keep the adrenaline pumped up, but you have to rely on the track announcer to understand what's happening. It's very much the way it was all those years I listened to it on the radio, but with a lot of special effects thrown in. I'm aware that Johncock, who had jumped into a commanding lead at the start, has dropped out. It's a five-hundred-mile race. Running away with the early laps may please the crowd and momentarily put a driver in the limelight, but the chances are he'll be all but forgotten when the checkered flag falls. Foyt and Rutherford are swapping the lead now, though I'm seldom certain who has it at any given moment. As the cars scream out of turn two it all seems effortless, though they're fighting the limit of adhesion. They pass so close it almost seems I could touch them. In twos and threes, the engines surge down the back straight like aircraft engines out of sync.

There's a yellow light and most of the cars head for the pits. For a full ten seconds no cars pass, and the silence is startling. I'm keeping my camera ready, watching what's coming out of turn two and trying to answer the questions of the distractingly pretty woman who has taken the seat next to me. Our conversation is disjointed, broken sentences sequenced in the brief intervals between passing cars. Occasionally a whiff of her perfume mingles with and subsumes the perspiration and burning rubber. She's a young Grace Kelly type from somewhere in Pennsylvania. It's difficult to hear, let alone remember, details in these circumstances. She seems unaffected by the heat, which at the moment is causing large drops of sweat to trickle over my ribs. They tickle, and I know if I touch them they'll show through my shirt. I want to appear to be as cool as she is. I lean closer for her next question, but not too close. At the same time I'm reminding myself to keep my lens and my attention on turn two.

Several times I stand up to watch some passing action down the back straight. Tom Sneva is running a highly respectable fifth and is still very much in contention. He pulls to the inside to lap several slower cars and the precision of his judgment keeps me standing. It seems he won't have time to get past them and back into the groove to set up for turn three, and I realize that at that point he's traveling at about 220 mph. He's deep, almost too deep, but in the last few feet, he cuts back to the outside, clear of the traffic and right in the groove. Then I remember how it always looks more impressive from the outside than it does from the driver's seat. Once at Mosport, during practice for the Canadian Grand Prix, I walked over to watch at turn one while my car was being worked on. I was frightened and astounded at how ragged and perilous it seemed, the cars skidding and vibrating through the reverse camber downhill turn. *Jesus, that's scary,* I thought. *How can they do it?* Then a half hour later I went and qualified on the pole for the G. T. Race. I didn't know how to do it. I just did it.

More laps, more questions, more fragmented answers: "They're limited to"—two cars scream through the turn, nose to tail, and I wait for the noise to fade—"280 gallons, which means that"—another car passes and I can feel the heat from its exhaust "at the mileage they're getting that they"—this time we're interrupted by the track announcer calling attention to Wally Dallenbach, who started in twenty-first position and is now moving up toward the lead at an alarming rate—"they couldn't finish the race if they didn't do at least"—another car—"a few laps under the yellow."

I've been watching Dallenbach. His engine sounds stronger, higher pitched and wound tighter than the other cars, and another strange thing is that though he's gobbling up the field, his line through the corners isn't following the groove. He's running through the middle of turn two each time he passes, not drifting wide and using the whole track the way other cars do when they're turning hot laps. Each time he passes, it seems he's operating on a separate principle of physics, as if the laws governing centrifugal force have been suspended for him. Later I would hear rumbling that he had a small tank of nitrous oxide (laughing gas) that was being injected directly into the cylinders, giving him an extra 150 horsepower with no increase in boost, and that his unorthodox line was to compensate for the extra sensitivity under his right foot. It occurred to me that if that were true, it might be possible that the nitrous oxide was being injected directly into Dallenbach and that his extra speed was the result of an altered consciousness. Whatever the facts, Dallenbach was laughing on the sixtieth lap when he passed Foyt and went on to open up a twenty-two-second lead.

One hundred and twenty-six laps and almost two hours of racing. Senses are beginning to numb and the stream of cars is beginning to have a hypnotic effect on the afternoon. I have a mild headache, my throat's getting sore, and fortunately, or unfortunately, Grace Kelly is asking fewer questions. The tension begins to dissolve into monotony. I'm less attentive with my lens and have pretty well determined that I won't have to shoot any action on this turn today. Somebody taps me on the shoulder and as I turn to my right, I hear a scream from the crowd, followed by a loud, dull thud. I turn back to my left and there, not forty feet away, and twenty feet in the air, just about eye level, is the top of Tom Sneva's helmet. Flames have engulfed the rear half of his car and it's cartwheeling horizontally along the wire-retaining fence. I have a stop-action image, looking at the car as if from above as it hurtles toward me, but not on film. I've forgotten about my camera. For an instant I am certain I'm witnessing a man's death and that it will also be my own. Things have gone too smoothly, the atmosphere has been deceptively benign, and it now seems this track has demanded another catastrophe. I leap over the now vacant chair to my right, and as I turn toward the suite, I see the reflection of the flames in the sliding glass doors and feel the heat sweep across my back. The instant of danger has passed and I turn back toward the track just in time to see the disembodied engine tumble by in a ball of flame. Debris fills the air like a flight of sand grouse. The Nikon takes over, zipping off exposures, one last somersault before the car comes to rest, right side up and on fire. It really doesn't resemble a car anymore, just a burning tub of metal, not thirty feet away, a driver's helmet protruding from the flames. The original fire had been from burning oil, but now the methanol has ignited and can be seen only as intense heat waves blurring the edges of the wreckage.

The fire marshall is herding everyone off the balconies and into the suite. He sees my camera and press badge and lets me stay, though I've finished the roll and have to change film. At this point, I'm certain Sneva is dead. It's the most brutal, spectacular, and horrifying crash I've ever seen, and I've seen at least a dozen that were fatal. The scene in the suite couldn't be more macabre or more comic. All these people know Sneva in some capacity. Several of them are sponsors of his car, and he's crashed and apparently been annihilated right in their laps. Sneva's wife has gone into hysterics and has been hustled out to the balcony overlooking the golf course on the far side of the building. Grace Kelly, who had been fixing a drink at the time, has fallen backward into a tray of chocolate brownies. The chairman of the bank, in nervous relief, tells me how delighted he is that I've been able to get some good pictures. Though I'm sure it isn't his intention, it sounds as if, in his role as gracious host, he has arranged the crash for my photographic convenience. Everyone looks sick to their stomach, and I am changing film.

"Did you get it?" I look up into the wide eyes of a young executive type.

"Yeah, I think so."

"Did you get Mrs. Sneva?"

"What?" I'm certain I've misunderstood.

"Did you get pictures of Mrs. Sneva?"

I choke on my own saliva and shake my head. "I didn't hear that. No."

"Good for you," he says earnestly, "good for you."

The fire marshall lets me back out on the balcony to photograph the work of the fire crew. There are clouds of chemical vapors, flashing lights, scattered detritus, and crash crews diverting traffic to the grass verge inside the track. Then I see something that, for a moment, I am certain is an illusion. Sneva moves. His helmet is wiggling back and forth and he's put his arms down on the fuselage. He's trying to push himself up and out of the cockpit, but he appears to be stuck. Another driver has abandoned his car and is trying to help the emergency crew get Sneva out of the wreckage. The struggle goes on for several minutes, till they finally free him, dragging him up and out by his armpits. Not only is he alive, but he walks, with help, to the waiting ambulance, lies down on the stretcher, and is taken to the infield hospital. Still, I'm not confident he'll recover. I remember how two years ago Swede Savage rode into the infield hospital sitting up, but died of his injuries a month later.

The emergency crew finishes clearing the debris, and I sit down to try and sort out what has happened. It is at that moment that I realize that two weeks ago to the hour, I had been sitting on this balcony interviewing Tom Sneva, the day after he had qualified. He told me he had been a junior high school principal in Lamont, Washington, and had raced as a hobby until the racing began to be more profitable and more time-consuming than teaching. He was enthusiastic, boyish, and articulate, and appeared to regard Roger Penske with almost the same reverence that a University of Alabama quarterback might hold for Bear Bryant. "We'd like to be racing more than just the Championship Trail," he tells me, "but Roger's got a lot invested in this series, and he doesn't want to take any chances." He reminded me how the previous year Penske had lost his driver in midseason when Gary Bettenhausen was seriously injured in a minor dirt-track race in Syracuse. I asked him about his relationship with the established superstars, like Foyt and Unser. "That's a funny thing," he said. There was surprise in his voice, as if he were only discovering the irony as he told me about it. "I guess they just thought of us as another kid who wanted to be a racing driver. Anyway, they barely paid any attention to us, hardly said hello, until we began to become a threat to them." I asked him why he referred to himself in the plural, and he said it was a habit. "It's a team effort. If we win I don't want to take all the credit, and if we lose I don't want all the blame." I'm sure this *organization man* attitude is largely the result of driving for a no-nonsense, quasi-military business organization like Penske's, but there also seems to be a certain element of the affectionate plurality with which a show jumper will refer to himself and his horse as one being. "Anyway," Sneva continued, "when we started showing them something, that indifference seemed to change; not that they got friendly or anything, but they knew we were there."

I had first become aware of Sneva while watching a television broadcast of the Phoenix 150 several years ago. I remembered having been quite impressed watching this then unknown driver pass Foyt to take the lead. As we sat there that overcast afternoon, he told me the story. "Foyt was having a little momentary problem with his car. He bobbled, and I shot by him like he was standing still. It was no big deal. He was having trouble for a second, and I took advantage of it and got by. But they played it up big on television, as if I'd really pulled something off. Anyway, Foyt wasn't upset about it after the race but later, when people, friends of his who'd watched it on TV, razzed him about it, 'Boy, that Sneva kid really blew you off, didn't he?' he began to get pissed. Then one day he walked up to me in the garage—I mean it was just like something out of the movies—and told me that I'd gotten away with it once, but that if I tried anything like it again, he could bump me right out of the park. It was unbelievable."

The ABC slow-motion replays show Sneva passing Eldon Rasmussen and running just ahead of Foyt in the short chute between turns one and two. Sneva's right rear tire touches Rasmussen's left front, and Sneva finds himself upside down and airborne, heading for the outside wall at almost two hundred miles an hour. Sneva's car slams into the wall tail first, the wing, engine, and rear wheels separating, in a protracted dance with the flames and scattering fragments of metal and fiberglass; the remains of the car cartwheel three times along the wall, then somersault three times down the asphalt to come to rest, on fire, in the middle of the track. It's the kind of accident usually associated with dirt tracks at less than half these speeds.

Three weeks later, Sneva is recovering from his burns and practicing to qualify for the 500 at Pocono when I talk to him on the telephone. "It was like a dream," he tells me. "We watched the TV replays and it looked like it was all happening to somebody else. We passed Rasmussen in the first turn and thought we were by him in turn two. We glanced in the mirrors and he wasn't there; he was right beside us and we saw that the wheels were going to touch. From there on it was as if we were dreaming, as if we were lying in bed dreaming we were flying through the air upside down. After we first made contact with the wall, we don't remember anything till we woke up in the track hospital and wondered how the car was." I ask him how it's going at Pocono and he tells me that the first day out he was pretty cautious. "The second day we started running hard through the corners, but I noticed that we still weren't trying to prove anything in traffic. It takes a little while," he concludes. "It makes you realize you really could get hurt doing this kind of thing."

After Sneva's crash, the 500 begins an anticlimactic slide toward a rain-shortened conclusion. Dallenbach, who has maintained his lead, drops out thirty-six laps later, claiming his air intakes have gotten clogged with litter from the wreckage, causing him to burn a piston. Some drivers have other theories about what caused the burned piston, but it is a sad end to what had been one of the most spectacular, come-from-behind drives in the history of the race.

The sky darkens radically, the wind begins to whip up hot dog wrappers and dust devils in the infield, and within minutes the 500 has been transformed into a hydroplane race. The checkered and red flags appear simultaneously and cars spume rooster tails, trying to make the start-finish line. There are multiple and relatively harmless spins and crashes, cars sliding, looping lazily down the straights, up the pit lane, and through the corners. It is Bobby Unser's good fortune to be leading when the sky splits open, and in a delicate ballet with his now tractionless tires, he creeps toward the start-finish line. There are twenty-six more laps that will never be run and there will be seemingly endless theories and arguments by and for Rutherford and Foyt that had the race run its full course, they would have certainly won. It is the luck of the draw. It's made heroes and corpses without discretion.

Back in my motel room, I fix myself a drink and watch the rain pour down on the policemen channeling the postrace traffic on Sixteenth Street. I notice that the hair on the back of my arms has been singed; it balls and crumbles off like melted plastic. This whole month in

Indianapolis seems like an abruptly ended dream. Two weeks from now, most of these drivers will be racing at Milwaukee, and it won't much matter who won today. The race has been important only because 400,000 paying spectators and millions more by their radios and TV sets have, by agreement, made it so. But now it is all over and another "agreement" is in force. The following day's sports section will carry the news that the Golden State Warriors have beaten the Washington Bullets for the National Basketball Association championship, and the cover of *Sports Illustrated* will carry a picture of Billy Martin, "Baseball's Fiery Genius." I have an autographed picture of the winner for my son, and I'm beginning to get drunk.

The next morning there's a photograph of Sneva's crash on the front page of the *Indianapolis Star*, and I recognize my own figure, fleeing ignominiously from the flames. On my way to the airport I drive past the Speedway, and all I can see is litter, two feet deep, in every tunnel, passageway, and concourse, more than six million pounds of it. I stop for a red light and notice one more thing: the corpse of a huge tomcat lying next to the chain-link fence. Someone has considerately propped its head up on a crushed beer can and crossed its paws in repose. There's my story, I think. After twenty-five years of listening and dreaming, I've seen my first Indianapolis 500, and this is the one picture that will stick. Another great event chronicled in trash, another discarded container.

from Riding the Demon
by Peter Chilson

Peter Chilson (born 1961) went to Niger with the Peace Corps during the 1980s. He was terrified and fascinated by the standard mode of travel, makeshift vehicles-for-hire called bush taxis. Chilson returned to Niger in 1992 to study bush taxi culture.

In northern Nigeria, I saw a Peugeot station wagon and a petrol tanker immersed in fire and smoke. The tanker lay on its side, hidden behind gushing clouds of bright orange and black—a gasoline fire. Clouds as big as Volkswagens shot up in dense stacks while the fire expanded into the fields of corn and millet on both sides of the road like slowly spreading wings.

I remember the sound of fire and smoke whispering under a barely audible, stuttering thunder, as if a distant storm were passing. The scene shocked the eyes but soothed the ears. I could not immediately see the demolished Peugeot for the inferno. And I recall realizing that I too had just been riding in a Peugeot station wagon, a bush taxi headed north to the city of Kaduna, where I would get a car to Niger.

I stood on the road beside our car, twenty yards from the fire, and watched as orange flashes at the base of the wreck mushroomed and dissolved in smoke that pushed almost straight up hundreds of feet, where stronger winds carried it south. I could feel the fire's pulse, a hot and warm probing in the breezeless air. Settling ash from the burning fields turned my white T-shirt splotchy gray and smeared my face, neck, and arms. Even without the heat from the fire, the temperature must have been near one hundred degrees. People milled about, dozens at first, and later hundreds, all road travelers.

A man told me the accident had happened twenty minutes earlier. No survivors. The tanker crashed in the pocket of a long curve—made blind by high, thorny prosopis bushes hugging the shoulder—into a bush taxi crowded with people. The impact had turned the Peugeot to paste and scattered it in pieces. A few yards away, a tan chunk of car door lay in a ditch with its window frame intact; nearby, a lump of bloody clothing. A lot more of this sort of thing lay around, more than enough for me. Most of the bodies, the man said, were on the other side of the wreck.

I started to back away and bumped into a small boy, a passenger from another car. Transfixed by the fire, he did not look at me but instinctively clutched at my trousers, standing behind me as if for protection. I was dimly aware of other people, and later realized that very few were watching the wreck as I was. A woman picked up the boy and carried him off the road. More vehicles pulled up, forming a long line. With my eyes on the wreckage, I retreated with slow backward steps, captivated by the feeling that I was witnessing something alive and horrible. A demon feast.

Then I turned away, numbed, and headed for the shade of a tree to try and collect myself. Sitting down, I drew my knees against my chest and put my face against them, hands clasped tightly behind my head, trying to blot out sight and sound. Trying to think.

It was late morning of a day in March 1993. I had been on the road since October. Before dawn, in the city of Ibadan, southern Nigeria, I had bought the last available seat in a white Peugeot station wagon, the four-cylinder model known as a 504. It was a bush taxi, one of the patchwork secondhand cars that define West Africa's public transport. This one carried nine passengers: two men in front with the driver, four men across the middle row (where I sat), and three women in the rear, a cramped space even with two people. The car had no intact windows except for the windshield, and the door on the middle-row right "window" seat, my place, was gone. For hundreds of miles I sat braced against the open air, without a seat belt to restrain me, my left arm thrown across the seat's shoulder so I could grasp the top, my right hand tightly holding the seat in front of me. I had to guess at the driver's speed—always very high—because none of the dashboard gauges worked. And the engine hood would not close. The driver had looped rope through the under latch and tied the hood down to the front fender.

A bush taxi.

Vehicles just like it had filled the Ibadan motor park that morning—bush taxis with no windows, no hoods, no shocks; with balding tires and brakes that whined and screeched. So I took my chances with this one. We left at 6:30 a.m. on the 240-mile trip north to Kaduna. All day the car flew along Nigeria's narrow, crowded arterial north-south highway at speeds around a hundred miles per hour. We sat together, passengers and driver, grim-faced and silent, not uttering a word to one another. Occasionally I heard a soft exclamation, *"Allah!"* or a gasp. Much of the time I kept my eyes closed to protect them from the wind blasting through the door space—and because of the driving. We played chicken on blind curves in the inside lane, passing five, six cars at a time, and always seemed to regain our own lane with only a few feet to spare before we would have smashed into the oncoming traffic.

Regardless of nationality, everyone who drives in Africa drives like this—with heat-inspired, desperate, pedal-to-the-floor insanity, heedless of reason, of their own or anyone else's desire to live beyond the next turn. The driver becomes his vehicle, soaking up the power—enjoying it mentally and physically—lusting for the freedom of unregulated roads. Speed limits are not enforced. He drives as if life must be chased mercilessly to its end and finished in a bright flash.

Our driver that morning stood about six feet five, two hundred muscular pounds of bulk with large, pudgy hands that seemed to grasp the whole top of the steering wheel. He worked in a clean, well-pressed, navy blue wide-collared cotton tunic and matching trousers. A red fez covered his bald head. He handled the car with impatient bravado, the way a teenager might operate a pinball machine, slamming the thing from gear to gear, grumbling and laughing, making turns with wild jerks. With the palm of his right hand he thumped a staccato protest on the top of the dashboard when traffic frustrated him. That habit made it all the more difficult for me to endure this driver, whom I felt certain had lost his mind.

Or maybe I was losing mine to paranoia. Not far south of Kaduna we witnessed, from miles away, the sudden rising of a plume of black smoke. The sight alarmed us instantly. Against a hazy sky, the smoke formed a sharp silhouette over tired, sandy terrain, the West African Sahel, where lingering savanna struggles against invading desert. I had seen many such sights across West Africa, smoke from burning tires and garbage, from farmers clearing fields to prepare for a new crop. Yet this smoke, so dark and ascending so quickly, unnerved me. I thought of the road demons my driver friends in Niger had described to me, beings that appeared on the road suddenly, often in black and in virtually any form, to distract and frighten drivers—to kill them, in fact, and all those with them. An old woman in dark rags, a black bull, a goat, a dog, the silhouette of a horse and its rider, a leviathan black truck covering the whole road and bearing down from the opposite direction. My friends drove with talismans they called *gris-gris* hung from rear and side-view mirrors and steering wheel. Some wore them as necklaces beneath their shirts, like our driver on this trip, a Hausa from northern Nigeria near the border with Niger. His two leather *gris-gris* hung on a cord just below his neck. All of this recalls Nigerian writer Ben Okri's words in his novel *The Famished Road:* "The road swallows people and sometimes at night you can hear them calling for help, begging to be freed from inside its stomach."

Now, under a tree, I sat hugging my knees, feeling that I had been left without an escape route. I thought of fate—the fact that the tanker and Peugeot had collided not long before we arrived on the scene. Fear changes things, stirs up mind and body. I tried to focus on mundane subjects but failed. I could not recall what I'd had for breakfast that morning or what clothes I had worn the day before. I was left suddenly with only bits of myself—a fleeting tangle of thoughts: family, friends, failures, ambitions—as if I were paper shredding in a whirlwind. My abdomen ached, my temples felt numb, my scalp hurt.

I was not involved, knew none of the dead, but fear held me anyway. For months I'd been traveling on roads dominated by predatory soldiers and lined by wrecks, some still burning when I passed. The day before, I had seen a tiny hamlet in southern Nigeria—just four or five mud homes—hours after a single careening eighteen-wheeler had razed it, every house.

There were roads in Niger that suddenly vanished into walls of blowing sand, like a soda straw dunked into chocolate milk. I met and traveled with drivers there who paid homage to the unseen beings controlling the roads. They spent huge sums on protective talismans and sacrifices and then drove with homemade petrol tanks—plastic jugs—sitting in the lap of a passenger, me. I heard people talk of demons of the road, and of the road itself as a fickle god, a compassionate, jealous, violent, hungry being.

In Nigeria, I heard and read of Ogun, the vengeful Yoruba god of iron and the road. One day a Nigerian newspaper headline caught my eye: "Seven Pregnant Women Roasted to Death." The report of the auto accident beneath the headline began with these words: "Thursday January 21, 1993 will always be remembered as a day Ogun decided to feast on the Ukwa Kin Highway."

Months earlier, in Niger, I had bought my own *gris-gris*: three eyeball-sized goatskin pouches filled, perhaps, with Koranic prayers written in Arabic on bits of paper. I could only guess their contents from things I had heard. Issoufou Garba, a driver I came to know well in Niger, told me that *gris-gris* are also filled with grains of blessed soil. Mine were sewn shut and given me by a marabout, a teacher and holy man of Islam, who forbade me to open them so as to protect their sacred value. He told me to keep the *gris-gris* separated from one another in pockets of my pants or my bag. "Be careful," he added, "not to put money in with them."

In my time in Niger I cultivated a sort of road neurosis, beginning with the *gris-gris*. Even when paying for passage in a bush taxi, I argued passionately and bribed shamelessly for the same spot, which I had convinced myself was lucky—the right window seat in the middle row. I don't know why exactly, but that particular seat felt right, far enough away from the front to keep my legs from being pinned and cut off in a head-on collision; and maybe sitting next to the window helped my claustrophobia. I inspected brakes, steering, and tires, pushing drivers and mechanics to exasperation; and I always insisted on seeing the papers of the car and driver, believing this would somehow ensure my safety. Drivers would stare at me in puzzlement, as if I had attacked their integrity, which I had. They would ask, "Don't you trust us?" Other people, even passengers, would laugh at me and say, "He is afraid of death." My neurotic rituals never erased my fears, but they helped control the anguish of travel.

I had to talk myself through every trip with every driver, dozens of journeys, long and short, all the time building a case that traveling in a bush taxi and challenging the odds against dying in a high-speed crash worked to my story's favor. On the road, I scribbled notes—bits of dialogue, landscape details, or lines like, "crazy bastard's going to kill us"—as if the display of hard work would prove the importance of my task to a higher authority, and thus somehow excuse me from death or maiming. A kind of draft deferment owing to my indispensable journalistic existence.

That morning, as we hurtled toward Kaduna and the billowing smoke, my mind was fragmenting. I was thinking I did not know the Nigerian driver's name and did not want to know it. Then, on impulse, I took out my notebook and wrote, "See big plume black smoke not far off. I don't like this."

As we approached that rising black smoke, I saw a clearer shape: a thick, leaning column like a giant tether to the sky. The driver kept an eye on the smoke and uttered a prayer to himself in Arabic, not his language or mine, but it was a prayer I had heard before and understood:

"*Belsfemallah Arahman Arahim*"—a plea for God's protection. Then he struck his chest lightly with his right fist and fell quiet. A moment later, as the plume of smoke got closer, higher, blacker, he mumbled and frowned, shook the index finger of his right hand at the smoke as if he had just identified a thing he'd rather not encounter, and made a sound: "*Yai, yai, yai.*"

The next minute we rounded a curve to see five cars backed up behind flames and smoke on the road, as if the asphalt demon itself had reared up to reveal its face. We were just in time to see a burst of flame as part of the petrol load ignited. The sight sickened me, already fatigued by fear. I could feel myself going up in the flames, wishing it would just happen, finally conclude in a spectacular, painless explosion that would turn my life to vapor and end the fear and uncertainty of the road. When I began traveling, I had not expected this risk, this emotion.

As I sat in the shade of that tree, risk consumed my thoughts. I was nauseous, in need of a walk to clear my head but afraid of what I might find lying on the ground: human remains that might have been mine had I left earlier that morning, reminders of the terrible fate that might lay ahead for me. I didn't think to just walk away from the wreck. Clear thought didn't come. All I knew was on that spot of earth, off the road, I felt safe.

Transport in Africa is a free-for-all system so chaotic that few travelers, even Africans, agree on a precise definition of the bush taxi. Consider this broad interpretation: Bush taxis are dangerous, dilapidated, slow, crowded, demoralizing, and suffocating; they are also fast, intimate, exciting, equalizing, and enlightening. They are bowls of human soup, microscope slides of society, mobile windows on the raw cultural, economic, and political vitality of Africa. Most bush taxis are Peugeot or Toyota station wagons, minibuses, or pickups, but big semis and cars of other makes do the job as well: Renaults, Mercedes, Mitsubishis, Hondas. More specifically, bush taxis are private cars rented out to transport goods and people. They are unregulated; they leave when they are full and arrive whenever. Bush taxis are cheap, are used by all levels of society, and are an important means of transporting trade goods. Any automobile can qualify, but most come secondhand from Europe.

Few Africans own cars, and African governments cannot support large transport systems. Bush taxis fill the void, making up most of the rural motor traffic. Much of what is manufactured, smuggled, or grown in Africa passes weekly through vast, seething outdoor car depots—the motor parks—in cities, and through smaller parks in villages. Similar systems exist in many countries where private car owners are comparatively few, from the Middle East to Southeast Asia, from Africa to South America. In other words, those who own cars cash in on them.

I spoke about bush taxis with John Riverson, a civil engineer from Ghana who studies African rural transport for the World Bank, in Washington, D.C. Riverson views bush taxis as tools of reality. We talked in his cramped office amid shelves of technical reports and photos of road projects.

"There is such a deprivation of transport that people are grateful to have anything that moves," he told me, pointing out that in rural areas most vehicles, government owned or private, serve as bush taxis at some point. Riverson's words called to mind a government ambulance driver in Niger who took on passengers at four dollars a head while delivering medicine to villages in a Land Rover ambulance. Riverson acknowledged the difficulty of defining the bush taxi, but offered this rough guideline: "If we're looking at bush taxis as something identifiable, we're looking at vehicles in the range of three tons' weight"—starting with heavier minibuses, then pickups, station wagons, and sedans. But the number and kinds of vehicles used as bush taxis fluctuate between countries.

Our conversation came down to this: bush taxis are the legacy of an overburdened but vital freelance rural transport network that supports West Africa's economies—a network starved of motor vehicles, spare parts, fuel, mechanics, drivers, and decent roads. Whatever rolls, works.

• • •

It occurred to me that the growing crowd on both sides of the wreck was remarkably calm. I hadn't noticed where my fellow passengers had gone, but I realized that only I seemed to be alone. All around me people sat in the shade, sleeping, talking, or eating. Children played and traveling merchants laid out their products on the ground or on small folding wooden tables—clothes, vegetables, cheap jewelry. The scene looked as if all these people, perhaps two hundred by now, were traveling together in one big group. Only small clusters of drivers and a few children paid the burning wreck close attention. This was not a festive crowd, but rather a respectful and patient one that seemed to know better than to argue or complain about something they could not control. Being held up on the road by a calamity was a common event, something not to obsess about but to deal with. Why not sleep or do a little business during the wait?

A man sitting with a woman and a baby a few yards away from me rose to his feet and approached, carrying something wrapped in newspaper. I looked up and smiled, though we had never met.

"Have you got food?" he asked.

"No, I'm not hungry, thank you."

"You will be hungry. You must eat. God knows how long we will be here." He watched me for a moment and then handed me the object in the newspaper. "It's meat, take it."

I was embarrassed but grateful, and I knew better than to refuse a food offering. I shook his hand and took the meat, which turned out to be roasted chicken breast. "Thank you, sir."

"It's nothing, my friend." The man walked back to his family.

In Africa, there are fewer than twenty million motor vehicles to serve 700 million people. The number of cars that actually work is far less. Car accidents in Africa, according to the World Bank, number eight to ten times higher, proportionately, than in developed nations and are a leading cause of death. In Nigeria, home to 90 million people, road accidents consume 2 percent of the gross national product in destroyed vehicles, material, and lives—around 100,000 people injured and ten thousand deaths a year, according to Nigeria's Federal Road Safety Commission. In contrast, in the United States, with its 250 million people and 145 million passenger cars, the figure hovers around forty thousand deaths each year.

Niger has sixteen thousand passenger vehicles and eighteen thousand commercial cars to serve its 9 million people. There are eight thousand miles of roads, two thousand miles of them paved; the rest are packed dirt road and sandy track. Almost 2,000 people are reported injured annually in road accidents; some 300 of them die. Many, many more injuries and deaths go unreported. Niger's national highway, Route Nationale I, absorbs half the carnage on its thousand-mile east-west odyssey from Mali to Chad.

Bad driving, poor road and vehicle maintenance, and chaotic traffic are the primary factors to blame for Africa's road deaths, according to a 1990 World Bank study entitled "Transport Policy Issues in Sub-Saharan Africa." The language of this paper employs the wordy bureaucratese of international development documents: "The deterioration of the road networks is causing heavy losses to both the road system itself and to its users and requires urgent action."

On lawless roads the problem is obvious. The human impulse to speed, the desire to get there quickly, takes over. And the bush taxi, more than any other form of transport, rules West Africa's roads.

I have come to know many bush taxi drivers, to like them and sympathize with how they work and live, if not to completely understand their point of view. They see themselves as transporters, honest professionals, survivors forced by circumstances to use guerrilla methods. So, during my travels, I was careful not to express my fears and concerns too bluntly; the drivers do not appreciate hearing about their roguish image. "People think we are irresponsible or thieves," my driver friend Issoufou Garba from Niger once told me. "But they don't understand the difficulty of our work."

In the 1980s, bush taxi drivers struck me as a dashing, reckless male elite, akin to the image of early airplane pilots. The drivers worked blindly and intuitively, vulnerable to technology and the will of a hostile environment: sun, wind, sand, demons, darkness, and checkpoint soldiers. Today, the African bush taxi driver still strikes me as a rogue folk hero: adventurous, kind, cruel, and selfless all at once. A bit like the contradictions inherent in the American cowboy myth—the free-spirited, big-hearted soul with a malicious edge. The drivers, too, are struggling to survive.

It was probably half an hour later, though I'm unsure of the passage of time that day. The tanker was still burning fiercely. No police or emergency services had arrived, and they would not before I left that day. I sat and watched without really seeing. *Can I walk to Kaduna?* I asked myself. *Fifty miles. Three days and I'll be there, still alive. I'll just follow the road and sleep in villages.*

The heat made me think again. In March, even the night offers little temperature relief.

My gaze fell on our driver. When we arrived at the accident, he had huddled with other drivers in discussion. But now he was standing alone, as close to the tanker—perhaps fifteen yards away—as the heat would allow. He stood with folded arms and feet planted a little apart. I'm not sure how long he had been standing there, studying the burning wreck. He stood for fifteen minutes more, moving only to shift his weight from one leg to the other. After a while, I realized what he was thinking, and it scared me. I had seen him scouting detour possibilities just after we arrived at the wreck, but the bush was too thick to drive through. Now, I understood that he wanted to challenge the gods.

He turned around, arms swinging with determination, and strode back to the car. This was both a game and a performance to this man, a career opportunity.

He understood other drivers were observing him, waiting to see what he would do.

He opened the door and leaned against the roof, looking first at the fire and then around at his audience. He pursed his lips, raised his shoulders and hands, palms skyward, as if he were asking God for help.

He got into the car, moved it onto the road, and backed up a hundred yards or so. And then we heard him yell: "EEEOOOHHWW!" The wheels of the car spit dirt. He shot forward, aiming for the left side of the wreck, which was pulsing with just as much smoke and fire as when we first arrived. He had seen what others had not: that the haze masked a gap between the rear of the wreck and the bush about the width of his Peugeot.

Issoufou Garba, I thought, would never have risked this—a point to his credit. But I found myself glad this driver had tried. I badly wanted to be gone from this scene, and this man was obliging me.

The taxi disappeared into the smoke and reappeared seconds later on the other side of the wreck where the road began a low ascent. It lifted gently out of the curve where the wreck lay and then stopped.

No one cheered when the driver stepped out from behind the wheel and looked around for his passengers. Time was wasting. Nor did he seem to encourage cheering. Maybe he didn't want to taunt the gods any further. He leaned against the roof, braced by the outstretched palm of his left hand. All at once, drivers and passengers scrambled for vehicles, sprinting to make the run themselves. Hundreds of cars, trucks, and buses lined up on both sides of the wreck to take advantage of that small gap. I thought of an hourglass, but with jumping grains of sand fighting and trampling each other from both sides in their efforts to get through the narrow middle before it closed.

I made my way to the car by going through the bush, around the fire and wreckage. Looking back, I saw a fight start between two drivers, a pushing and shouting match. One man threw a punch to the face of the other, who went down. I heard more shouting in several languages, the rhythmic slap of sandals on cement, engines starting, doors slamming, the soft rumble of flames eating gasoline, and, finally, a siren wailing from the south.

We drove away.

from Malaria Dreams:
An African Adventure
by Stuart Stevens

Stuart Stevens in the 1980s agreed to drive his friend Lucien's Land Rover from the Central African Republic to Paris. Stevens and his companion—a former fashion model named Ann—soon discovered that locals figured Lucien for a spy or a diamond smuggler. The Central African Republic's minister of mines appropriated the Land Rover. Stevens managed to buy a Toyota Land Cruiser, and set out with Ann to cross the Sahara.

There are two main routes across the Sahara. On the Michelin map they appear as comforting red lines, bisecting the yellow emptiness of the map like superhighways. The most popular, known as the Hoggar (named for the spectacular Hoggar mountain region of Algeria, which it bisects), actually has stretches of pavement, though this only makes the driving more difficult. As the *Sahara Handbook* explains, "Long stretches of once beautiful new asphalt roads have deteriorated rapidly. . . . Traffic soon establishes myriads of pistes on either side of the former road with deep ruts, or ornières, and terrible corrugations. This can turn a two-day journey into a long frustrating ordeal." The Hoggar runs from Algiers south to Tamanrasset and into Niger.

The more direct route from Gao is the Tanezrouft. "It's more rugged than the Route du Hoggar," reads the guidebook from Lonely Planet, "takes considerably longer, and there's far less transport along the way."

We decided not to take either one, at least not for the entire distance.

Our plan was to drive first to Timbuktu, then slant northeast across the desert to Tamanrasset and pick up the Hoggar. It was a less direct way to reach the Mediterranean but it was the shortest distance from Timbuktu to Tamanrasset, Algeria. And Tamanrasset was a place I had to be—by the twenty-second of December. That was when my wife was arriving from America. Air Algerie promised—though I was dubious in the extreme—that it was possible to fly to Tamanrasset from Algiers; one flight a week but it could be done. We left Gao on the ninth: almost two weeks to make it to Tamanrasset, more than enough time if the tires didn't blow (we were down to one spare tube), the four-wheel drive expire (the gearshift still had to be strapped down), the rear springs collapse (the same springs that had been diagnosed terminally ill in Chad), the wheels fall off (the car vibrated so fiercely I had to tighten the lug nuts each evening) or, of course, the gearbox glue dissolve.

There is no road to Timbuktu. One finds it the same way people have for the last ten centuries or so—by following the River Niger. *Africa Overland* reports, "We had to find our way to Timbuctoo through 200 miles of untamed desert, using only the stars and our compass. . . . This was going to be the toughest section of the desert."

The navigation was fairly simple: northwest for 95 kilometers to Bourem (here there was even a sign: "To Timbuktu") then west along the river for 292 more kilometers. Counting the kilometers was essential. Since the river had shifted course leaving Timbuktu inland by a dozen kilometers or so, it was possible to drive right past the town, always expecting to see it over the next rise. Eventually you ran out of gas. (The question of whether or not diesel fuel was available in Timbuktu was an open one. Sometimes there was, truck drivers told us; sometimes there wasn't. Without it, we had problems.)

In *News from Tartary*, Peter Fleming's tale of a journey from Beijing to India in 1935, he describes a Tibetan village as having "more than the usual fairie tale look." I felt the same way about the settlements along the Niger, though these jumbles of black African and Arab cultures made for a very different sort of fairy tale than do the peaked roofs and prayer wheels of Tibet. Here there were mud brick huts, some quite large, and the distinctive lopsided Tuareg tents that always looked as if they were about to fall down. Children and goats played together in the ruins of huts long abandoned and broken walls blown over with sand. It gave one the sense that these were places where civilization had been attempted and then abandoned for lack of interest.

In a final touch of mocking irony, the River Niger gleamed in the background, with sandy beaches straight out of a tropical vacation brochure.

At night we always tried to camp by the river. If its meandering curves hid it from view, we left the track and bushwhacked south, knowing that eventually we had to hit water. Invariably we waited too late in the day (hoping the river would appear along our route, as it did from time to time), so that we found ourselves driving through the scrub brush and acacia thorns in failing light. The terrain, to my surprise, was rolling, complicating both the navigation and the driving.

Searching for the river the second night after leaving Gao, we were startled to find ourselves suddenly driving not on sand but across black rocks. The light was flat and dim; it was like skiing on a hazy day. We dropped down into a gully, bucked our way across and up the other side. I was thinking about the rocks and how our tires left no imprint on the hard surface. I glanced at the compass hanging from the dash, trying to fix our direction. Tomorrow we wouldn't be able to retrace our tracks—there were no tracks. Something—peripheral vision? mental radar?—made me glance up from the compass.

"There's the river," Ann said.

It hung in front of us, glinting in the muted sunset. But there was an oddness to the way it looked, as if the river were *down* there and we were up here.

That was it. I slammed the brakes to the floor.

We got out of the car and walked forward. A few feet in front of us the black pebbles ended in a sudden cliff that plummeted twenty or thirty feet to the level of the river. The cliff was composed of a curious black rock, porous as lava.

Off to the left we spotted a gully running down to the river. We followed it to the water and made camp on the shore.

I woke up at first light and brewed coffee on the little gas stove. The mornings were the best time of day, when it was cool enough to forget, at least for a little while, the strangling heat of the upcoming hours. A pirogue floated through the mist, a graceful craft with bow and stern rising upward like outstretched arms. There were two teenagers poling the boat. They landed and hoisted out a bulky fish, mouth gaping. It was a capitaine, a breed of giant perch I'd first seen pulled from the Ubangi River in Bangui.

We talked, in the way people do with only a few words of shared language. They wanted to sell the fish and I wanted to eat it in the worst way. But there was nothing I could do with the ten or fifteen pounds of fresh meat that would be left after even the most heroic eating efforts. So we drank coffee and looked at each other, waiting peacefully for the day formally to begin. Tiny red birds darted between the thorn bushes, perfect little things that looked like Christmas tree ornaments.

When Ann rose up from the Cruiser roof wrapped in her sleeping bag, the fishermen—who hadn't realized there was a person inside all that blue nylon on the roof—gasped in surprise and backed protectively toward their pirogue.

She reassured them with a soft laugh. We drank more coffee.

It is customary for Westerners to speak of their disappointment on reaching Timbuktu. René Caillié, the first European to see Timbuktu and return alive, wrote of his visit in 1828:

> I looked around and found that the sight before me did not answer my expectations. I had formed a totally different idea of the grandeur and wealth of Timbuctoo. The city presented, at first view, nothing but a mass of ill-looking houses, built of earth. Nothing was to be seen in all directions but immense plains of sand of a yellowish white color. The sky was a pale red as far as the horizon; all nature

wore a dreary aspect, and the most profound silence prevailed; not even the warbling of a bird was to be heard.

The third European to visit Timbuktu, the German explorer Heinrich
Barth, wrote a detailed description of the town as he found it in 1853,
including a map with descriptions of every major building. Little is
changed today. Timbuktu is still "a mass of ill-looking houses," full of
"profound silences."

I visited most of those houses searching for a barrel.

Travel has a charmingly sneaky way of making the unexpected terribly important. Never would I have imagined that the acquisition of a
barrel—a fifty-gallon drum, more precisely—would be important. But
in Timbuktu, thanks to a German we ran into, it was a task bestowed
with a compelling imperative.

"Friends, friends, friends," the German announced solemnly as we
hovered over the map, "from here"—he pointed to Timbuktu—"to
there,"—his finger traced the breadth of the Sahara—"there is no certainty of fuel supplies. You must carry your own stores." He had the
vocabulary of a military commander—fuel supplies, stores—and the
look of a sixties refugee: long black hair, tattered beard sprinkled with
gray, shorts and sandals.

"For ten days," he continued, "I once waited here"—his finger
stabbed a point in the middle of the desert—for a truck to pass with
fuel. I had water for eleven days. On the tenth a truck came and I
bought fifty liters of fuel. It cost me three hundred dollars. But it was
better I think than dying." He said the last as if he had truly pondered
the question, weighing both sides of the equation.

The German, Hernst Whitney, was one of those perpetual graduate
students forever working on their doctorate. His thesis for his anthropology degree was on Tuareg blacksmiths. He knew a great deal about
Tuareg blacksmiths, and about crossing the Sahara, a tour (his description) he'd made over a half dozen times.

We met him at our hotel in Timbuktu, though hotel is a grandiose
description for that collection of dusty mud brick rooms with collapsing

ceilings and walls decorated with slithering lizards. I took one glance at the bed, with its gray sheets and tortured mattress, and decided to sleep on the roof of the Cruiser parked out front in the sand. It was the hotel's shower we were really after, that halfhearted stream of tepid brown liquid where all the fashionable lizards hung out.

Hernst had floated down the Niger from Bamako, the capital of Mali, to Timbuktu on one of the river steamers that still plied the trade route. He'd traveled with two French soldiers and a Tahitian woman; she was the wife of the soldiers' comrade-in-arms, who had not been able to make the trip. She was also exceedingly beautiful, a fact not lost on the German or on the French soldiers, who spoke openly of the anguish imposed upon them by the obligations of loyalty to their friend. Apparently they felt no such restrictions toward Ann, though she seemed to find their charms resistible.

Having completed the drive from Gao to Timbuktu without disaster, I felt quite sanguine about negotiating the Sahara. But the German changed all that in a hurry. It started with his question about our maps. "You have good ones?" he asked in his perfect English.

I beamed confidently and fetched from the Cruiser my bulky carto-graphic collection. In Paris before leaving for Africa, I had discovered a map store that specializes in West Africa and bought what I assumed was a world-class collection. Ann groaned when she saw the bundle. All across Africa I had bragged about the maps and pored over them with a pleasure bordering on the fetishistic.

"Umm," the German asked, thumbing through the package, "you have no aircraft charts?" This he said in a deeply disappointed voice.

"Aircraft charts?"

"No? How about topographical maps. Any of those?"

I shook my head in shame.

"Well," he said. "Well."

We were sitting in Timbuktu's only restaurant, the front room of a two-room mud house next to the market. The location was significant as the chef took orders then sent his son out to buy the ingredients. Unfortunately, the child was a ferocious bargainer who held out to the bitter end for the best price, so the process—from ordering to eating—took at least two hours. This is, I would venture, a record for omelets. As the sounds of the rapacious negotiations—shouts of scorn, laughter—wafted in the open doorway, the chef put on a proud "That's-my-boy!" grin and poured rounds of bubbling sweet tea.

Using my woefully inadequate maps, the German went over our route stage by stage, warning us about stretches of deep sand, the location and quality of wells, and areas where it was easy to get lost. (There seemed to be a chilling number of these.)

"How much petrol can you carry?" he asked.

"We have six jerricans." It was understood that all jerricans held twenty liters.

"And does your Land Cruiser have double petrol tanks?"

"No."

He made calculations in the notebook he carried everywhere. Anthropologists always carry notebooks. "In the deep sand," he asked, "you use what, twenty liters per hundred kilometers?" This was how everyone in Africa talked about fuel consumption, not "how many liters to the kilometer" but "how many liters per hundred kilometers."

I nodded. Actually the Cruiser used slightly more fuel but I remained silent out of loyalty to the vehicle.

"You must travel at least fifteen hundred kilometers to cross the desert. More if you are lost. It is best to plan for two thousand kilometers. If you are wrong you die," he observed cheerfully, "so caution is best. For two thousand kilometers you need . . ." He divided some figures.

"At least four hundred liters of fuel," Ann spoke up.

The German smiled. "Yes. Math and anthropology do not mix so well, I think."

I did some figuring of my own. With the six jerricans we carried and the 90 liters that the Toyota's tank held, we had only 210 liters, about half of what the German estimated we needed. This was not good.

"I don't know how we could fit ten more jerricans in the car," Ann said.

"I don't know how we could afford ten more jerricans," I said. Each can cost almost fifty dollars at the inflated prices of the desert oasis.

"What you need," the German observed sagely, "is a barrel."

It made sense. A single 200-liter oil drum would solve our storage problems—if we could fit it in the Cruiser. And if we could find one.

For the better part of a day, we roamed through the sand streets of Timbuktu looking for a barrel. I became a student of the 200-liter metal drum.

It is quite astonishing the number of uses one can invent for the basic oil drum. I saw drums used as stoves, usually with the top half decapitated. I saw water collection drums, mud mortar-mixing drums, grain drums, cooking fuel drums, drum tables, drum lanterns, drum jacks (hoisting ailing Land Rovers), trash drums and even latrine drums. The problem was, most had been altered to suit their converted purpose (ruining their original fuel-toting ability) and were hopelessly contaminated by their new role; this was particularly true of the mud and latrine barrels.

As the word went forth that we were in barrel-buying mode, eager salesmen chased us down the narrow sand alleys rolling their merchandise in hot pursuit. We finally settled on an old Shell oil drum that we located in the courtyard of a house near the great mosque.

A mad scene ensued. With a crowd jamming the alley, we unloaded everything from the Cruiser and struggled to squeeze the drum onto the back seat. After much sweating, swearing and ripping of upholstery (what little was left), we succeeded and then faced the challenge of repacking the car with about a third less available space. The loading process greatly entertained the gathered multitudes and made me question my sanity. Was I really contemplating driving across the Sahara in a vehicle that looked like something out of *The Grapes of Wrath*?

"California or bust," Ann said, sharing my thoughts.

"Right."

We drove from Timbuktu back to Gao.

There was no choice. It was a question of fuel—or a lack of fuel, to be accurate. After the great barrel hunt, we turned up at Timbuktu's only gas pump to discover the diesel tanks were dry. The situation, I had to admit, reeked of the sort of irony that thrives in Africa. Great energy is expended to solve one problem only to discover the basic premise of the effort is flawed. Why find the perfect diesel drum if there is no diesel? Why import relief food if it only rots on the dock because there are no delivery trucks?

In Gao we could fill the two-hundred-liter drum. So we went to Gao. The delay was only a few days.

Only a few days. I thought, bemused, of the times in my pre-Africa life I had fumed and ranted over late planes and traffic jams. An hour— hell, *a half hour*—was intolerably painful. Now I accepted with a shrug a few days' detour just *to buy gas.*

And anyway, it was good to drop by the little omelet shack in Gao and find our pal Bob coolly spinning deals. "You want diesel?" His eyes brightened. "I control diesel in Gao!"

We spent a day and night in Gao, long enough to buy black-market diesel and get arrested for camping in a military zone. (It was a horrible night. While snoozing peacefully in my sleeping bag, I was attacked by dogs, then nearly run over by an armored car on some kind of drunken maneuver and finally, when dawn came at last, arrested before my first cup of coffee. It took five Polaroid photos and a box of Cameroonian cigars to buy our freedom.)

We also had enough time to hire a guide.

Bob found him for us. Of course.

"You want guide? I control guide!"

He was a tall, skinny teenager with buck teeth and a hipster's nonchalance. "Water for the journey? Oh, you don't need much."

His name was something like Sidramma Muhammad. Ann called him Siddhartha; I called him Sid. He seemed to like both and did not take our inability to pronounce his name as an insult. (Indeed, he called me Stu.)

Sid lived in Tessalit, the last town in Mali before entering Algeria. He claimed to be intimately familiar with the route from Tessalit to Tamanrasset—the *"piste dangereuse,"* as the Michelin map proclaimed—

and was anxious to travel to Tamanrasset in the way all country boys want to visit the big city. That he seemed to think of the desert outpost Tamanrasset as a major metropolis should have made me question whether he had ever actually been there, but after being attacked by dogs, almost crushed under a half-track's treads and arrested as a spy, I was not thinking too clearly. Sid said he knew the way, requested a reasonable fee, and that, as it were, seemed to be that.

In retrospect, warnings abounded that Sid might be, well, problematic. Like when we noticed him trying to crawl under the fuel drum on the back seat when we approached the first of three checkpoints leaving Gao.

"Siddhartha," Ann asked levelly, "what are you doing?"

Like the best comedic straight man, Sid asked, "Me?"

"Yes, Siddhartha. Why are you hiding?"

"A little problem . . ."

"Yes, Siddhartha?"

He dug further under the barrel.

"Sid?" I tried to sound friendly but firm. "Oh, Sid?" I could see the first checkpoint a hundred yards ahead. I slowed down.

"Papers," he finally said.

"What about papers?"

"There is a problem. A little problem." He held his thumb and index finger close together to stress just how little a problem.

By now the guard at the checkpoint was watching us curiously; his automatic weapon beckoned us forward.

"Well, Siddhartha," Ann said, "explain it to him."

And he did, or he tried to. The sticking point involved some irregularity in Sid's identity papers. Such matters are invariably so complex that I doubt any official, much less a hapless guard on a checkpoint to nowhere, could understand the details. But however perplexing problems with African paperwork may be, there is always one reliable solution: money.

"*Patron*," Sid began, "this is a great injustice. This is very much wrong. This man says I can not go home to Tessaht and be your guide.

Please, we must give him something." Sid had traded his usual sly grin for the pout of a persecuted child.

I groaned, knowing my choices all too well. We could argue, which would only increase the final price, or try to wait the guard out, hoping he would change his mind—but who had more time than a roadblock guard on the edge of the Sahara?—or, yes, pay the bribe.

"How much, Sid?"

"A little money, that is all."

"Sid?"

"Five thousand CFA."

"Fine."

Sid seemed shocked at my ready agreement.

"But it comes out of your fee. Do you understand, Sid? I asked you yesterday. You said all your papers were in order." This was true.

Sid looked horrified but nodded. His ready agreement shocked *me* until I watched him pocket four of the five thousand-CFA notes, the other going to the guard. Clever boy, this Sid.

An hour beyond Gao we hit deep sand and slowed to a few miles per hour. It was windy and uncommonly bright, the sun glaring off the sand as bright as klieg lights at a Hollywood opening. I wore my darkest mountaineering glasses and wished for goggles.

Our slow pace troubled Sid as we neared a Tuareg encampment. "Go faster," he urged, genuinely nervous. "These are bad people. Go faster!"

There was no more speed to be had in the sand. We poked along, a perfect target for a Tuareg lance or a dagger wielded by a courageous hijacker.

But there were only women waving and children running alongside, as kids did everywhere in Africa. Camels and goats wandered among the dark cloth tents. The few men we saw sat in the tents' open door-ways, looking as if we had awakened them from long naps. Tuaregs are famed for surprise attacks, but if this was an act, it was a very good one indeed. Ann pointed this out to Sid.

"Yes," he agreed, now not so nervous, "they are very lazy people."

Somehow, coming from Sid this touch of moral indignation was less than convincing.

Late in the afternoon we came to a tiny village called Aguelhok. Because it appeared on our maps, it was a reassuring sight: the first convincing indication since leaving Gao that we were not lost. A bridge over a dry riverbed was destroyed, forcing us to negotiate the stony river bottom strewn with boulders. A tall, skinny man greeted us on the other side, his white gown flapping in the wind. His eagerness oozed into the unctuous. "Come eat with me, please," he kept repeating. "I have a restaurant. Please."

Sitting around the cistern of a dry well next to his one-room restaurant, we ate macaroni mixed with greasy lamb. The man wanted to talk deals. What did we have to trade? Did we want to sell the car?

I was exhausted from the day spent in deep sand; my sun-induced headache was fierce.

"We have a whole car full of stuff to trade," I said, trying to pick up a piece of the lamb. There were no forks or spoons. "The question is, what do *you* have to trade?"

He laughed and, as if to let us know he was not a small-town operator, said confidentially, "I keep cars for Maurice."

"Maurice?"

"From Marseilles."

Oh, *that* Maurice, I thought.

The man gestured toward a mud building on the other side of the restaurant. "There is a Range Rover in there this very minute. He brings the cars down from France and I keep them for a while. Do you want to sell your car?"

It was such an odd question, as if we could sell the car and then catch a bus or plane back to Europe. Short of camels, I hadn't seen *any* transportation since leaving Gao.

"How much would you give me for the Cruiser?"

"Two million CFA," he said instantly.

I laughed. "But I paid more than that in Yaounde and there are many cars in Yaounde. Here you can not be so tough."

"But Maurice sells a Range Rover for only two million!"

"Yes, but my car is not stolen."

He nodded. "I know." His voice was sad. "That is not good. It is much better price if stolen. Maurice steals all his cars."

This he said with a certain pride. I felt as if I should apologize for not stealing mine.

"All cars in Africa are stolen." He shrugged. "Do you have shoes like these?" he asked suddenly, thrusting out his feet. From under his white robe jutted tennis shoes with Velcro straps instead of laces.

"No, but they are very nice."

He nodded, pleased that he had something I didn't. "It is much faster with these," he explained, opening and fastening the Velcro several times. It was indeed very fast. "It saves time."

I nodded, wondering what in the world he did with the extra time he saved not having to tie shoelaces. Everyone else in the village was barefoot.

"Two million two hundred!" he shouted, waving his arms at the Land Cruiser. "No more!"

We spent two nights on the road traveling to Tessalit, Sid's hometown. Both nights Sid expressed extreme displeasure with our choice of camping sites. The first night he thought the ground was too rocky (it was, but so was every spot for a hundred miles in either direction), and the second campsite he feared was too close to a Tuareg encampment. "We die!" he repeated numerous times.

This concerned me at first, but after Sid vetoed several possible sites due to the Tuareg threat, I began to understand there was a hidden agenda at work. Sid did not want to camp at all. He wanted to keep driving until we reached Tessalit so he could sleep at home. Perfectly understandable as this was, driving after dark in this terrain was akin in danger and difficulty to a night landing on a carrier deck.

We were passing through the Tilemsi Valley, following not a *road* but compass bearings, landmarks and tracks from other vehicles, none of which were worth a damn after sunset. The headlights on the Cruiser were sad little beams of yellow light, only slightly brighter than, say, a refrigerator bulb. Surrounded by crumbling hills, our route through the valley floor abounded with dry riverbeds offering an unexpected plunge at any moment and car-crunching boulders strewn about haphazardly.

We camped at dark; Sid insisted he was going to walk the rest of the way to Tessalit. Ann asked to take his photograph so that she would have it as a remembrance when the Tuaregs killed him. He stayed and slept so soundly, I had trouble waking him the next morning. A Tuareg would have found him easy pickings.

We drove to Tessalit for breakfast.

Sid's hometown had the look of a classic French foreign legion outpost: a hilltop fort of brown walls towering above a warren of sandy streets. It took about ten minutes in Tessalit to realize that Sid's guiding days—at least for us—were over. Not only did he not have an identity card, Sid didn't have a passport.

This became clear when we parked at the base of the hill and hiked up to the fort, which was now the police station. A kindly official in a cardigan sweater treated Sid like a favorite nephew. He was short and round, a mix of Arab and black.

He laughed when we explained that Sid was guiding us to Tamanrasset. "That boy." He shook his head, grinning. "He told you that?"

"Well, yes. Why?"

"Are you a smuggler?"

"Well, no."

"That boy can't leave Tessalit—but he does. He has no papers! No papers!" He laughed as if this were the greatest joke in the world.

"No passport?"

"Of course not! Would you give him a passport?" He pulled Sid to him and squeezed him in a sudden hug. Sid looked appropriately chagrined.

"You go to Tamanrasset?" the official asked.

"Yes."

"Do you know the way?"

"No, that's why we wanted Sid."

"You think that boy has been to Tamanrasset?" He chuckled. "Good luck." He wasn't laughing when he said this last bit.

We walked back down the hill to Tessalit's only restaurant to think things over. A large van with Dutch plates sat in front, an emaciated blond figure stretched out on the hood. He was middle-aged, with long hair, a mustache and a tie-dyed shirt.

"Are you okay?" I asked.

"No. Not really."

His name was Peter Jokal and he had a chilling story to tell.

Two weeks before he had left Tamanrasset. *Two weeks.* Normally it was a three-day trip, possibly shorter. Four at the maximum.

Two weeks.

"On the second day I get very sick. Diarrhea. Dysentery. I have three hitchhikers with me. Two German boys and a girl. They drive and I lay in the back.

"It was very bad. The road—there is no road. Up and down. Bumps. Horrible. Finally I say to the Germans, 'We must stop.' But they do not want to stop. They say, 'We will drive, you rest.' But the pain, it is too much. I say to the Germans, 'We must stop!' They keep driving.

"So I get my knife"—he showed us a two-foot bayonet—"and grab the keys and tell these Germans, 'After you kill me, you drive truck. But maybe I kill one or two of you first.' They were true Germans, cowards in the end."

For eight days, Peter Jokal held the Germans at bay.

"Why didn't the Germans hitch a ride with another car?" I asked.

He laughed. "You do not understand. We were not on the autobahn. Out there"—he gestured toward Tamanrasset—"there is nothing there. A car or truck maybe twice a month, no more."

He paused, as if gathering his strength. "Where are you going?"

We drank sweet tea and told him about Sid and our plans to drive to Tamanrasset. For two weeks he had been living on bits of bread and tea. His bones looked as if they might puncture his skin.

"You have a good car," he said, looking over at the Cruiser. "You should have no problems." He shook his head and looked suddenly as tired as anyone I'd ever seen. "But you never know about cars. You never know. And on that route, if you have a problem, you could be there for two or three weeks. Easy."

There were now eight days until my wife flew to Tamanrasset. I thought of her arriving and not finding us. I thought of her sitting in a hotel in Tamanrasset wondering what had happened.

On the small table we unfolded our now-tattered Michelin map. "If you do not go directly to Tamanrasset from Tessalit," the Dutch traveler suggested, "you can go north on the Tanezrouft across the Sahara and then go across and down the Hoggar to Tamanrasset. It is longer but there are more people on this route. If something happens, you can get help very quickly. Maybe just a few days."

A few days. I silently counted our water supplies. One hundred liters. It seemed like a lot but . . .

We decided to take the longer, safer route. Peter Jokal looked at the map wistfully. "I wish I could go with you. Two vehicles is always safer. But I have no strength. I must stay here." He motioned toward the door that led to the public bathroom, a hole in a concrete floor. "In a few days, maybe I can drive to Gao and then Niamey. In Niamey I sell the truck and catch the first plane to Europe."

We gave him diarrhea pills and left him sitting in the sun near the bathroom door.

We tromped back up the hill to the police station to retrieve our passports, which we'd left for stamping. Our favorite uncle who'd explained Sid's problems took me aside. I sighed, expecting a request for a bribe.

"You go to Bordj-Moktar now," he said, naming the Algerian border town due north of Tessalit.

I nodded.

"There is a man. He travels to Bordj-Moktar." The official nodded toward a tall, impressive figure across the room. He wore a green army jacket and had the detached air of a high-ranking officer.

"He needs a ride?" I asked, getting to the inevitable.

"Yes. He could be helpful."

It was not far to Bordj-Moktar, perhaps one day and a night, no more. Traveling with an official could speed our way through the remaining Malian customs posts as well as the upcoming Algerian border, reputed to be among the toughest in Africa. Algeria had very strict currency regulations and fierce searches were routine.

I agreed to take the official. He walked down the hill with us to the Cruiser carrying a small gym bag. I felt almost smug, delighted with the increased status our new passenger imparted.

At the last Malian posts, the officers greeted our passenger with friendly banter and waved us through. This was definitely the way to travel.

A rocky track led north toward Algeria through the low hills surrounding Tessalit. Ann and I were arguing; she had wanted to stay in Tessalit for lunch and I had insisted we needed to depart at once. Our new route would take considerably longer and I was worried about reaching Tamanrasset. We had, I figured, just enough time to make the journey.

The track split off in two directions. We stopped arguing to ask the officer in the back seat which route was correct. He nodded to the right.

A few miles later we came to a large fenced compound containing a cluster of buildings. A few men in green uniforms stared at us. I waved and kept driving. But just beyond the compound the road appeared to end. I circled back to ask directions.

A short uniformed figure strode out of one of the buildings. He stopped and stared at us with a disbelieving look on his face. Ann asked directions.

"What are you doing here?" he barked.

She explained that we were driving to Bordj-Moktar. Could he tell us please if this was the route?

He stared incredulously then blew a long, piercing note on a whistle hanging from his neck. Within seconds five guards rushed out of a nearby building to surround the car. Their automatic weapons pointed directly at us.

"Passports!" the martinet screamed.

I tried to explain.

"Passports!"

Desperately, I turned to our passenger. Surely he could explain or pull rank and end this misunderstanding.

But what I saw in the back seat was hardly a comfort. The expression on our passenger's face was that of a terrified child. He looked as if he were about to burst into tears.

"Tell them something!" I pleaded. He shook his head, his eyes opening even wider.

"Passports!" The martinet took a step forward, placing his hand on his holstered gun. There was nothing to do. We dug out our passports. In the back seat, our passenger began to sob. I couldn't believe it.

"Return to Tessalit and report to the police. Now!"

"But our passports?" we sputtered.

"We keep them! Leave!"

All the way back to Tessalit, the man in the rear seat sobbed.

"Why did you listen to this boy?" the police captain implored. "Why?"

"We asked him directions, that's all! He lives here, he should know which road goes to Bordj-Moktar and which road goes to an army camp!"

"But why?" The police captain, who still resembled a kindly uncle albeit an annoyed one, stepped closer to me and lowered his voice. We were in the hilltop fort turned police station; voices echoed through the empty room as if in a deep cave. "This boy is . . ." He touched his head.

"Crazy?" I whispered.

He shrugged and gestured with his palms up. "A little."

I looked across the room and saw the figure that only a short while ago I had pegged as an important military official. He was huddled in a chair, his eyes red. A more pathetic figure was difficult to imagine.

"So what do we do now?" Ann asked.

The police officer shrugged, a gesture I was coming to loathe. "You must wait," he said eventually. "Tell me, did you not see the sign that says 'No Entry' on this road?"

"No."

He shifted his eyes between the red-eyed figure slumped across the room and myself, as if trying to judge who was the greater idiot. "It is a large sign," he said softly with an indigenous politeness.

"We were arguing," I explained.

"About what?" He leaned forward, eager to gossip. It was clear he welcomed this break in the routine of Tessalit life.

"Nothing as important as being stuck at the Malian border without a passport," Ann rightly surmised.

"Well," the officer said, disappointed, "we must wait. But do not worry. Let us have tea. The army will bring your passports."

Ann and I relaxed and followed him over to a low table next to a small gas stove. He asked me for a match, lit the stove and pocketed the unused matches. They were hard to find in Tessalit. Like most things.

"When do you think our passports will be returned?" I asked. I was hungry and wondered if we had time to eat at the town's single restaurant.

He shrugged. That gesture.

"An hour, two hours?" I asked.

He laughed now, his voice bouncing off the red walls of the fort.

"Two weeks if we are lucky. Perhaps longer."

Two weeks. Ann and I drank our tea in silence then walked out through the open doorway. Below us, Tessalit in all its grandeur baked under an impossibly hot sun. Two weeks.

There were, of course, no phones in Tessalit. Two weeks. My wife would arrive in Tamanrasset. We would be waiting in Tessalit. Two weeks.

We walked down the hill to the café.

"What happened?" Peter Jokel, emerging from the bathroom, asked. "Change your mind? You like Tessalit too much to leave?"

• • •

Solidarity, the Polish labor organization, and a few rock-and-roll cassettes reduced our sentence in Tessalit to two days. This may not seem like very long. It is. There are nice people in Tessalit. We now know every one. We now know a great deal about their families.

Though he welcomed our company, our patron in the police station was quite willing to help us retrieve our passports. "I would go talk to the commandant," he told us over a delicious pot of couscous our first evening in town.

"But there is a problem. I have no car."

"Take our Land Cruiser," I quickly offered.

He was profuse in his thanks but refused. "If the army sees your car again they will think you have returned and will shoot it very quickly, before they see I am driving. This will not be good."

As much as I hated to, I had to agree with his conclusion.

So we waited until help arrived, and from a most unlikely source: Polish auto smugglers.

They came in two new Peugeot 504s, a punkish, good-looking couple with spiked hair and heavy Eastern European wing tip shoes. They had Polish passports but no visas for Mali, no insurance, and car registration papers of the most flimsy sort. Our friend in the police station sniffed blood from the very start.

"So," he said when they had made the long hike up the hill to pay homage at his station, "you would like to enter my country, yes? With your cars, yes? These are your papers? Really?"

A deal was slowly crafted over many glasses of frothy tea. He would allow their entrance into Mali if they would drive him to the army camp. He also wanted a fair slice of their cassette collection (which mainly consisted of Eastern European heavy-metal bands).

"We sell the cars and give the money to Solidarity!" the couple boasted to Ann and me, expecting all Americans to have a soft spot for Walesa and company.

Passports regained, we left Tessalit for the second time. We did not take any passengers and we did not miss the proper road.

I felt liberated, thrilled to embark on the final stretch. There was just enough time to reach Tamanrasset by the twenty-second.

The next morning, an hour or two before dawn, I woke up in the desert vomiting uncontrollably.

Ann looked down from the roof of the Cruiser. "Can I ask what you're doing?" she said in a sleepy voice.

I had a needle and syringe in my right hand and with my left I was rubbing a wet towel on my bare thigh. Alcohol is the standard preinjection cleanser but there was none of that to be had.

What I was doing was shooting four milligrams of Compazine into my leg. When a doctor friend had given me the vials and a handful of needles back in the States, he'd laughed at my avowed squeamishness over self-injection. "Don't worry, if you really need this stuff you'll do it in a second."

He was right. "This is the strongest antivomiting medicine I can give you," he told me. "I hope you don't need it."

I did.

We were in the desert somewhere near the Mali-Algerian border. This was the real Sahara, with no road at all but only an odd marker—an old refrigerator, an oil drum—every ten or fifteen kilometers to show the way. It was a flat, exhilarating expanse of open vistas to the horizon and rocky, firm sand.

"I didn't think this was possible," I gasped to Ann between seizures. "I mean, I really didn't."

The Compazine helped, increasing the time between heaves. As the sun bolted upward, Ann drove us toward Algerian customs in Bordj-Moktar.

Ahead was reputedly the worst customs post in West or North Africa. For the first time, we actually had something to hide: cash. French francs and U.S. dollars tucked away to trade on the black market. I had intended to put on one of my usual "Charm the Customs Officials" shows to counter a serious search.

"Maybe you can just vomit all over the customs officers and they'll be too busy to search the car," Ann suggested. "This really could be a lucky break."

I groaned.

In a way she proved to be right. Not that I vomited on anyone, but the officials quickly realized I was ill in a most unpleasant way and responded with the basic decency and grace that is quintessentially Algerian. The rough-looking, bearded officials in their drab olive uniforms shook their heads like the best Jewish mothers and hurried us through their office.

"There is a doctor here. You must go see him."

"A doctor?" It was hard to believe. A real doctor?

There were two, actually: a doctor and a dentist. They found me asleep on the cot in the one-room medical center. Both were recent med school graduates sent to Bordj-Moktar for their mandatory national service.

They asked me the usual questions, poking and probing. "Have you taken any medication?"

When I told them Compazine, they grew very excited.

"You have Compazine? Really? How much?"

The state of medical facilities in Bordj-Moktar was such that in my little kit of pharmaceutical odds and ends I had more medicine than the army clinic. Too polite to ask, the doctors looked on my unused vials of Compazine with undisguised envy.

But what they did have was a two-bed infirmary and enough kindness to fill a major hospital. We spent a day and night under their care; mostly I slept while the two doctors engaged in intense intellectual discussions with Ann. For several hours they analyzed in detail the differences between the films *Platoon* and *Apocalypse Now*, with a corollary comparison of the Vietnam War to the Algerian battle for independence. Outside the window, the Sahara stretched for over a thousand miles.

The next morning they implored us to stay for another day, a week, a month. They said they'd send a military plane to Tamanrasset to retrieve my wife. Their final words were, "Be very careful. Crossing the Sahara, people still die. Every week a corpse is brought here. People get careless."

Late that afternoon, hours into the desert, the Cruiser died. We were stranded.

The demise of the Cruiser was quite undramatic: no flames, no grinding, just a quiet rolling to a halt. One minute we were chugging over the stony sand at thirty kilometers an hour and then there was nothing. The engine still roared mightily but no power reached the wheels.

We got out and walked around, staring in disbelief. The Cruiser had served us well. We loved the Cruiser. The Cruiser would not abandon us.

Particularly not in the middle of the Sahara Desert. This was uncalled for.

My feeble powers of automotive deduction pointed me toward a transmission problem. I thought about the epoxy sealing the gearbox.

All afternoon we tried to revive the Cruiser. We added oil to the gearbox, fluid to the clutch. We topped off the fuel tank. Nothing worked.

As the sun slipped away, a hot wind kicked up from the north; the blowing sand made cooking impossible. We laid our sleeping bags behind a wheel and fell asleep.

To be stuck in the Sahara with a dead car is never a pleasant prospect. But our situation was far from desperate. We had one hundred liters of water and food; we were traveling on or close to one of the major north-south routes of the desert. As these things go, we were in good shape. Someone, we figured, would pass us. It had to happen.

And it did: two Italians in a strange dune buggy vehicle bombing over the sand. Two Italian *mechanics*.

It was a stroke of extraordinary luck. In all of North and West Africa there were perhaps ten people capable of fixing the Land Cruiser—at least without spare parts. The problem was a dead clutch and the obvious solution was a replacement clutch. We didn't have one, nor did the Italians.

The two, Giancarlo and Marco, were the picture of Italian chic. Young and good-looking, they wore fashionable jeans and Polo shirts that would have done them proud in Milano. They approached the Cruiser's sad state as a great challenge, a puzzle plunked down in the Sahara for their amusement. For hours they worked under the car while I handed them cigars and coffee.

At first they feared it was hopeless. The clutch plate was completely worn. We discussed what to do: Ann would ride with them back to Bordj-Moktar and I would stay with the Cruiser.

But Giancarlo refused to accept defeat. After a cup of coffee and a discussion of Italian rugby tournaments (we discovered we had both played in the same tournament near Venice), he charged under the Cruiser and, after much cursing and banging of wrenches, proposed a solution.

"I think I can jam the car into gear. One gear, no clutch. You would have one gear. It might work."

Marco was dubious. "It is not easy to drive in the desert with *four* gears. With one . . ." He shrugged and threw up his hands.

But the alternatives were bleak. Even if Ann mustered a tow truck in Bordj-Moktar, it was doubtful there was a clutch to be had. We would have to leave the Cruiser there and catch a ride across the Sahara with a truck driver, buy a clutch then return. It was also questionable whether there was a mechanic in Bordj-Moktar who could install the clutch. It was, after all, a town of nine buildings.

And there was the question of my wife's arrival in Tamanrasset. I had concluded that we could never reach there in time, but I held hopes of finding a phone on the other side of the Sahara. There were, of course, no phones in Bordj-Moktar.

So we decided to risk the single gear. We debated for a long time the proper gear: should it be second or third? Marco and Giancarlo disagreed, each presenting eloquent arguments for his favorite gear.

In the end, third gear won. Marco did the deed. We restarted the Cruiser and it lumbered immediately forward, shuddering at the work of starting in third gear.

"Don't stop!" Marco and Giancarlo shouted, jumping up and down in glee. I drove around them in a tight circle so we could talk. "Drive straight. Drive fast! Do not stop!!"

We left them puffing on the last of my Dannemann cigars, waving furiously.

Hundreds of kilometers lay between us and Reggane, the Algerian town on the northern edge of the Sahara.

The ride was the wildest of my life. With no gears to shift, speed was our only hope of making it through the soft stretches of sand. The Cruiser bucked and snorted like a wild mustang. As we flew over the sand ridges, all four wheels often left the ground, landing with a shuddering crash that felt as if a giant were beating on the roof with a sledgehammer. I tried not to think about the rear springs.

The wind continued to build into a sandstorm. We drove by compass directions, praying we wouldn't happen onto a parked truck convoy or a string of camels.

We drove all through the night, aided by a full moon. The wind died and we could see for miles in the pale light. It was strangely peaceful: the screech of the motor protesting its third-gear imprisonment, the white light spilling over the desert, the simplicity of our goal. Don't stop. Reach Reggane.

Just before dawn exploded on the desert, we saw the faint lights of a town hovering on the horizon.

It was watching the engine lift out that really scared me. I felt a deep, wrenching sensation as Yusuf and I hung from the chain pulley, raising the diesel heart of the Cruiser toward the tin roof of his garage. Wires and hoses dangled like arteries. One thought ran through my head: *What have I done? My God, what have I done?*

"Ahhh!" Yusuf screeched triumphantly. He released the chain and climbed into the hood cavity where the pistons once throbbed so powerfully. This left me holding the chain supporting the engine.

"Now we can begin!" he crowed.

I wondered if he intended for me to stay attached to the chain for the duration.

Cheik-ben wandered into the garage with Ann, followed by Habib, the Palestinian. They gathered around the disemboweled Cruiser offering advice to Yusuf. No one seemed to notice me holding on to the chain.

"I had no idea," Ann said in an academic tone I found all too aloof, "that the entire engine had to come out so the clutch can be replaced. How interesting."

"Would somebody please tie off this chain!" I finally shouted.

We were in Adrar, the first sizable town north of Reggane. Still in third gear, the cruiser had limped into town on a Thursday afternoon. This proved unfortunate timing as it coincided with the beginning of the Muslim weekend. All of this was explained by the policeman who stopped us as soon as we entered the town. The sand ladders mounted on the front—my beloved battering ram—had caught his eye.

"You don't need that here," he insisted with some indignation, as if we had insulted the progressive state of his hometown. "We have roads here. Good roads."

He warmed up to us when he realized we weren't French. (Adrar had been very close to the site of the French atomic bomb tests in the 1950s—*aboveground* tests. The leukemia rate was exceptional.) When we explained our predicament, he directed us to the town's best garage: Yusuf's.

"He is gone now," the policeman explained, "but I will go look for him." So we waited.

That's how Cheik-ben Bou Djemaa found us: waiting, parked in front of the big metal doors to Yusuf's garage. A gregarious fellow in his mid-thirties, Cheik-ben was short with a big belly and a scraggly black beard. His jewelry store adjoined the closed garage.

Immediately Cheik-ben expressed outrage that his town had treated us so poorly. "It is terrible you must wait here," he said. "What is happening that two visitors all the way from America must wait in the street!"

When we told him that the policeman had departed in search of Yusuf, he scoffed. "I know Yusuf. I take you to him."

His insistence was irresistible, as was his suggestion that Ann accompany him. "You must wait with the car," he explained to me, "so that if Yusuf returns you can tell him what is wrong."

"Of course," I agreed. It wasn't until a few minutes after Cheik-ben and Ann departed in his tiny Toyota that I wondered why it was necessary for Ann to accompany him. This I thought about more when two hours had passed and there was no sight of anyone: Ann, Yusuf or Cheik-ben.

Well, now, I thought, this is just great. Ann is probably headed for the auction block in Tangiers, I'm here with a dead car in a closed town, and my wife arrives in forty-eight hours. This is just swell.

But in truth I found it pleasant to lie back on the hood of the Cruiser with nothing to do. My body still tingled with the jolts of the desert crossing. In a vague way I thought about what I would need to do if Ann did not return shortly: make inquires in Cheik-ben's store, look for Yusuf (if Yusuf really existed), find a policeman. I drifted to sleep.

Habib woke me up. "Can I help you?" he asked politely, like the steward on a cruise ship at teatime. He was a portly fellow wearing a tweed jacket and rep tie with a scarf thrown over his neck. His accent was English, his manner that of an amiable Oxford don.

"I'm waiting for a friend," I explained, trying to sound as casually elegant as he looked.

"I see." He peered at me through thick glasses. "You have friends in Adrar. How nice."

I told him the whole story. He chuckled when I expressed concern over Ann and Cheik-ben's lengthy absence. "They probably take coffee at Yusuf's home. It would be impossible for Yusuf not to insist that a foreign visitor take refreshment in his home. It would be a great insult."

I thought about Ann's fondness for refreshments and our lack thereof for quite some time. I was certain it would require little insistence on Yusuf's part.

Habib was a Palestinian, a teacher by profession, forced to Algeria with his family after 1948. With little prompting, he launched into an astoundingly intricate analysis of the Israeli-Palestinian situation. At regular intervals he interrupted the erudite lecture to grasp my arm, encrusted with a grimy layer of oil and sand, imploring, "You see? You must help us!"

Eventually I realized that he meant the United States government, rather than myself. I nodded vaguely, trying to come up with words befitting my new diplomatic status. It had been so long, however, since I had discussed anything more elaborate than a dead clutch or a flat tire that the best I could muster was a gravely, if ludicrously, uttered, "I see."

In fact this was probably not a bad start for a diplomat.

Just as Habib was demanding I explain the true relevance of UN Resolution 242, Ann and Cheik-ben returned with Yusuf in tow.

"You have problem?" Yusuf asked.

"We had tea," Ann spoke up before I could answer. "And cakes. Wonderful sweet cakes."

Yusuf wanted French francs, not Algerian dinars. "Our money," he said cheerfully, "it is no good."

This was true. Algeria, unlike the former French colonies of West Africa, had strict currency regulations. Travelers declared all foreign funds upon entering the country and Algerian citizens were strictly limited in the amount of money they could take with them when leaving the country. As Algerians were a sophisticated lot with a keen interest in international travel and trade, they evolved numerous ingenious schemes to circumvent these annoying currency restrictions.

"There is a thriving black market both inside and outside the country," explains the Lonely Planet guide. "French francs are the preferred currency. The Algerian authorities are well aware of these rates, so they're very keen on preventing you from using the black market and, as a result, there are heavy baggage and body searches (shoes off, a quick look in your underpants, etc.). If you're taking in black market money, you'll need to hide it very well. If they find the money it will be confiscated."

Ever the good student, I followed this advice with great enthusiasm.

Convinced my cleverness would win me a place in the Smuggler's Hall of Fame, I secreted a small fortune in French francs inside the hollow aluminum poles of my mountain tent.

But what had seemed so brilliant on conception had one resounding difficulty: I couldn't get the money out.

I discovered this after Yusuf and I negotiated a price for the new clutch, payment to be made in francs. While he worked in the empty cavity of the engine compartment, I unfolded the tent on the garage floor and set about to retrieve my artfully hidden funds.

Like Robinson Crusoe constructing his first canoe too far from the water, my clever planning had a rather basic flaw. I had assumed, to the degree I had considered the question, that the francs would simply slide out of the hollow poles. This proved inaccurate.

Habib and Cheik-ben watched while I whipped the tent poles through the air, trying to force the francs out of the open end.

"My people have suffered like no American can imagine," Habib droned.

"Please, Habib," I begged. "I am suffering. Believe me."

"But you are an American. Americans have no problems!"

I flailed the tent poles against the cinder-block floor.

"Habib, Please. I am in Adrar with a car that has no clutch—"

"Yusuf replaces your clutch! No problem!"

"With all my money stuffed down these damn tent tubes."

"I believe that is Yusuf's problem," Cheik-ben chuckled.

"And my wife arrives in Algiers in two days."

"Algiers is a beautiful city. A city more greater than Paris!"

"And once she is in Algiers, she will get on a plane to Tamanrasset expecting to meet Ann and me and I will be sitting here in Yusuf's garage still trying to get my money out of these tent poles!"

"It was a very smart hiding place," Cheik-ben said thoughtfully. "I must remember it the next time I go to France."

"But why would you take a tent to France?" Habib, the scholar, asked. "The hotels in France are excellent. After the 1986 PLO council meeting in Tangiers, the old man and I traveled to Saint-Tropez."

I had one end of the pole in my mouth, alternately blowing and sucking. This caused the francs to ruffle teasingly but they remained firmly lodged.

"You should call your wife," Yusuf shouted from the depths of the Cruiser. "It is not good to keep your wife waiting!"

It was, of course, good advice. But telephoning from Adrar to America was a daunting challenge.

Complicating the procedure was Cheik-ben's fervent insistence that we use the telephone in his house, not the post office. "It is logical," he asserted, "because you must stay at my home."

I demurred. Adrar actually had a hotel, a rather decent-looking one. It was such a rarity, I was looking forward to a night between real sheets.

"For you to stay in the hotel and not my home would be a terrible, terrible insult. We cannot even talk about this." He scowled, and then broke into a huge grin when we accepted with thanks, embracing each of us in a crushing bear hug.

"You will like my mother," he promised.

Cheik-ben was the only man in a houseful of women: his mother, two sisters and a young black woman who seemed part servant, part family member. "She is very poor," Cheik-ben explained. "We take care of her since birth."

"She's a slave," Ann whispered. "A slave!"

This may have been true but then the same could have been said for Cheik-ben's mother and sisters. They hovered in the background of the four-room house, awaiting Cheik-ben's commands. These came with decided regularity.

Cheik-ben held court in the largest room in the house, decorated with thick pillows and rugs; the centerpiece of the room was a television resting on an orange crate. It was a comfortable, cozy space. Cheik-ben's life greatly resembled that of a stereotypical American teenage girl: he spent all spare moments watching television and talking on the telephone to his friends. The phone rang constantly. His callers apparently were situated in similar circumstances, as the favorite topic of conversation was a running commentary on the television show of the moment and what their mothers and sisters had just brought them to eat.

Cheik-ben and his pals were all Muslims; they also drank prodigious quantities of scotch. Friday night was the highlight of their week, not for religious but rather entertainment reasons. "Disco on television!" Cheik-ben shouted happily. "Tonight! Every Friday!"

A half dozen of his friends dropped by during the long American dance show dubbed in Arabic. They squatted around the delicious couscous prepared by the household's female contingent and debated fiercely the relative appeal of the dancing girls on television.

"If I come to America, she will marry me, yes?" he frequently inquired.

While the music blared, I tried continually to telephone my wife in America or the Air France office in Algiers to leave a message. The operators were gracious in the extreme but our efforts were futile. "Do you like disco?" my favorite female operator asked, hearing the music in the background. "I love to dance! I would love to dance this minute! I'm sorry, I feel sadness for your wife."

It was that same operator who telephoned near dawn. "Have you heard?" she asked excitedly.

"Heard?"

"There is a strike in Algiers! That is why we could not get a circuit. A big strike!"

"I see." I started to fall asleep.

"But this is very good news for your wife!"

"It is?"

"The airport is closed! Her flight from America will be delayed. You will have time to finish your car repairs and drive to Algiers. Everything will be happy!"

I thanked her and hung up the phone. The disco show was over, replaced by a red and green test pattern. Cheik-ben and two of his friends snored loudly, wrapped in each other's arms like kittens. Scotch bottles and plates of dried couscous littered the floor.

"Is there any food left?" Ann asked sleepily. She was across the room, as far from Cheik-ben and his friends as possible. Toward the end of the evening they had been very interested in trying some of the American dances with a real American girl.

"In the kitchen," I said. "A big pot of *couscous.*"

"I'm starved."

"Let's eat some couscous and then walk over to the hotel for coffee." We were still enthralled by the novelty of the hotel.

"And then we have to work on the poles," Ann reminded me. There were still several hundred dollars in the tent poles.

"I've got a new idea," she said. "What if we poured motor oil down the tubes and—"

"Oil?"

That afternoon, Yusuf finished the clutch repair. I paid him in francs, as agreed.

"But these francs, they are sticky! What has happened?" he cried, but slipped them into his pocket with alacrity.

As we were leaving, he handed me a large box of motor parts.

"What's this?" I asked.

"We had these parts left over after we put the engine back in."

I stared at the heavy box. "All these parts?"

He nodded happily. "It is much better. The car is lighter now and runs better. You can sell these in Algiers."

I started to stay something but didn't. I put the box in the car.

"How much do you think we can get for the parts?" Ann asked as we drove out of town.

We talked about it all the way to Algiers.

from The Last American Hero
by Tom Wolfe

Junior Johnson was stock-car racing's first super-star. Tom Wolfe (born 1931) in 1964 profiled Johnson in an Esquire article that became the basis for a 1973 film. Wolfe celebrates Johnson as a kind of archetypal American: "... one of the last of those sports stars who is not just an ace at the game itself, but a hero a whole people or class of people can identify with."

Starting time! Linda Vaughn, with the big blonde hair and blossomy breasts, puts down her Coca-Cola and the potato chips and slips off her red stretch pants and her white blouse and walks out of the officials' booth in her Rake-a-cheek red showgirl's costume with her long honeydew legs in net stockings and climbs up on the red Firebird float. The Life Symbol of stock car racing! Yes! Linda, every luscious morsel of Linda, is a good old girl from Atlanta who was made Miss Atlanta International Raceway one year and was paraded around the track on a float and she liked it so much and all the good old boys liked it so much, Linda's flowing hair and blossomy breasts and honeydew legs, that she became the permanent glamor symbol of stock car racing, and never mind this other modeling she was doing . . . this, she liked it. Right before practically every race on the Grand National circuit Linda Vaughn puts down her Coca-Cola and potato chips. Her momma is there, she generally comes around to see Linda go around the track on the float, it's such a nice spectacle seeing Linda looking so lovely, and the applause and all. "Linda, I'm thirstin', would you bring me a Coca-Cola?" "A lot of them think I'm Freddie Lorenzen's girl friend, but I'm not any of 'em's girl friend, I'm real good friends with 'em all, even Wendell," he being Wendell Scott, the only Negro in big-league stock car racing. Linda gets up on the Firebird float. This is an extraordinary object, made of wood, about twenty feet tall, in the shape of a huge bird, an eagle or something, blazing red, and Linda, with her red showgirl's suit on, gets up on the seat, which is up between the wings, like a saddle, high enough so her long honeydew legs stretch down, and a new car pulls her—Miss Firebird!—slowly once around the track just before the race. It is more of a ceremony by now than the national anthem. Miss Firebird sails slowly in front of the stands and the good old boys let out some real curdle Rebel yells, "Yaaaaaaaaaaaaghhh-hoooooo! Let me at that car!" "Honey, you sure do start my motor, I swear to God!" "Great God and Poonadingdong, I mean!"

And suddenly there's a big roar from behind, down in the infield, and then I see one of the great sights in stock car racing. That infield! The cars have been piling into the infield by the hundreds, parking in there on the clay and the grass, every which way, angled down and angled up, this way and that, where the ground is uneven, these beautiful blazing brand-new cars with the sun exploding off the windshields and the baked enamel and the glassy lacquer, hundreds, thousands of cars, stacked this way and that in the infield with the sun bolting down and no shade, none at all, just a couple of Coca-Cola stands out there. And already the good old boys and girls are out beside the cars, with all these beautiful little buds in short shorts already spread-eagled out on top of the car roofs, pressing down on good hard slick automobile sheet metal, their little cupcake bottoms aimed up at the sun. The good old boys are lollygagging around with their shirts off and straw hats on that have miniature beer cans on the brims and buttons that read, "Girls Wanted—No Experience Required." And everybody, good old boys and girls of all ages, are out there with portable charcoal barbecue ovens set up, and folding tubular steel terrace furniture, deck chairs and things, and Thermos jugs and coolers full of beer—and suddenly it is not the upcountry South at all but a concentration of the modern suburbs, all jammed into that one space, from all over America, with blazing cars and instant goodies, all cooking under the bare blaze—inside a strange bowl. The infield is like the bottom of a bowl. The track around it is banked so steeply at the corners and even on the straightaways, it is like the steep sides of a bowl. The wall around the track, and the stands and the bleachers are like the rim of a bowl. And from the infield, in this great incredible press of blazing new cars, there is no horizon but the bowl, up above only that cobalt-blue North Carolina sky. And then suddenly, on a signal, thirty stock car engines start up where they are lined up in front of the stands. The roar of these engines is impossible to describe. They have a simultaneous rasp, thunder and rumble, that goes right through a body and fills the whole bowl with a noise of internal combustion. Then they start around on two build-up runs, just to build up speed, and then they come around the fourth turn and onto the straightaway in front of the stands at—here, 130 miles an hour, in Atlanta, 160 miles an hour, at Daytona, 180 miles an hour— and the flag goes down and everybody in the infield and in the stands is up on their feet going mad, and suddenly here is a bowl that is one great orgy of everything in the way of excitement and liberation the automobile has meant to Americans. An orgy!

The first lap of a stock car race is a horrendous, a wildly horrendous spectacle such as no other sport approaches. Twenty, thirty, forty automobiles, each of them weighing almost two tons, 3700 pounds, with 427-cubic-inch engines, 600 horsepower, are practically locked together, side to side and tail to nose, on a narrow band of asphalt at 130, 160, 180 miles an hour, hitting the curves so hard the rubber, burns off the tires in front of your eyes. To the driver, it is like being inside a car going down the West Side Highway in New York City at rush hour, only with everybody going literally three to four times as fast, at speeds a man who has gone eighty-five miles an hour down a highway cannot conceive of, and with every other driver an enemy who is willing to cut inside of you, around you or in front of you, or ricochet off your side in the battle to get into a curve first.

The speeds are faster than those in the Indianapolis 500 race, the cars are more powerful and much heavier. The prize money in Southern stock car racing is far greater than that in Indianapolis-style or European Grand Prix racing, but few Indianapolis or Grand Prix drivers have the raw nerve required to succeed at it.

Although they will deny it, it is still true that stock car drivers will put each other "up against the wall"—cut inside on the left of another car and ram it into a spin—if they get mad enough. Crashes are not the only danger, however. The cars are now literally too fast for their own parts, especially the tires. Firestone and Goodyear have poured millions into stock car racing, but neither they nor anybody so far have been able to come up with a tire for this kind of racing at the current speeds. Three well-known stock car drivers were killed last year, two of them champion drivers, Joe Weatherly and Fireball Roberts, and another, one of the best new drivers, Jimmy Pardue, from Junior Johnson's own home territory, Wilkes County, North Carolina. Roberts was the only one killed in a crash. Junior Johnson was in the crash but was not injured. Weatherly and Pardue both lost control on curves. Pardue's death came during a tire test. In a tire test, engineers from Firestone or Goodyear try out various tires on a car, and the driver, always one of the top competitors, tests them at top speed, usually on the Atlanta track. The drivers are paid three dollars a mile and may drive as much as five or six hundred miles in a single day. At 145 miles an hour average that does not take very long. Anyway, these drivers are going at speeds that, on curves, can tear tires off their casings or break axles. They practically run off from over their own wheels.

Junior Johnson was over in the garden by the house some years ago, plowing the garden barefooted, behind a mule, just wearing an old pair of overalls, when a couple of good old boys drove up and told him to come on up to the speedway and get in a stock car race. They wanted some local boys to race, as a preliminary to the main race, "as a kind of side show," as Junior remembers it.

"So I just put the reins down," Junior is telling me, "and rode on over 'ere with them. They didn't give us seat belts or nothing, they just roped us in. H'it was a dirt track then. I come in second."

Junior was a sensation in dirt-track racing right from the start. Instead of going into the curves and just sliding and holding on for dear life like the other drivers, Junior developed the technique of throwing himself into a slide about seventy-five feet before the curve by cocking the wheel to the left slightly and gunning it, using the slide, not the brake, to slow down, so that he could pick up speed again halfway through the curve and come out of it like a shot. This was known as his "power slide," and—yes! of course!—every good old boy in North Carolina started saying Junior Johnson had learned that stunt doing those goddamned *about-faces* running away from the Alcohol Tax agents. Junior put on such a show one night on a dirt track in Charlotte that he broke two axles, and he thought he was out of the race because he didn't have any more axles, when a good old boy came running up out of the infield and said, "Goddamn it, Junior Johnson, you take the axle off my car here, I got a Pontiac just like yours," and Junior took it off and put it on his and went out and broke *it* too. Mother dog! To this day Junior Johnson loves dirt track racing like nothing else in this world, even though there is not much money in it. Every year he sets new dirt track speed records, such as at Hickory, North Carolina, one of the most popular dirt tracks, last spring. As far as Junior is concerned, dirt track racing is not so much of a mechanical test for the car as those long five- and six-hundred-mile races on asphalt are. Gasoline, tire and engine wear aren't so much of a problem. It is all the driver, his skill, his courage—his willingness to mix it up with the other cars, smash and carom off of them at a hundred miles an hour or so to get into the curves first. Junior has a lot of fond recollections of mixing it up at places like Bowman Gray Stadium in Winston-Salem, one of the minor league tracks, a very narrow track, hardly wide enough for two cars. "You could always figure Bowman Gray was gonna cost you two fenders, two doors and two quarter panels," Junior tells me with nostalgia.

Anyway, at Hickory, which was a Saturday night race, all the good old boys started pouring into the stands before sundown, so they wouldn't miss anything, the practice runs or the qualifying or anything. And pretty soon, the dew hasn't even started falling before Junior Johnson and David Pearson, one of Dodge's best drivers, are out there on practice runs, just warming up, and they happen to come up alongside each other on the second curve, and—the thing is, here are two men, each of them driving $15,000 automobiles, each of them standing to make $50,000 to $100,000 for the season if they don't get themselves killed, and they meet on a curve on a goddamned practice run on a dirt track, and neither of them can resist it. Coming out of the turn they go into a wildass race down the backstretch, both of them trying to get into the third turn first, and all the way across the infield you can hear them ricocheting off each other and bouncing at a hundred miles an hour on loose dirt, and then they go into ferocious power slides, red dust all over the goddamned place, and then out of this goddamned red-dust cloud, out of the fourth turn, here comes Junior Johnson first, like a shot, with Pearson right on his tail, and the good old boys in the stands going wild, and the *qualifying* runs haven't started yet, let alone the race.

Junior worked his way up through the minor leagues, the Sportsman and Modified classifications, as they are called, winning championships in both, and won his first Grand National race, the big leagues, in 1955 at Hickory, on dirt! He was becoming known as "the hardest of the hard chargers," power sliding, rooting them out of the groove, raising hell, and already the Junior Johnson legend was beginning.

He kept hard-charging, power sliding, going after other drivers as though there wasn't room on the track but for one, and became the most popular driver in stock car racing by 1959. The presence of Detroit and Detroit's big money had begun to calm the drivers down a little. Detroit was concerned about Image. The last great duel of the dying dog-eat-dog era of stock car racing came in 1959, when Junior and Lee Petty, who was then leading the league in points, had it out on the Charlotte raceway. Junior was in the lead, and Petty was right on his tail, but couldn't get by Junior. Junior kept coming out of the curves faster. So every chance he got, Petty would get up right on Junior's rear bumper and start banging it, gradually forcing the fender in to where the metal would cut Junior's rear tire. With only a few laps to go, Junior had a blowout and spun out up against the guardrail. That is Junior's version. Petty claimed Junior hit a pop bottle and spun out. The fans in Charlotte were always throwing pop bottles and other stuff onto the track late in the race, looking for blood. In any case, Junior eased back into the pits, had the tire changed, and charged out after Petty. He caught him on a curve and—well, whatever really happened, Petty was suddenly "up against the wall" and out of the race, and Junior won.

What a howl went up. The Charlotte chief of police charged out onto the track after the race, according to Petty, and offered to have Junior arrested for "assault with a dangerous weapon," the hassling went on for weeks—

"Back then," Junior tells me, "when you got into a guy and racked him up, you might as well get ready, because he's coming back for you. H'it was dog eat dog. That straightened Lee Petty out right smart. They don't do stuff like that anymore, though, because the guys don't stand for it."

Anyway, the Junior Johnson legend kept building up and building up, and in 1960 it got hotter than ever when Junior won the biggest race of the year, the Daytona 500, by discovering a new technique called "drafting." That year stock car racing was full of big powerful Pontiacs manned by top drivers, and they would go like nothing else anybody ever saw. Junior went down to Daytona with a Chevrolet.

"My car was about ten miles an hour slower than the rest of the cars, the Pontiacs," Junior tells me. "In the preliminary races, the warmups and stuff like that, they was smoking me off the track. Then I remember once I went out for a practice run, and Fireball Roberts was out there in a Pontiac and I got in right behind him on a curve, right on his bumper. I knew I couldn't stay with him on the straightaway, but I came out of the curve fast, right in behind him, running flat out, and then I noticed a funny thing. As long as I stayed right in behind him, I noticed I picked up speed and stayed right with him and my car was going faster than it had ever gone before. I could tell on the tachometer. My car wasn't turning no more than 6000 before, but when I got into this drafting position, I was turning 6800 to 7000. H'it felt like the car was plumb off the ground, floating along."

"Drafting," it was discovered at Daytona, created a vacuum behind the lead car and both cars would go faster than they normally would. Junior "hitched rides" on the Pontiacs most of the afternoon, but was still second to Bobby Johns, the lead Pontiac. Then, late in the race, Johns got into a drafting position with a fellow Pontiac that was actually one lap behind him and the vacuum got so intense that the rear window blew out of Johns' car and he spun out and crashed and Junior won.

This made Junior the Lion Killer, the Little David of stock car racing, and his performance in the 1963 season made him even more so.

Junior raced for Chevrolet at Daytona in February, 1963, and set the all-time stock car speed record in a hundred-mile qualifying race, 164.083 miles an hour, twenty-one miles an hour faster than Parnelli Jones's winning time at Indianapolis that year. Junior topped that at Daytona in July of 1963, qualifying at 166.005 miles per hour in a five-mile run, the fastest that anyone had ever averaged that distance in a racing car of any type. Junior's Chevrolet lasted only twenty-six laps in the Daytona 500 in 1963, however. He went out with a broken push rod. Although Chevrolet announced they were pulling out of racing at this time, Junior took his car and started out on the wildest performance in the history of stock car racing. Chevrolet wouldn't give him a cent of backing. They wouldn't even speak to him on the telephone. Half the time he had to have his own parts made. Plymouth, Mercury, Dodge and Ford, meantime, were pouring more money than ever into stock car racing. Yet Junior won seven Grand National races out of the thirty-three he entered and led most others before mechanical trouble forced him out.

All the while, Junior was making record qualifying runs, year after year. In the usual type of qualifying run, a driver has the track to himself and makes two circuits, with the driver with the fastest average time getting the "pole" position for the start of the race. In a way this presents stock car danger in its purest form. Driving a stock car does not require much handling ability, at least not as compared to Grand Prix racing, because the tracks are simple banked ovals and there is almost no shifting of gears. So qualifying becomes a test of raw nerve—of how fast a man is willing to take a curve. Many of the top drivers in competition are poor at qualifying. In effect, they are willing to calculate their risks only against the risks the other drivers are taking. Junior takes the pure risk as no other driver has ever taken it.

"Pure" risk or total risk, whichever, Indianapolis and Grand Prix drivers have seldom been willing to face the challenge of Southern stock car drivers. A. J. Foyt, last year's winner at Indianapolis, is one exception. He has raced against the Southerners and beaten them. Parnelli Jones has tried and fared badly. Driving "Southern style" has a quality that shakes a man up. The Southerners went on a tour of northern tracks last fall. They raced at Bridgehampton, New York, and went into the corners so hard the marshals stationed at each corner kept radioing frantically to the control booth: "They're going off the track. They're all going off the track!"

But this, Junior Johnson's last race in a Dodge, was not his day, neither for qualifying or racing. Lorenzen took the lead early and won the 250-mile race a lap ahead of the field. Junior finished third, but was never in contention for the lead.

"Come on, Junior, do my hand—"

Two or three hundred people come out of the stands and up out of the infield and onto the track to be around Junior Johnson. Junior is signing autographs in a neat left-handed script he has. It looks like it came right out of the Locker book. The girls! Levis, stretch pants, sneaky shorts, stretch jeans, they press into the crowd with lively narbs and try to get their hands up in front of Junior and say:

"Come on, Junior, do my hand!"

In order to do a hand, Junior has to hold the girl's hand in his right hand and then sign his name with a ball-point on the back of her hand.

"Junior, you got to do mine, too!"

"Put it on up here."

All the girls break into . . . smiles. Junior Johnson does a hand. Ah, sweet little cigarette-ad blonde! She says:

"Junior, why don't you ever call me up?"

"I 'spect you get plenty of calls 'thout me."

"Oh, Junior! You call me up, you hear now?"

But also a great many older people crowd in, and they say:

"Junior, you're doing a real good job out there, you're driving real good."

"Junior, when you get in that Ford, I want to see you pass that Freddie Lorenzen, you hear now?"

"Junior, you like that Ford better than that Dodge?"

And:

"Junior, here's a young man that's been waiting sometime and wanting to see you—" and the man lifts up his little boy in the middle of the crowd and says: "I told you you'd see Junior Johnson. This here's Junior Johnson!"

The boy has a souvenir racing helmet on his head. He stares at Junior through a buttery face. Junior signs the program he has in his hand, and then the boy's mother says:

"Junior, I tell you right now, he's beside you all the way. He can't be moved."

And then:

"Junior, I want you to meet the meanest little girl in Wilkes County."

"She don't look mean to me."

Junior keeps signing autographs and over by the pits the other kids are all over his car, the Dodge. They start pulling off the decals, the ones saying Holly Farms Poultry and Autolite and God knows whatall. They fight over the strips, the shreds of decal, as if they were totems.

All this homage to Junior Johnson lasts about forty minutes. He must be signing about 250 autographs, but he is not a happy man. By and by the crowd is thinning out, the sun is going down, wind is blowing the Coca-Cola cups around, all one can hear, mostly, is a stock car engine starting up every now and then as somebody drives it up onto a truck or something, and Junior looks around and says:

"I'd rather lead one lap and fall out of the race than stroke it and finish in the money."

"Stroking it" is driving carefully in hopes of outlasting faster and more reckless cars. The opposite of stroking it is "hard-charging." Then Junior says:

"I hate to get whipped up here in Wilkes County, North Carolina."

Wilkes County, North Carolina! Who was it tried to pin the name on Wilkes County, "The bootleg capital of America"? This fellow Vance Packard. But just a minute. . . .

The night after the race Junior and his fiancée, Flossie Clark, and myself went into North Wilkesboro to have dinner. Junior and Flossie came by Lowes Motel and picked us up in the dreamboat white Pontiac. Flossie is a bright, attractive woman, *saftig*, well-organized. She and Junior have been going together since they were in high school. They are going to get married as soon as Junior gets his new house built. Flossie has been doing the decor. Junior Johnson, in the second-highest income bracket in the United States for the past five years, is moving out of his father's white frame house in Ingle Hollow at last. About three hundred yards down the road. Overlooking a lot of good green land and Anderson's grocery. Junior shows me through the house, it is almost finished, and when we get to the front door, I ask him, "How much of this land is yours?"

Junior looks around for a minute, and then back up the hill, up past his three automated chicken houses, and then down into the hollow over the pasture where his $3100 Santa Gertrudis bull is grazing, and then he says:

"Everything that's green is mine."

Junior Johnson's house is going to be one of the handsomest homes in Wilkes County. Yes. And—such complicated problems of class and status. Junior is not only a legendary figure as a backwoods boy with guts who made good, he is also popular personally, he is still a good old boy, rich as he is. He is also respected for the sound and sober way he has invested his money. He also has one of the best business connections in town, Holly Farms Poultry. What complicates it is that half the county, anyway, reveres him as the greatest, most fabled night-road driver in the history of Southern bootlegging. There is hardly a living soul in the hollows who can conjure up two seconds' honest moral indignation over "the whiskey business." That is what they call it, "the whiskey business." The fact is, it has some positive political overtones, sort of like the I.R.A. in Ireland. The other half of the county—well, North Wilkesboro itself is a prosperous, good-looking town of 5,000, where a lot of hearty modern business burghers are making money the modern way, like everywhere else in the U.S.A., in things like banking, poultry processing, furniture, mirror, and carpet manufacture, apple growing, and so forth and so on. And one thing these men are tired of is Wilkes County's reputation as a center of moonshining. The U.S. Alcohol and Tobacco Tax agents sit over there in Wilkesboro, right next to North Wilkesboro, year in and year out, and they have been there since God knows when, like an Institution in the land, and every day that they are there, it is like a sign saying, Moonshine County. And even that is not so *bad*—it has nothing to do with it being immoral and only a little to do with it being illegal. The real thing is, it is—raw and hill-billy. And one thing thriving modern Industry is not is hillbilly. And one thing the burghers of North Wilkesboro are not about to be is hill-billy. They have split-level homes that would knock your eyes out. Also swimming pools, white Buick Snatchwagons, flagstone *terrasse*-porches enclosed with louvered glass that opens wide in the summertime, and built-in brick barbecue pits and they give parties where they wear Bermuda shorts and Jax stretch pants and serve rum collins and play twist and bossa nova records on the hi-fi and tell Shaggy Dog jokes about strange people ordering martinis. Moonshining . . . just a minute—the truth is, North Wilkesboro. . . .

So we are all having dinner at one of the fine new restaurants in North Wilkesboro, a place of suburban plate-glass elegance. The manager knows Junior and gives us the best table in the place and comes over and talks to Junior a while about the race. A couple of men get up and come over and get Junior's autograph to take home to their sons and so forth. Then toward the end of the meal a couple of North Wilkesboro businessmen come over ("Junior, how are you, Junior. You think you're going to like that fast-backed Ford?") and Junior introduces them to me.

"You're not going to do like that fellow Vance Packard did, are you?"

"Vance Packard?"

"Yeah, I think it was Vance Packard wrote it. He wrote an article and called Wilkes County the bootleg capital of America. Don't pull any of that stuff. I think it was in *American* magazine. The bootleg capital of America. Don't pull any of that stuff on us."

I looked over at Junior and Flossie. Neither one of them said anything. They didn't even change their expressions.

The next morning I met Junior down in Ingle Hollow at Anderson's Store. That's about fifteen miles out of North Wilkesboro on County Road No. 2400. Junior is known in a lot of Southern newspapers as "the wild man from Ronda" or "the lead-footed chicken farmer from Ronda," but Ronda is only his post-office-box address. His telephone exchange, with the Wilkes Telephone Membership Corporation, is Clingman, North Carolina, and that isn't really where he lives either. Where he lives is just Ingle Hollow, and one of the communal centers of Ingle Hollow is Anderson's Store. Anderson's is not exactly a grocery store. Out front there are two gasoline pumps under an overhanging roof. Inside there are a lot of things like a soda-pop cooler filled with ice, Coca-Colas, Nehi drinks, Dr. Pepper, Double Cola, and a gumball machine, a lot of racks of Red Man chewing tobacco, Price's potato chips, OKay peanuts, cloth hats for working outdoors in, dried sausages, cigarettes, canned-goods, a little bit of meal and flour, fly swatters, and I don't know what all. Inside and outside of Anderson's there are good old boys. The young ones tend to be inside, talking, and the old ones tend to be outside, sitting under the roof by the gasoline pumps, talking. And on both sides, cars; most of them new and pastel.

Junior drives up and gets out and looks up over the door where there is a row of twelve coon tails. Junior says:

"Two of them gone, ain't they?"

One of the good old boys says, "Yeah," and sighs.

A pause, and the other one says, "Somebody stole 'em."

Then the first one says, "Junior, that dog of yours ever come back?"

Junior says, "Not yet."

The second good old boy says, "You looking for her to come back?"

Junior says, "I reckon she'll come back."

The good old boy says, "I had a coon dog went off like that. They don't ever come back. I went out 'ere one day, back over yonder, and there he was, cut right from here to here. I swear if it don't look like a coon got him. Something. H'it must of turned him every way but loose."

Junior goes inside and gets a Coca-Cola and rings up the till himself, like everybody who goes into Anderson's does, it seems like. It is dead quiet in the hollow except for every now and then a car grinds over the dirt road and down the way. One coon dog missing. But he still has a lot of the black and tans, named Rock. . . .

. . . Rock, Whitey, Red, Buster are in the pen out back of the Johnson house, the old frame house. They have scars all over their faces from fighting coons. Gypsy has one huge gash in her back from fighting something. A red rooster crosses the lawn. That's a big rooster. Shirley, one of Junior's two younger sisters, pretty girls, is out by the fence in shorts, pulling weeds. Annie May is inside the house with Mrs. Johnson. Shirley has the radio outside on the porch aimed at her, The Four Seasons! "Dawn!—ahhhh, ahhhhh, ahhhhhh!" Then a lot of electronic wheeps and lulus and a screaming disc jockey, yessss! WTOB, the Vibrant Mothering Voice of Winston-Salem, North Carolina. It sounds like WABC in New York. Junior's mother, Mrs. Johnson, is a big, good-natured woman. She comes out and says, "Did you ever see anything like that in your life? Pullin' weeds listenin' to the radio." Junior's father, Robert Glenn Johnson, Sr.—he built this frame house about thirty-five years ago, up here where the gravel road ends and the woods starts. The road just peters out into the woods up a hill. The house has a living room, four bedrooms and a big kitchen. The living room is full of Junior's racing trophies, and so is the piano in Shirley's room. Junior was born and raised here with his older brothers, L. P., the oldest, and Fred, and his older sister, Ruth. Over yonder, up by that house, there's a man with a mule and a little plow. That's L. P. The Johnsons still keep that old mule around to plow the vegetable gardens. And all around, on all sides, like a rim are the ridges and the woods. Well, what about those woods, where Vance Packard said the agents come stealing over the ridges and good old boys go crashing through the underbrush to get away from the still and the women start "calling the cows" up and down the hollows as the signal *they were coming.* . . .

Junior motions his hand out toward the hills and says, "I'd say nearly everybody in a fifty-mile radius of here was in the whiskey business at one time or another. When we growed up here, everybody seemed to be more or less messing with whiskey, and myself and my two brothers did quite a bit of transporting. H'it was just a business, like any other business, far as we was concerned. H'it was a matter of survival. During the Depression here, people either had to do that or starve to death. H'it wasn't no gangster type of business or nothing. They's nobody that ever messed with it here that was ever out to hurt anybody. Even if they got caught, they never tried to shoot anybody or anything like that. Getting caught and pulling time, that was just part of it. H'it was just a business, like any other business. Me and my brothers, when we went out on the road at night, h'it was just like a milk run, far as we was concerned. They was certain deliveries to be made and. . . ."

A milk run—yes! Well, it was a business, all right. In fact, it was a regional industry, all up and down the Appalachian slopes. But never mind the Depression. It goes back a long way before that. The Scotch-Irish settled the mountains from Pennsylvania down to Alabama, and they have been making whiskey out there as long as anybody can remember. At first it was a simple matter of economics. The land had a low crop yield, compared to the lowlands, and even after a man struggled to grow his corn, or whatever, the cost of transporting it to the markets from down out of the hills was so great, it wasn't worth it. It was much more profitable to convert the corn into whiskey and sell that. The trouble started with the Federal Government on that score almost the moment the Republic was founded. Alexander Hamilton put a high excise tax on whiskey in 1791, almost as soon as the Constitution was ratified. The "Whiskey Rebellion" broke out in the mountains of western Pennsylvania in 1794. The farmers were mad as hell over the tax. Fifteen thousand Federal troops marched out to the mountains and suppressed them. Almost at once, however, the trouble over the whiskey tax became a symbol of something bigger. This was a general enmity between the western and eastern sections of practically every seaboard state. Part of it was political. The eastern sections tended to control the legislatures, the economy, and the law courts, and the western sections felt shortchanged. Part of it was cultural. Life in the western sections was rougher. Religions, codes, and styles of life were sterner. Life in the eastern capitals seemed to give off the odor of Europe and decadence. Shay's Rebellion broke out in the Berkshire hills of western Massachusetts in 1786 in an attempt to shake off the yoke of Boston, which seemed as bad as George III's. To this day people in western Massachusetts make proposals, earnestly or with down-in-the-mouth humor, that they all ought to split off from "Boston." Whiskey—the mountain people went right on making it. Whole sections of the Appalachians were a whiskey belt, just as sections of Georgia, Alabama and Mississippi were a cotton belt. Nobody on either side ever had any moral delusions about why the Federal Government was against it. It was always the tax, pure and simple. Today the price of liquor is 60 per cent tax. Today, of course, with everybody gone wild over the subject of science and health, it has been much easier for the Federals to persuade people that they crack down on moonshine whiskey because it is dangerous, it poisons, kills and blinds people. The statistics are usually specious.

Moonshining was *illegal*, however, that was also the unvarnished truth. And that had a side effect in the whiskey belt. The people there were already isolated, geographically, by the mountains and had strong clan ties because they were all from the same stock, Scotch-Irish. Moonshining isolated them even more. They always had to be careful who came up there. There are plenty of hollows to this day where if you drive in and ask some good old boy where so-and-so is, he'll tell you he never heard of the fellow. Then the next minute, if you identify yourself and give some idea of why you want to see him, and he believes you, he'll suddenly say, "Aw, you're talking about *so-and-so*. I thought you said—" With all this isolation, the mountain people began to take on certain characteristics normally associated, by the diffident civilizations of today, with tribes. There was a strong sense of family, clan and honor. People would cut and shoot each other up over honor. And physical courage! They were almost like Turks that way.

In the Korean War, there were seventy-eight Medal of Honor winners. Thirty-two of them were from the South, and practically all of the thirty-two were from small towns in or near the Appalachians. The New York metropolitan area, which has more people than all these towns put together, had three Medal of Honor winners, and one of them had just moved to New York from the Appalachian region of West Virginia. Three of the Medal of Honor winners came from within fifty miles of Junior Johnson's side porch.

Detroit has discovered these pockets of courage, almost like a natural resource, in the form of Junior Johnson and about twenty other drivers. There is something exquisitely ironic about it. Detroit is now engaged in the highly sophisticated business of offering the illusion of Speed for Everyman—making their cars go 175 miles an hour on racetracks—by discovering and putting behind the wheel a breed of mountain men who are living vestiges of a degree of physical courage that became extinct in most other sections of the country by 1900. Of course, very few stock car drivers have ever had anything to do with the whiskey business. A great many always lead quiet lives off the track. But it is the same strong people among whom the whiskey business developed who produced the kind of men who could drive the stock cars. There are a few exceptions, Freddie Lorenzen, from Elmhurst, Illinois, being the most notable. But, by and large, it is the rural Southern code of honor and courage that has produced these, the most daring men in sports.

Cars and bravery! The mountain-still operators had been running white liquor with hopped-up automobiles all during the thirties. But it was during the war that the business was so hot out of Wilkes County, down to Charlotte, High Point, Greensboro, Winston-Salem, Salisbury, places like that; a night's run, by one car, would bring anywhere from $500 to $1000. People had money all of a sudden. One car could carry twenty-two to twenty-five cases of white liquor. There were twelve half-gallon fruit jars full per case, so each load would have 132 gallons or more. It would sell to the distributor in the city for about ten dollars a gallon, when the market was good, of which the driver would get two dollars, as much as $300 for the night's work.

The usual arrangement in the white liquor industry was for the elders to design the distillery, supervise the formulas and the whole distilling process and take care of the business end of the operation. The young men did the heavy work, carrying the copper and other heavy goods out into the woods, building the still, hauling in fuel—and driving. Junior and his older brothers, L. P. and Fred, worked that way with their father, Robert Glenn Johnson, Sr.

Johnson, Senior, was one of the biggest individual copperstill operators in the area. The fourth time he was arrested, the agents found a small fortune in working corn mash bubbling in the vats.

"My Daddy was always a hard worker," Junior is telling me. "He always wanted something a little bit better. A lot of people resented that and held that against him, but what he got, he always got h'it by hard work. There ain't no harder work in the world than making whiskey. I don't know of any other business that compels you to get up at all times of night and go outdoors in the snow and everything else and work. H'it's the hardest way in the world to make a living, and I don't think anybody'd do it unless they had to."

Working mash wouldn't wait for a man. It started coming to a head
when it got ready to and a man had to be there to take it off, out there
in the woods, in the brush, in the brambles, in the muck, in the snow.
Wouldn't it have been something if you could have just set it all up inside
a good old shed with a corrugated metal roof and order those parts like
you want them and not have to smuggle all that copper and all that sugar
and all that everything out here in the woods and be a coppersmith and
a plumber and a copper and a carpenter and a pack horse and every
other goddamned thing God ever saw in this world, all at once.

And live decent hours—Junior and his brothers, about two o'clock
in the morning they'd head out to the stash, the place where the liquor
was hidden after it was made. Sometimes it would be somebody's
house or an old shed or some place just out in the woods, and they'd
make their arrangements out there, what the route was and who was
getting how much liquor. There wasn't anything ever written down.
Everything was cash on the spot. Different drivers liked to make the
run at different times, but Junior and his brother always liked to start
out from 3 to 4 a.m. But it got so no matter when you started out you
didn't have those roads to yourself.

"Some guys liked one time and some guys liked another time,"
Junior is saying, "but starting about midnight they'd be coming out of
the woods from every direction. Some nights the whole road was full
of bootleggers. It got so some nights they'd be somebody following
you going just as fast as you were and you didn't know who h'it was,
the law or somebody else hauling whiskey."

And it was just a business, like any other business, just like a milk
route—but this funny thing was happening. In those wild-ass times,
with the money flush and good old boys from all over the country running that white liquor down the road ninety miles an hour and more
than that if you try to crowd them a little bit—well, the funny thing
was, it got to be competitive in an almost aesthetic, a pure sporting
way. The way the good old boys got to hopping up their automobiles—
it got to be a science practically. Everybody was looking to build a car
faster than anybody ever had before. They practically got into industrial

espionage over it. They'd come up behind one another on those wild-ass nights on the highway, roaring through the black gulches between the clay cuts and the trees, pretending like they were officers, just to challenge them, test them out, race . . . *pour le sport*, you mothers, careening through the darkness, old Carolina moon. All these cars were registered in phony names. If a man had to abandon one, they would find license plates that traced back to . . . nobody at all. It wasn't anything, particularly, to go down to the Motor Vehicle Bureau and get some license plates, as long as you paid your money. Of course, it's rougher now, with compulsory insurance. You have to have your insurance before you can get your license plates, and that leads to a lot of complications. Junior doesn't know what they do about that now. Anyway, all these cars with the magnificent engines were plain on the outside, so they wouldn't attract attention, but they couldn't disguise them altogether. They were jacked up a little in the back and had 8.00 or 8.20 tires, for the heavy loads, and the sound—

"They wasn't no way you could make it sound like an ordinary car," says Junior.

God-almighty, that sound in the middle of the night, groaning, roaring, humming down into the hollows, through the clay gulches— yes! And all over the rural South, hell, all over the South, the legends of wild-driving whiskey running got started. And it wasn't just the plain excitement of it. It was something deeper, the symbolism. It brought into a modern focus the whole business, one and a half centuries old, of the country people's rebellion against the Federals, against the seaboard establishment, their independence, their defiance of the outside world. And it was like a mythology for that and for something else that was happening, the whole wild thing of the car as the symbol of liberation in the postwar South.

"They was out about every night, patroling, the agents and the State Police was," Junior is saying, "but they seldom caught anybody. H'it was like the dogs chasing the fox. The dogs can't catch a fox, he'll just take 'em around in a circle all night long. I was never caught for transporting. We never lost but one car and the axle broke on h'it."

The fox and the dogs! Whiskey running certainly had a crazy game-like quality about it, considering that a boy might be sent up for two years or more if he were caught transporting. But these boys were just wild enough for that. There got to be a code about the chase. In Wilkes County nobody, neither the good old boys or the agents, ever did anything that was going to hurt the other side physically. There was supposed to be some parts of the South where the boys used smoke screens and tack buckets. They had attachments in the rear of the cars, and if the agents got too close they would let loose a smoke screen to blind them or a slew of tacks to make them blow a tire. But nobody in Wilkes County ever did that because that was a good way for somebody to get killed. Part of it was that whenever an agent did get killed in the South, whole hordes of agents would come in from Washington and pretty soon they would be tramping along the ridges practically inch by inch, smoking out the stills. But mainly it was—well, the code. If you got caught, you went along peaceably, and the agents never used their guns. There were some tense times. Once was when the agents started using tack belts in Iredell County. This was a long strip of leather studded with nails that the agents would lay across the road in the dark. A man couldn't see it until it was too late and he stood a good chance of getting killed if it got his tires and spun him out. The other was the time the State Police put a roadblock down there at that damned bridge at Millersville to catch a couple of escaped convicts. Well, a couple of good old boys rode up with a load, and there was the roadblock and they were already on the bridge, so they jumped out and dove into the water. The police saw two men jump out of their car and dive in the water, so they opened fire and they shot one good old boy in the backside. As they pulled him out, he kept saying.

"What did you have to shoot at me for? What did you have to shoot at me for?"

It wasn't pain, it wasn't anguish, it wasn't anger. It was consternation. The bastards had broken the code.

Then the Federals started getting radio cars.

"The radios didn't do them any good," Junior says. "As soon as the officers got radios, then *they* got radios. They'd go out and get the same radio. H'it was an awful hard thing for them to radio them down. They'd just listen in on the radio and see where they're setting up the roadblocks and go a different way."

And such different ways. The good old boys knew back roads, dirt roads, up people's backlanes and every which way, and an agent would have to live in the North Carolina hills a lifetime to get to know them. There wasn't hardly a stretch of road on any of the routes where a good old boy couldn't duck off the road and into the backcountry if he had to. They had wild detours around practically every town and every intersection in the region. And for tight spots—the legendary devices, the "bootleg slide," the siren and the red light. . . .

It was just a matter of keeping up with the competition. You always have to have the latest equipment. It was a business thing, like any other business, you have to stay on top—"They was some guys who was more dependable, they done a better job"—and it may have been business to Junior, but it wasn't business to a generation of good old boys growing up all over the South. The Wilkes County bootleg cars started picking up popular names in a kind of folk hero worship—"The Black Ghost," "The Grey Ghost," which were two of Junior's, "Old Mother Goose," "The Midnight Traveler," "Old Faithful."

And then one day in 1955 some agents snuck over the ridges and caught Junior Johnson at his daddy's still. Junior Johnson, the man couldn't *any*body catch!

The arrest caught Junior just as he was ready to really take off in his career as a stock car driver. Junior says he hadn't been in the whiskey business in any shape or form, hadn't run a load of whiskey for two or three years, when he was arrested. He says he didn't need to fool around with running whiskey after he got into stock car racing, he was making enough money at that. He was just out there at the still helping his daddy with some of the heavy labor, there wasn't a good old boy in Ingle Hollow who wouldn't help his daddy lug those big old cords of ash wood, it doesn't give off much smoke, out in the woods. Junior was sentenced to two years in the Federal reformatory in Chillicothe, Ohio.

"If the law felt I should have gone to jail, that's fine and dandy," Junior tells me. "But I don't think the true facts of the case justified the sentence I got. I never had been arrested in my life. I think they was punishing me for the past. People get a kick out of it because the officers can't catch somebody, and this angers them. Soon as I started getting publicity for racing, they started making it real hot for my family. I was out of the whiskey business, and they knew that, but they was just waiting to catch me on something. I got out after serving ten months and three days of the sentence, but h'it was two or three years I was set back, about half of fifty-six and every bit of fifty-seven. H'it takes a year to really get back into h'it after something like that. I think I lost the prime of my racing career. I feel that if I had been given the chance I feel I was due, rather than the sentence I got, my life would have got a real boost."

But, if anything, the arrest only made the Junior Johnson legend hotter.

And all the while Detroit kept edging the speeds up, from 150 m.p.h, in 1960 to 155 to 165 to 175 to 180 flat out on the longest straightaway, and the good old boys of Southern stock car racing stuck right with it. Any speed Detroit would give them they would take right with them into the curve, hard-charging even though they began to feel strange things such as the rubber starting to pull right off the tire casing. And God! Good old boys from all over the South roared together after the Stanchion—Speed! Guts!—pouring into Birmingham, Daytona Beach, Randleman, North Carolina; Spartanburg, South Carolina; Weaverville, Hillsboro, North Carolina; Atlanta, Hickory, Bristol, Tennessee, Augusta, Georgia; Richmond, Virginia; Asheville, North Carolina; Charlotte, Myrtle Beach—tens of thousands of them. And still upper- and middle-class America, even in the South, keeps its eyes averted. Who cares! They kept on heading out where we all live, after all, out amongst the Drive-ins, white-enameled filling stations, concrete aprons, shopping-plaza apothecaries, show-window steak houses, Burger-Ramas, Bar-B-Cubicles and Miami aqua-swimming-pool motor inns, on out the highway . . . even outside a town like Darlington, a town of 10,000 souls, God, here they come, down route 52, up 401, on 340, 151 and 34, on through the South Carolina lespedeza fields. By Friday night already the good old boys are pulling the infield of the Darlington raceway with those blazing pastel dreamboats stacked this way and that on the clay flat and the tubular terrace furniture and the sleeping bags and the Thermos jugs and the brown whiskey bottles coming on out. By Sunday—the race!—there are 65,000 piled into the racetrack at Darlington. The sheriff, as always, sets up the jail right there in the infield. No use trying to haul them out of there. And now—the *sound* rises up inside the raceway, and a good old boy named Ralph goes mad and starts selling chances on his Dodge. Twenty-five cents and you can take the sledge he has and smash his car anywhere you want. How they roar when the windshield breaks! The police could interfere, you know, but they are busy chasing a good old girl who is playing Lady Godiva on a hogbacked motorcycle, naked as sin, hauling around and in and out of the clay ruts.

Eyes averted, happy burghers. On Monday the ads start appearing—for Ford, for Plymouth, for Dodge—announcing that we gave it to you, speed such as you never saw. There it was! At Darlington, Daytona, Atlanta—and not merely in the Southern papers but in the albino pages of the suburban women's magazines, such as *The New Yorker*, in color—the Ford winners, such as Fireball Roberts, grinning with a cigar in his mouth in *The New Yorker* magazine. And somewhere, some Monday morning, Jim Pascal of High Point, Ned Jarrett of Boykin, Cale Yarborough of Timmonsville and Curtis Crider from Charlotte, Bobby Isaac of Catawba, E. J. Trivette of Deep Gap, Richard Petty of Randleman, Tiny Lund of Cross, South Carolina; Stick Elliott of Shelby—and from out of Ingle Hollow—

And all the while, standing by in full Shy, in alumicron suits—there is Detroit, hardly able to believe itself what it has discovered, a breed of good old boys from the fastnesses of the Appalachian hills and flats—a handful from this rare breed—who have given Detroit . . . speed . . . and the industry can present it to a whole generation as . . . yours. And the Detroit P.R. men themselves come to the tracks like folk worshipers and the millions go giddy with the thrill of speed. Only Junior Johnson goes about it as if it were . . . the usual. Junior goes on down to Atlanta for the Dixie 400 and drops by the Federal penitentiary to see his Daddy. His Daddy is in on his fifth illegal distillery conviction; in the whiskey business that's just part of it; an able craftsman, an able businessman, and the law kept hounding him, that was all. So Junior drops by and then goes on out to the track and gets in his new Ford and sets the qualifying speed record for Atlanta Dixie 400, 146.301 m.p.h.; later on he tools on back up the road to Ingle Hollow to tend to the automatic chicken houses and the road-grading operation. Yes.

Yet how can you tell that to . . . anybody . . . out on the bottom of that bowl as the motor thunder begins to lift up through him like a sigh and his eyeballs glaze over and his hands reach up and there, riding the rim of the bowl, soaring over the ridges, is Junior's yellow Ford . . . which is his white Chevrolet . . . which is a White Ghost, forever rousing the good old boys . . . hard-charging! . . . up with the automobile into their America, and the hell with arteriosclerotic old boys trying to hold onto the whole pot with arms of cotton seersucker. Junior!

from On the Road
by Jack Kerouac

Cars mean excitement and escape to Sal and Dean, protagonists of Jack Kerouac's (1922–1969) 1957 novel On the Road. *The two men meet up in San Francisco and hatch a plan to get to Europe by way of New York— with a stop-off in Denver to drop in on Sal's friend Frankie.*

Nothing happened that night; we went to sleep. Everything happened the next day. In the afternoon Dean and I went to downtown Denver for our various chores and to see the travel bureau for a car to New York. On the way home in the late afternoon we started out for Okie Frankie's, up Broadway, where Dean suddenly sauntered into a sports-goods store, calmly picked up a softball on the counter, and came out, popping it up and down in his palm. Nobody noticed; nobody ever notices such things. It was a drowsy, hot afternoon. We played catch as we went along. "We'll get a travel-bureau car for sure tomorrow."

A woman friend had given me a big quart of Old Granddad bourbon. We started drinking it at Frankie's house. Across the cornfield in back lived a beautiful young chick that Dean had been trying to make ever since he arrived. Trouble was brewing. He threw too many pebbles in her window and frightened her. As we drank the bourbon in the littered living room with all its dogs and scattered toys and sad talk, Dean kept running out the back kitchen door and crossing the cornfield to throw pebbles and whistle. Once in a while Janet went out to peek. Suddenly Dean came back pale. "Trouble, m'boy. That gal's mother is after me with a shotgun and she got a gang of high-school kids to beat me up from down the road."

"What's this? Where are they?"

"Across the cornfield, m'boy." Dean was drunk and didn't care. We went out together and crossed the cornfield in the moonlight. I saw groups of people on the dark dirt road.

"Here they come!" I heard.

"Wait a minute," I said. "What's the matter, please?"

The mother lurked in the background with a big shotgun across her arm. "That damn friend of yours been annoying us long enough. I'm not the kind to call the law. If he comes back here once more I'm gonna shoot and shoot to kill." The high-school boys were clustered with their fists knotted. I was so drunk I didn't care either, but I soothed everybody some.

I said, "He won't do it again. I'll watch him; he's my brother and listens to me. Please put your gun away and don't bother about anything."

"Just one more time!" she said firmly and grimly across the dark. "When my husband gets home I'm sending him after you."

"You don't have to do that; he won't bother you any more, understand. Now be calm and it's okay." Behind me Dean was cursing under his breath. The girl was peeking from her bedroom window. I knew these people from before and they trusted me enough to quiet down a bit. I took Dean by the arm and back we went over the moony cornrows.

"Woo-hee!" he yelled. "I'm gonna git drunk tonight." We went back to Frankie and the kids. Suddenly Dean got mad at a record little Janet was playing and broke it over his knee: it was a hillbilly record. There was an early Dizzy Gillespie there that he valued—"Congo Blues," with Max West on drums. I'd given it to Janet before, and I told her as she wept to take it and break it over Dean's head. She went over and did so. Dean gaped dumbly, sensing everything. We all laughed. Everything was all right. Then Frankie-Maw wanted to go out and drink beer in the roadhouse saloons. "Lessgo!" yelled Dean. "Now dammit, if you'd bought that car I showed you Tuesday we wouldn't have to walk."

"I didn't like that damn car!" yelled Hankie. Yang, yang, the kids started to cry. Dense, mothlike eternity brooded in the crazy brown parlor with the sad wallpaper, the pink lamp, the excited faces. Little Jimmy was frightened; I put him to sleep on the couch and trussed the dog on him. Frankie drunkenly called a cab and suddenly while we were waiting for it a phone call came for me from my woman friend. She had a middle-aged cousin who hated my guts, and that earlier afternoon I had written a letter to Old Bull Lee, who was now in Mexico City, relating the adventures of Dean and myself and under what circumstances we were staying in Denver. I wrote: "I have a woman friend who gives me whisky and money and big suppers."

I foolishly gave this letter to her middle-aged cousin to mail, right after a fried-chicken supper. He opened it, read it, and took it at once to her to prove to her that I was a con-man. Now she was calling me tearfully and saying she never wanted to see me again. Then the triumphant cousin got on the phone and began calling me a bastard. As the cab honked outside and the kids cried and the dogs barked and Dean danced with Frankie I yelled every conceivable curse I could think over that phone and added all kinds of new ones, and in my drunken frenzy I told everybody over the phone to go to hell and slammed it down and went out to get drunk.

We stumbled over one another to get out of the cab at the road-house, a hillbilly roadhouse near the hills, and went in and ordered beers. Everything was collapsing, and to make things inconceivably more frantic there was an ecstatic spastic fellow in the bar who threw his arms around Dean and moaned in his face, and Dean went mad again with sweats and insanity, and to add still more to the unbearable confusion Dean rushed out the next moment and stole a car right from the driveway and took a dash to downtown Denver and came back with a newer, better one. Suddenly in the bar I looked up and saw cops and people were milling around the driveway in the headlights of cruisers, talking about the stolen car. "Somebody's been stealing cars left and right here!" the cop was saying. Dean stood right in back of him, listening and saying, "Ah yass, ah yass." The cops went off to check. Dean came in the bar, and rocked back and forth with the poor spastic kid who had just gotten married that day and was having a tremendous drunk while his bride waited somewhere. "Oh, man, this guy is the greatest in the world!" yelled Dean. "Sal, Frankie, I'm going out and get a real good car this time and we'll all go and with Tony too" (the spastic saint) "and have a big drive in the mountains." And he rushed out. Simultaneously a cop rushed in and said a car stolen from downtown Denver was parked in the driveway. People discussed it in knots. From the window I saw Dean jump into the nearest car and roar off, and not a soul noticed him. A few minutes later he was back in an entirely different car, a brand-new convertible. "This one is a beaut!" he whispered in my ear. "The other one coughed too much—I left it at the crossroads, saw that lovely parked in front of a farmhouse. Took a spin in Denver. Come on, man, let's *all* go riding." All the bitterness and madness of his entire Denver life was blasting out of his system like daggers. His face was red and sweaty and mean.

"No, I ain't gonna have nothing to do with stolen cars."

"Aw, come on, man! Tony'll come with me, won't you, amazing darling Tony?" And Tony—a thin, dark-haired, holy-eyed moaning foaming lost soul—leaned on Dean and groaned and groaned, for he was sick suddenly and then for some odd intuitive reason he became terrified of Dean and threw up his hands and drew away with terror writhing in his face. Dean bowed his head and sweated. He ran out and drove away. Frankie and I found a cab in the driveway and decided to go home. As the cabby drove us up the infinitely dark Alameda Boulevard along which I had walked many and many a lost night the previous months of the summer, singing and moaning and eating the stars and dropping the juices of my heart drop by drop on the hot tar, Dean suddenly hove up behind us in the stolen convertible and began tooting and tooting and crowding us over and screaming. The cabby's face grew white.

"Just a friend of mine," I said. Dean got disgusted with us and suddenly shot ahead at ninety miles an hour, throwing spectral dust across the exhaust. Then he turned in at Frankie's road and pulled up in front of the house; just as suddenly he took off again, U-turned, and went back toward town as we got out of the cab and paid the fare. A few moments later as we waited anxiously in the dark yard, he returned with still another car, a battered coupe, stopped it in a cloud of dust in front of the house, and just staggered out and went straight into the bedroom and flopped dead drunk on the bed. And there we were with a stolen car right on our doorstep.

I had to wake him up; I couldn't get the car started to dump it somewhere far off. He stumbled out of bed, wearing just his jockey shorts, and we got in the car together, while the kids giggled from the windows, and went bouncing and flying straight over the hard alfalfa-rows at the end of the road whomp-ti-whomp till finally the car couldn't take any more and stopped dead under an old cottonwood near the old mill. "Can't go any farther," said Dean simply and got out and started walking back over the cornfield, about half a mile, in his shorts in the moonlight. We got back to the house and he went to sleep. Everything was in a horrible mess, all of Denver, my woman friend, cars, children, poor Frankie, the living room splattered with beer and cans, and I tried to sleep. A cricket kept me awake for some time. At night in this part of the West the stars, as I had seen them in Wyoming, are big as roman candles and as lonely as the Prince of the Dharma who's lost his ancestral grove and journeys across the spaces between points in the handle of the Big Dipper, trying to find it again. So they slowly wheeled the night, and then long before actual sunrise the great red light appeared far over the dun bleak land toward West Kansas and the birds took up their trill above Denver.

Horrible nauseas possessed us in the morning. First thing Dean did was go out across the cornfield to see if the car would carry us East. I told him no, but he went anyway. He came back pale. "Man, that's a detective's car and every precinct in town knows my fingerprints from the year that I stole five hundred cars. You see what I do with them, I just wanta ride, man! I gotta go! Listen, we're going to wind up in jail if we don't get out of here this very instant."

"You're damned right," I said, and we began packing as fast as our hands could go. Dangling neckties and shirttails, we said quick good-byes to our sweet little family and stumbled off toward the protective road where nobody would know us. Little Janet was crying to see us, or me, or whatever it was, go—and Frankie was courteous, and I kissed her and apologized.

"He sure is a crazy one," she said. "Sure reminds me of my husband that run away. Just exactly the same guy. I sure hope my Mickey don't grow up that way, they all do now."

And I said good-by to little Lucy, who had her pet beetle in her hand, and little Jimmy was asleep. All this in the space of seconds, in a lovely Sunday morning dawn, as we stumbled off with our wretched baggage. We hurried. Every minute we expected a cruising car to appear from around a country bend and come sloping for us.

"If that woman with the shotgun ever finds out, we're cooked," said Dean. "We *must* get a cab. Then we're safe." We were about to wake up a farm family to use their phone, but the dog drove us away. Every minute things became more dangerous; the coupe would be found wrecked in the cornfield by an early-rising country man. One lovely old lady let us use her phone finally, and we called a downtown Denver cab, but he didn't come. We stumbled on down the road. Early-morning traffic began, every car looking like a cruiser. Then we suddenly saw the cruiser coming and I knew it was the end of my life as I had known it and that it was entering a new and horrible stage of jails and iron sorrows. But the cruiser was our taxi, and from that moment on we flew east.

At the travel bureau there was a tremendous offer for someone to drive a '47 Cadillac limousine to Chicago. The owner had been driving up from Mexico with his family and got tired and put them all on a train. All he wanted was identification and for the car to get there. My papers assured him everything would come off right. I told him not to worry. I told Dean, "And don't scrounge with this car." Dean was jumping up and down with excitement to see it. We had to wait an hour. We lay on the grass near the church where in 1947 I had passed some time with panhandling hobos after seeing Rita Bettencourt home, and there I fell asleep from sheer horror exhaustion with my face to the afternoon birds. In fact they were playing organ music somewhere. But Dean hustled around town. He talked up an acquaintance with a waitress in a luncheonette, made a date to take her driving in his Cadillac that afternoon, and came back to wake me with the news. Now I felt better. I rose to the new complications.

When the Cadillac arrived, Dean instantly drove off with it "to get gas," and the travel-bureau man looked at me and said, "When's he coming back? The passengers are all ready to go." He showed me two Irish boys from an Eastern Jesuit school waiting with their suitcases on the benches.

"He just went for gas. He'll be right back." I cut down to the corner and watched Dean as he kept the motor running for the waitress, who had been changing in her hotel room; in fact I could see her from where I stood, in front of her mirror, primping and fixing her silk stockings, and I wished I could go along with them. She came running out and jumped in the Cadillac. I wandered back to reassure the travel-bureau boss and the passengers. From where I stood in the door I saw a faint flash of the Cadillac crossing Cleveland Place with Dean, T-shirted and joyous, fluttering his hands and talking to the girl and hunching over the wheel to go as she sat sadly and proudly beside him. They went to a parking lot in broad daylight, parked near the brick wall at the back (a lot Dean had worked in once), and there, he claims, he made it with her, in nothing flat; not only that but persuaded her to follow us east as soon as she had her pay on Friday, come by bus, and meet us at Ian MacArthur's pad on Lexington Avenue in New York. She agreed to come; her name was Beverly. Thirty minutes and Dean roared back, deposited the girl at her hotel, with kisses, farewells, promises, and zoomed right up to the travel bureau to pick up the crew.

"Well, it's about time!" said the Broadway Sam travel-bureau boss. "I thought you'd gone off with that Cadillac."

"It's my responsibility," I said, "don't worry"—and said that because Dean was in such obvious frenzy everybody could guess his madness. Dean became businesslike and assisted the Jesuit boys with their baggage. They were hardly seated, and I had hardly waved good-by to Denver, before he was off, the big motor thrumming with immense birdlike power. Not two miles out of Denver the speedometer broke because Dean was pushing well over 110 miles an hour.

"Well, no speedometer, I won't know how fast I'm going. I'll just ball that jack to Chicago and tell by time." It didn't seem we were even going seventy but all the cars fell from us like dead flies on the straight-away highway leading up to Greeley. "Reason why we're going northeast is because, Sal, we must absolutely visit Ed Wall's ranch in Sterling, you've got to meet him and see his ranch and this boat cuts so fast we can make it without any time trouble and get to Chicago long before that man's train." Okay, I was for it. It began to rain but Dean never slackened. It was a beautiful big car, the last of the old-style limousines, black, with a big elongated body and whitewall tires and probably bulletproof windows. The Jesuit boys—St. Bonaventura—sat in the back, gleeful and glad to be underway, and they had no idea how fast we were going. They tried to talk but Dean said nothing and took off his T-shirt and drove barechested. "Oh, that Beverly is a sweet gone little gal—she's going to join me in New York—we're going to get married as soon as I can get divorce papers from Camille—everything's jumping, Sal, and we're off. Yes!" The faster we left Denver the better I felt, and we were doing it *fast*. It grew dark when we turned off the highway at Junction and hit a dirt road that took us across dismal East Colorado plains to Ed Wall's ranch in the middle of Coyote Nowhere. But it was still raining and the mud was slippery and Dean slowed to seventy, but I told him to slow even more or we'd slide, and he said, "Don't worry, man, you know me."

"Not this time," I said. "You're really going much too fast." And he was flying along there on that slippery mud and just as I said that we hit a complete left turn in the highway and Dean socked the wheel over to make it but the big car skidded in the grease and wobbled hugely.

"Look out!" yelled Dean, who didn't give a damn and wrestled with his Angel a moment, and we ended up backass in the ditch with the front out on the road. A great stillness fell over everything. We heard the whining wind. We were in the middle of the wild prairie. There was a farmhouse a quarter-mile up the road. I couldn't stop swearing, I was so mad and disgusted with Dean. He said nothing and went off to the farmhouse in the rain, with a coat, to look for help.

"Is he your brother?" the boys asked in the back seat. "He's a devil with a car, isn't he?—and according to his story he must be with the women."

"He's mad," I said, "and yes, he's my brother." I saw Dean coming back with the farmer in his tractor. They hooked chains on and the farmer hauled us out of the ditch. The car was muddy brown, a whole fender was crushed. The farmer charged us five dollars. His daughters watched in the rain. The prettiest, shyest one hid far back in the field to watch and she had good reason because she was absolutely and finally the most beautiful girl Dean and I ever saw in all our lives. She was about sixteen, and had Plains complexion like wild roses, and the bluest eyes, the most lovely hair, and the modesty and quickness of a wild antelope. At every look from us she flinched. She stood there with the immense winds that blew clear down from Saskatchewan knocking her hair about her lovely head like shrouds, living curls of them. She blushed and blushed.

We finished our business with the farmer, took one last look at the prairie angel, and drove off, slower now, till dark came and Dean said Ed Wall's ranch was dead ahead. "Oh, a girl like that scares me," I said. "I'd give up everything and throw myself on her mercy and if she didn't want me I'd just as simply go and throw myself off the edge of the world." The Jesuit boys giggled. They were full of corny quips and Eastern college talk and had nothing on their bird-beans except a lot of ill-understood Aquinas for stuffing for their pepper. Dean and I paid absolutely no attention to them. As we crossed the muddy plains he told stories about his cowboy days, he showed us the stretch of road where he spent an entire morning riding; and where he'd done fence-mending as soon as we hit Wall's property, which was immense; and where old Wall, Ed's father, used to come clattering on the rangeland grass chasing a heifer and howling, "Git im, git im, goddammit!" "He had to have a new car every six months," said Dean. "He just couldn't care. When a stray got away from us he'd drive right after it as far as the nearest waterhole and then get out and run after it on foot. Counted every cent he ever made and put it in a pot. A mad old rancher. I'll show you some of his old wrecks near the bunkhouse. This is where I came on probation after my last hitch in a joint. This is where I lived when I wrote those letters you saw to Chad King." We turned off the road and wound across a path through the winter pasture. A mournful group of whitefaced cows suddenly milled across our headlights. "There they are! Wall's cows! We'll never be able to get through them. We'll have to get out and whoop em up! Hee-hee-hee!!" But we didn't have to do that and only inched along through them, sometimes gently bumping as they milled and mooed like a sea around the car doors. Beyond we saw the light of Ed Wall's ranch house. Around this lonely light stretched hundreds of miles of plains.

The kind of utter darkness that falls on a prairie like that is inconceivable to an Easterner. There were no stars, no moon, no light whatever except the light of Mrs. Wall's kitchen. What lay beyond the shadows of the yard was an endless view of the world that you wouldn't be able to see till dawn. After knocking on the door and calling out in the dark for Ed Wall, who was milking cows in the barn, I took a short careful walk into that darkness, about twenty feet and no more. I thought I heard coyotes. Wall said it was probably one of his father's wild horses whinnying in the distance. Ed Wall was about our age, tall, rangy, spike-toothed, laconic. He and Dean used to stand around on Curtis Street corners and whistle at girls. Now he took us graciously into his gloomy, brown, unused parlor and fished around till he found dull lamps and lit them and said to Dean, "What in the hell happened to yore thumb?"

"I socked Marylou and it got infected so much they had to amputate the end of it."

"What in the hell did you go and do that for?" I could see he used to be Dean's older brother. He shook his head; the milk pail was still at his feet. "You always been a crackbrained sonofabitch anyhow."

Meanwhile his young wife prepared a magnificent spread in the big ranch kitchen. She apologized for the peach ice cream: "It ain't nothin but cream and peaches froze up together." Of course it was the only real ice cream I ever had in my whole life. She started sparsely and ended up abundantly; as we ate, new things appeared on the table. She was a well-built blonde but like all women who live in the wide spaces she complained a little of the boredom. She enumerated the radio programs she usually listened to at this time of night. Ed Wall sat just staring at his hands. Dean ate voraciously. He wanted me to go along with him in the fiction that I owned the Cadillac, that I was a very rich man and that he was my friend and chauffeur. It made no impression on Ed Wall. Every time the stock made sounds in the barn he raised his head to listen.

"Well, I hope you boys make it to New York." Far from believing that tale about my owning the Cadillac, he was convinced Dean had stolen it. We stayed at the ranch about an hour. Ed Wall had lost faith in Dean just like Sam Brady—he looked at him warily when he looked. There were riotous days in the past when they had stumbled around the streets of Laramie, Wyoming, arm-in-arm when the haying was over, but all this was dead and gone.

Dean hopped in his chair convulsively. "Well yes, well yes, and now I think we'd better be cutting along because we gotta be in Chicago by tomorrow night and we've already wasted several hours." The college boys thanked Wall graciously and we were off again. I turned to watch the kitchen light recede in the sea of night. Then I leaned ahead.

In no time at all we were back on the main highway and that night I saw the entire state of Nebraska unroll before my eyes. A hundred and ten miles an hour straight through, an arrow road, sleeping towns, no traffic, and the Union Pacific streamliner falling behind us in the moonlight. I wasn't frightened at all that night; it was perfectly legitimate to go 110 and talk and have all the Nebraska towns—Ogallala, Gothenburg, Kearney, Grand Island, Columbus—unreel with dreamlike rapidity as we roared ahead and talked. It was a magnificent car; it could hold the road like a boat holds on water. Gradual curves were its singing ease. "Ah, man, what a dreamboat," sighed Dean. "Think if you and I had a car like this what we could do. Do you know there's a road that goes down Mexico and all the way to Panama?—and maybe all the way to the bottom of South America where the Indians are seven feet tall and eat cocaine on the mountainside? Yes! You and I, Sal, we'd dig the whole world with a car like this because, man, the road must eventually lead to the whole world. Ain't nowhere else it can go—right? Oh, and are we going to cut around old Chi with this thing! Think of it, Sal, I've never been to Chicago in all my life, never stopped."

"We'll come in there like gangsters in this Cadillac!"

"Yes! And girls! We can pick up girls, in fact, Sal, I've decided to make extra-special fast time so we can have an entire evening to cut around in this thing. Now you just relax and I'll ball the jack all the way."

"Well, how fast are you going now?"

"A steady one-ten I figure—you wouldn't notice it. We've still got all Iowa in the daytime and then I'll make that old Illinois in nothing flat." The boys fell asleep and we talked and talked all night.

It was remarkable how Dean could go mad and then suddenly continue with his soul—which I think is wrapped up in a fast car, a coast to reach, and a woman at the end of the road—calmly and sanely as though nothing had happened. "I get like that every time in Denver now—I can't make that town any more. Gookly, gooky, Dean's a spooky. Zoom!" I told him I had been over this Nebraska road before in '47. He had too. "Sal, when I was working for the New Era Laundry in Los Angeles, nineteen forty-four, falsifying my age, I made a trip to Indianapolis Speedway for the express purpose of seeing the Memorial

Day classic, hitchhiking by day and stealing cars by night to make time. Also I had a twenty-dollar Buick back in LA, my first car, it couldn't pass the brake and light inspection so I decided I needed an out-of-state license to operate the car without arrest so went through here to get the license. As I was hitchhiking through one of these very towns, with the plates concealed under my coat, a nosy sheriff who thought I was pretty young to be hitchhiking accosted me on the main drag. He found the plates and threw me in the two-cell jail with a county delinquent who should have been in the home for the old since he couldn't feed himself (the sheriff's wife fed him) and sat through the day drooling and slobbering. After investigation, which included corny things like a fatherly quiz, then an abrupt turnabout to frighten me with threats, a comparison of my handwriting, et cetera, and after I made the most magnificent speech of my life to get out of it, concluding with the confession that I was lying about my car-stealing past and was only looking for my paw who was a farmhand hereabouts, he let me go. Of course I missed the races. The following fall I did the same thing again to see the Notre Dame–California game in South Bend, Indiana—trouble none this time and, Sal, I had just the money for the ticket and not an extra cent and didn't eat anything all up and back except for what I could panhandle from all kinds of crazy cats I met on the road and at the same time gun gals. Only guy in the United States of America that ever went to so much trouble to see a ballgame."

I asked him the circumstances of his being in LA in 1944. "I was arrested in Arizona, the joint absolutely the worst joint I've ever been in. I had to escape and pulled the greatest escape in my life, speaking of escapes, you see, in a general way. In the woods, you know, and crawling, and swamps—up around that mountain country. Rubber hoses and the works and accidental so-called death facing me I had to cut out of those woods along the ridge so as to keep away from trails and paths and roads. Had to get rid of my joint clothes and sneaked the neatest theft of a shirt and pants from a gas station outside Flagstaff, arriving LA two days later clad as a gas attendant and walked to the first station I saw and got hired and got myself a room and changed name (Lee Buliay) and spent an exciting year in LA, including a whole gang of new friends and some really great girls, that season ending when we were all driving on Hollywood Boulevard one night and I told my buddy to steer the car while I kissed my girl—I was at the wheel, see—and *he didn't hear me* and we ran smack into a post but only going twenty and I broke my nose. You've seen before my nose— the crooked Grecian curve up here. After that I went to Denver and met Marylou in a soda fountain that spring. Oh, man, she was only fifteen and wearing jeans and just waiting for someone to pick her up. Three days three nights of talk in the Ace Hotel, third floor, southeast corner room, holy memento room and sacred scene of my days—she was so sweet then, so *young*, hmm, ahh! But hey, look down there in the night thar, hup, hup, a buncha old bums by a fire by the rail, damn me." He almost slowed down. "You see, I never know whether my father's there or not." There were some figures by the tracks, reeling in front of a woodfire. "I never know whether to ask. He might be anywhere." We drove on. Somewhere behind us or in front of us in the huge night his father lay drunk under a bush, and no doubt about it—spittle on his chin, water on his pants, molasses in his ears, scabs on his nose, maybe blood in his hair and the moon shining down on him.

I took Dean's arm. "Ah, man, we're sure going home now." New York was going to be his permanent home for the first time. He jiggled all over; he couldn't wait.

"And think, Sal, when we get to Pennsy we'll start hearing that gone Eastern bop on the disk jockeys. Geeyah, roll, old boat, roll!" The magnificent car made the wind roar; it made the plains unfold like a roll of paper; it cast hot tar from itself with deference—an imperial boat. I opened my eyes to a fanning dawn; we were hurling up to it. Dean's rocky dogged face as ever bent over the dashlight with a bony purpose of its own.

"What are you thinking, Pops?"

"Ah-ha, ah-ha, same old thing, y'know—gurls gurls gurls."

I went to sleep and woke up to the dry, hot atmosphere of July Sunday morning in Iowa, and still Dean was driving and driving and had not slackened his speed; he took the curvy corndales of Iowa at a minimum of eighty and the straightaway 110 as usual, unless bothways traffic forced him to fall in line at a crawling and miserable sixty. When there was a chance he shot ahead and passed cars by the half-dozen and left them behind in a cloud of dust. A mad guy in a brand-new Buick saw all this on the road and decided to race us. When Dean was just about to pass a passel the guy shot by us without warning and howled and tooted his horn and flashed the tail lights for challenge. We took off after him like a big bird. "Now wait," laughed Dean, "I'm going to tease that sonofabitch for a dozen miles or so. Watch." He let the Buick go way ahead and then accelerated and caught up with it most impolitely. Mad Buick went out of his mind; he gunned up to a hundred. We had a chance to see who he was. He seemed to be some kind of Chicago hipster traveling with a woman old enough to be— and probably actually was—his mother. God knows if she was complaining, but he raced. His hair was dark and wild, an Italian from old Chi; he wore a sports shirt. Maybe there was an idea in his mind that we were a new gang from LA invading Chicago, maybe some of Mickey Cohen's men, because the limousine looked every bit the part and the license plates were California. Mainly it was just road kicks. He took terrible chances to stay ahead of us; he passed cars on curves and barely got back in line as a truck wobbled into view and loomed up huge. Eighty miles of Iowa we unreeled in this fashion, and the race was so interesting that I had no opportunity to be frightened. Then the mad guy gave up, pulled up at a gas station, probably on orders from the old-lady, and as we roared by he waved gleefully. On we sped, Dean bare-chested, I with my feet on the dashboard, and the college boys sleeping in the back. We stopped to eat breakfast at a diner run by a white-haired lady who gave us extra-large portions of potatoes as churchbells rang in the nearby town. Then off again.

"Dean, don't drive so fast in the daytime."

"Don't worry, man, I know what I'm doing." I began to flinch. Dean came up on lines of cars like the Angel of Terror. He almost rammed them along as he looked for an opening. He teased their bumpers, he eased and pushed and craned around to see the curve, then the huge car leaped to his touch and passed, and always by a hair we made it back to our side as other lines filed by in the opposite direction and I shuddered. I couldn't take it any more. It is only seldom that you find a long Nebraskan straightaway in Iowa, and when we finally hit one Dean made his usual 110 and I saw flashing by outside several scenes that I remembered from 1947—a long stretch where Eddie and I had been stranded two hours. All that old road of the past unreeling, dizzily as if the cup of life had been overturned and everything gone mad. My eyes ached in nightmare day.

"Ah hell, Dean, I'm going in the back seat, I can't stand it any more, I can't look."

"Hee-hee-hee!" tittered Dean and he passed a car on a narrow bridge and swerved in dust and roared on. I jumped in the back seat and curled up, to sleep. One of the boys jumped in front for the fun. Great horrors that we were going to crash this very morning took hold of me and I got down on the floor and closed my eyes and tried to go to sleep. As a seaman I used to think of the waves rushing beneath the shell of the ship and the bottomless deeps thereunder—now I could feel the road some twenty inches beneath me, unfurling and flying and hissing at incredible speeds across the groaning continent with that mad Ahab at the wheel. When I closed my eyes all I could see was the road unwinding into me. When I opened them I saw flashing shadows of trees vibrating on the floor of the car. There was no escaping it. I resigned myself to all. And still Dean drove, he had no thought of sleeping till we got to Chicago. In the afternoon we crossed old Des Moines again. Here of course we got snarled in traffic and had to go slow and I got back in the front seat. A strange pathetic accident took place. A fat colored man was driving with his entire family in a sedan in front of us; on the rear bumper hung one of those canvas desert waterbags they sell tourists in the desert. He pulled up sharp, Dean was talking to the boys in the back and didn't notice, and we rammed him at five miles an hour smack on the waterbag, which burst like a boil and squirted water in the air. No other damage except a bent bumper.

Dean and I got out to talk to him. The upshot of it was an exchange of addresses and some talk, and Dean not taking his eyes off the man's wife whose beautiful brown breasts were barely concealed inside a floppy cotton blouse. "Yass, yass." We gave him the address of our Chicago baron and went on.

The other side of Des Moines a cruising car came after us with the siren growling, with orders to pull over. "Now what?"

The cop came out. "Were you in an accident coming in?"

"Accident? We broke a guy's waterbag at the junction."

"He says he was hit and run by a bunch in a stolen car." This was one of the few instances Dean and I knew of a Negro's acting like a suspicious old fool. It so surprised us we laughed. We had to follow the patrolman to the station and there spent an hour waiting in the grass while they telephoned Chicago to get the owner of the Cadillac and verify our position as hired drivers. Mr. Baron said, according to the cop, "Yes, that is my car but I can't vouch for anything else those boys might have done."

"They were in a minor accident here in Des Moines."

"Yes, you've already told me that—what I meant was, I can't vouch for anything they might have done in the past."

Everything was straightened out and we roared on. Newton, Iowa, it was, where I'd taken that dawn walk in 1947. In the afternoon we crossed drowsy old Davenport again and the low-lying Mississippi in her sawdust bed; then Rock Island, a few minutes of traffic, the sun reddening, and sudden sights of lovely little tributary rivers flowing softly among the magic trees and greeneries of mid-American Illinois. It was beginning to look like the soft sweet East again; the great dry West was accomplished and done. The state of Illinois unfolded before my eyes in one vast movement that lasted a matter of hours as Dean balled straight across at the same speed. In his tiredness he was taking greater chances than ever. At a narrow bridge that crossed one of these lovely little rivers he shot precipitately into an almost impossible situation. Two slow cars ahead of us were bumping over the bridge; coming the other way was a huge truck-trailer with a driver who was making a close estimate of how long it would take the slow cars to negotiate the bridge, and his estimate was that by the time he got there they'd be over. There was absolutely no room on the bridge for the truck and any cars going the other direction. Behind the truck cars pulled out and peeked for a chance to get by it. In front of the slow cars other slow cars were pushing along. The road was crowded and everyone exploding to pass. Dean came down on all this at 110 miles an hour and never hesitated. He passed the slow cars, swerved, and almost hit the left rail of the bridge, went head-on into the shadow of the unslowing truck, cut right sharply, just missed the truck's left front wheel, almost hit the first slow car, pulled out to pass, and then had to cut back in line when another car came out from behind the truck to look, all in a matter of two seconds, flashing by and leaving nothing more than a cloud of dust instead of a horrible five-way crash with cars lurching in every direction and the great truck humping its back in the fatal red afternoon of Illinois with its dreaming fields. I couldn't get it out of my mind, also, that a famous bop clarinetist had died in an Illinois car-crash recently, probably on a day like this. I went to the back seat again.

The boys stayed in the back too now. Dean was bent on Chicago before nightfall. At a road-rail junction we picked up two hobos who rounded up a half-buck between them for gas. A moment before sitting around piles of railroad ties, polishing off the last of some wine, now they found themselves in a muddy but unbowed and splendid Cadillac limousine headed for Chicago in precipitous haste. In fact the old boy up front who sat next to Dean never took his eyes off the road and prayed his poor bum prayers, I tell you. "Well," they, said, "we never knew we'd get to Chicaga sa fast." As we passed drowsy Illinois towns where the people are so conscious of Chicago gangs that pass like this in limousines every day, we were a strange sight: all of us unshaven, the driver barechested, two bums, myself in the back seat, holding on to a strap and my head leaned back on the cushion looking at the country-side with an imperious eye—just like a new California gang come to contest the spoils of Chicago, a band of desperados escaped from the prisons of the Utah moon. When we stopped for Cokes and gas at a small-town station people came out to stare at us but they never said a word and I think made mental notes of our descriptions and heights in case of future need. To transact business with the girl who ran the gas-pump Dean merely threw on his T-shirt like a scarf and was curt and abrupt as usual and got back in the car and off we roared again. Pretty soon the redness turned purple, the last of the enchanted rivers flashed by, and we saw distant smokes of Chicago beyond the drive. We had come from Denver to Chicago via Ed Wall's ranch, 1180 miles, in exactly seventeen hours, not counting the two hours in the ditch and three at the ranch and two with the police in Newton, Iowa, for a mean average of seventy miles per hour across the land, with one driver. Which is a kind of crazy record.

from Road Fever:
A High-Speed Travelogue
by Tim Cahill

Professional long-distance driver Garry Sowerby and his writer friend Tim Cahill (born 1943) in 1987 set out to break a record by driving the length of the Americas in less than twenty-five days. The men headed north from Tierra del Fuego with a truck full of souvenirs and non-perishable milkshakes to hand out along the way. By Costa Rica, the pair had taken to describing themselves as "roto"—Spanish for "broken."

It is safe to drive at night in Costa Rica. There are no armed insurgencies, and the country long ago abolished its army. According to Oscar Arias, "in my homeland, you will not find a single tank, a single artillery piece, a single warship, or a single military helicopter." Costa Ricans are forever telling visitors that there are more teachers in the country than policemen; they point out that the country has the highest literacy rate in Central America and the best health-care system in the region.

The government attempts to remain neutral politically, though it has strong ties with the United States. It has been a democracy for over a hundred years, making it the oldest democracy in Latin America, and one of the oldest in the world.

In the 1850s, the government offered free land to those who would grow coffee. The crop brought near-instant prosperity, and the peasant class became landowners. Except for the town of Limón, where the people are primarily black, most of the people are white or mestizo. In recent years, Costa Rica has established several remarkable national parks, which are responsibly administered. (Many areas in South and Central America are designated national parks. These are usually remote, underpopulated areas where life goes on as always. People living on the land often do not know they are living in a national park. Mining, timbering, and petro development are all generally allowed, but the government can always point to national parks on its maps and talk about concern for the environment.)

Costa Rica is sometimes described as the Switzerland of Central America. On this day, when the president had been honored, we expected to see dancing in the streets when we hit the capital city of San José.

What could possibly go wrong?

The road to San José runs along the top of a ridge, through orchid-growing country, on a mountain called Buena Vista: good-view mountain. We would, of course, be driving through the orchids on good-view mountain in the middle of the night.

The road crosses the continental divide at about ten thousand feet. They say from that point, on a rare clear day, you can look in one direction and see the Atlantic Ocean, then turn 180 degrees and see the Pacific.

There is another, informal name for Buena Vista.

"Why," I asked a Costa Rican gas-station attendant, "do they call it the Mountain of Death?"

He was a short man of Italian ancestry and he wore the sleeves of his T-shirt rolled up to reveal bulging biceps.

"Why?"

He stared at me. "The road to San José," he said slowly, as if to a very young child, "is very steep, very narrow, very foggy, and very dangerous. Many have died."

We were used to people dying from gunshot wounds and I wanted to be sure about this: "They die in automobile accidents?"

The man jerked back, as if dumb questions were punches, like left jabs.

"In automobile accidents," he said very slowly, "many have died."

• • •

So Garry, who was still jittery and tense from the run to the Panamanian border, felt he should drive the Mountain of Death.

There was no one walking on the shoulder because there was no shoulder. Trees and foliage lined the road, and it was very dark. It had rained earlier, and the cooling mountain air was heavy with the sensual fragrance of orchids. A short time later, it was too cold to drive with the windows open. At six thousand feet, there was a customs check and the young officer was wearing a parka and wool cap.

We were rolling through long uphill climbs followed by short stretches of flatland that invariably led to another steep pitch. Pockets of thick fog sulked in the drainages of the rivers, on the mountain curves, in the flats.

It was slow, torturous driving through these areas the yellow road signs identified as ZONAS DE NEBLINA. I liked the word *neblina* for fog. Every time we saw one of these signs, we were plunged into a thick pewter-gray fog that limited our visibility to no more than ten feet.

"Another nebulous area," I'd tell Garry.

We were crawling through a fog as thick as porridge on an uphill stretch. There were three big trucks ahead of us and we were probably making all of six or seven miles an hour when a new Toyota pickup truck pulled out and passed all four of us on a blind uphill curve, in the fog. It had been a white truck, its side panels barely visible through the fog. Trees and foliage lined the road, but I had a sense that, just beyond the greenery, there were drop-offs everywhere. It felt like bus-plunge country.

"That guy must be drunk," I said.

"Either that or suicidal."

I was playing word games in my mind—*nebulous, neblina*—when we rounded another corner on a high ridge that was clear of the hellish fog. Two trucks and a car were pulled up on the side of the road. Men with flashlights were standing by a break in the foliage. A truck, they said, had come speeding around the corner, didn't make the turn, and had gone off the road here. It had just happened.

We were somewhere near the ten-thousand-foot level. Four or five of the thin trunked trees were broken off near the ground, the jagged stumps very white in the light of our flashlights.

I followed the beam of one of the lights down until the darkness swallowed it. There was no fire, nothing. I imagined this was one of the places where you could see both the Atlantic and Pacific oceans. The vehicle had sailed off the ridge on the Atlantic side.

"Was it a truck?" I asked one of the men.

"A white Toyota," he said.

So the driver who had passed on a blind uphill curve in the fog had taken a ten-thousand-foot dive into the Atlantic from the top of the Mountain of Death. There was a strange absence of emotion about this. I looked down into the black void and felt insubstantial, nebulous.

We pulled into San José, which was set in a mountain basin, like Quito. The weather was cool enough for a light jacket, and a woman who sold diesel at a convenience store that might have been an American 7-Eleven used her only phrase of English about a dozen times. "Welcome to Costa Rica, my friends," she said.

It was just after midnight, but people were indeed dancing in the streets, celebrating the honor their young president had brought to the country. We stopped on a corner to ask directions. People wanted to banter, to joke, to ask us what we thought of Costa Rica and Oscar Arias. It was a very good-natured crowd and we were handing out lapel pins, pledging eternal friendship and Pan-American unity when a flashy red Toyota truck pulled up in front of us and everyone disappeared. The truck was jacked up on monster tires and carried a lot of shiny chrome.

There were three men in the Toyota. All at once they were crouched behind the open doors of their vehicle like men expecting a gunfight.

Garry put his hands, both of them, on the wheel at eleven and one. I put mine flat on the dash. When the men saw we were unarmed, they moved out from behind their doors. One of them—a big man with a scar that ran from his ear to the tip of his chin—came at us from the passenger's side. Another approached from our left. He had a ponytail, a furious untrimmed beard, and wore a faded denim jacket which was open to the waist so you could see expensive gold chains against a black T-shirt. You tended to focus, however, on the gun tucked in the front of his pants. It was a big automatic, a nine millimeter that might carry a fourteen-shot clip.

Here we were in a country with no insurgencies; a country that had more teachers than policemen.

So who were these guys with the guns? Teachers?

The third man—younger than the other two—stood by the red truck. He wore a blue short-sleeved polo shirt that set off his brown leather shoulder holster and the wooden handle of a large revolver. Probably a forty-four. He never moved, and his eyes never left mine.

The man with the scar wore a light-beige rain jacket and there was a gun-sized bulge just under his left arm. He approached Garry, put his right hand into his jacket, and flashed a badge that was in his wallet along with a picture of the scar-faced man and some official-looking stamps. "Police," he said.

The man checked our papers. A few minutes later, he handed everything back and apologized for the inconvenience. The officers said they were looking for drug dealers. We had aroused their suspicions: two bearded strangers in a big truck talking with people after midnight in an unsavory section of town. There had been objects passed back and forth: the seemingly surreptitious exchange of what the officers now knew were lapel pins and milk shakes.

The big man with the scar spoke good English and suggested that we not park our truck on the street. We told him that we were pushing on for Nicaragua anyway. Well, he said, that was going to be a problem. "If you take the Pan-American, you'll drive for three hours and then be turned back."

The highway to the north, he explained, was blocked by a rock slide that would take several days to clear. There was however, a back road. It was gravel and dirt, very bad, but if we wanted to get to Nicaragua by eight the next morning, it was our only chance.

The man took our map from the suckerboard and, in consultation with the bearded man, traced a new route over a spiderweb of back roads.

"But look," he said, "even here in Costa Rica, if you're driving at night, don't ever stop for someone in an unmarked car."

"But you guys have an unmarked car," Garry pointed out.

"We're looking for drug dealers," the man explained. "It helps," he said, "not to look like a police officer."

"But what would you have done if we tried to run?" I asked.

The man shook his head slowly, and in a negative manner.

"Scarface," Garry said. "Guy tells us not to stop for unmarked cars. Don't stop for anybody unless he's driving a red pickup and has a badge. How are you supposed to know?"

We had found the Canadian embassy and picked up a manila envelope containing the letter from Honduras and the one from Nicaragua. I had opened the big three-ring binder that contained all our letters for all the countries we were driving through. Customs officers seemed to like to look through it, and the sheer volume of official correspondence, festooned with the great seals of various countries, often impressed them favorably. On the other hand, the Sandinista government in Nicaragua accused Honduras of harboring contra camps. If a Nicaraguan official saw a letter of recommendation from Honduras, we might be denied entry into the country. No friend of Honduras, the man might feel, is a friend of Nicaragua.

The letters were inside clear envelopes, one on one side, one on the other. I placed our letter from Honduras in one of the envelopes, between two letters from Argentina, so that it was reasonably well hidden.

We made coffee, but it turned out that I had not bought drinking water in Panama City. It was sparkling water. When you tried to make coffee with it, it foamed up like an experiment in the mad scientist's lab.

It was beginning to get roto on the down side of the Mountain of Death, and we drank our furiously foaming coffee cold, without pleasure, for the caffeine. It was the essence of roto.

• • •

The roads were bad and Garry was driving, as he had been since noon. It was now two in the morning.

"The road sign says eleven," Garry said. "Aren't we supposed to be on three?"

"I looked at the other map, the colored one. Three is marked eleven."

"What's the next town?"

"San Mateo. If we hit San Mateo, it doesn't matter what the road is called, we're going the right way."

There was an unmarked crossing and both roads plunged steeply downhill.

"These maps," I said, "say the road we want will run north."

We checked the compass. The road to the left looked to run more generally north. We drove for half an hour and the road jigged east for a time, then jagged west, but it never turned south, which was mildly encouraging.

"If the Pan-American is closed," Garry reasoned, "why don't we see any traffic? Wouldn't truck drivers know about this route?"

"Good point."

"Navi nightmare time."

"No, wait. There's a sign for San Mateo up there."

"Yeah," Garry said, "but where are the trucks?"

They were stacked up where the narrow winding road—all mud and loose gravel—dove through thick jungle foliage into the lowlands and Nicaragua. The drivers had set out flares: branches that they had broken off trees, doused in diesel, and set afire. We stopped in the back of a line of perhaps fifty semis.

Two of the big trucks, we were told, had had a mishap and were blocking the road. A small car could squeeze between them, but our Sierra was too big. We would have to wait. It would take twelve hours, at a minimum, before the road could be cleared.

We had to meet Chistita Caldera at the border in a little over five hours.

Garry fumed in silence. In the dashboard lights, his face looked feverish and, though it was cool enough for a jacket, he had begun to sweat copiously.

Suddenly he got out of the truck and walked down half a mile to the accident, carrying a flashlight. I made myself a cup of foaming roto coffee and when I had just about finished it, I saw Garry walking back uphill. He was moving fast, like an angry, determined man and I knew that we were going to go for it.

Garry folded our wide side mirrors into the truck. "We have," he said, "about five inches of clearance between those trucks."

"You measured it?"

"Eyeballed it."

He put the truck into four-wheel drive, low. "The problem is," he said, "that there are sheep guts all over the road. The stuff looks fresh and it's slippery as hell. I don't know why someone would do that, but there must have been a lot of animals. The road is ankle-deep in blood and intestines."

Garry drove past the line of trucks, and the drivers, who had nothing better to do, followed us down to the metal narrows that Garry had eyeballed. Two trucks blocked the road and were sitting back-to-back, one on the uphill side, one on the downhill. It was a very steep section there, and we'd have to try to drive across the road, at a right angle to its direction of travel, in order to squeeze between the back ends of both trucks. It looked too narrow to me. Worse, we would be traveling across the hillside, over a slippery carpet of gore.

The truck drivers stamped around in the foliage and found an area where Garry could back up to get in position. A very large crowd had gathered to watch the show.

"You'll never make it," one man called.

Another bet we would. Money began to change hands in the light of burning branches. Garry took it pretty fast, afraid that the truck might begin to slide where the sheep guts were thickest.

We were through in twenty seconds. There were three inches to spare on my side and two on Garry's. The truck drivers cheered: loud whistles and shouts in the jungle night.

• • •

We were in lowlands. After sixteen hard hours at the wheel, Garry crawled into the back and tried to sleep. I was driving a fine, straight asphalt road that looked red in the headlights.

We stopped for diesel not far from the border. We wouldn't be able to buy any in Nicaragua, where it was rationed.

Garry looked terrible.

"You know what we could do," I said. "We could market this drive as a board game. Shake the dice to see if you can get to the border on time. Pick cards that give you all sorts of contradictory information. Drive over the Mountain of Death, dodge the Costa Rican drug police, and slide through sheep guts in order to, ta-da, enter the war zone."

"I'm sick," Garry said. "I have a fever."

I felt his forehead. He was a little hot but his eyes were fever bright.

"You have a little fever," I said.

"I wonder if it's malaria?"

"No. It's not malaria," I said,

"I feel strange. Bad."

He spoke in a strained whisper and his eyes were burning, wild things trapped inside his head. They moved in a way that had no relation to anything he was saying.

We arrived at the border early and had to wait two hours until it opened at eight. I spoke with some truck drivers who said that things were very good through Nicaragua. People all over were celebrating the Arias peace plan. It was a fine time to drive through Central America, a very good time, the best.

Garry couldn't talk with anyone. He was walking back and forth, in the growing tropical heat, propelled by some internal demons that he wouldn't tell me about.

A grandmotherly Costa Rican lady placed herself in front of him and struck up a conversation. I saw her try to give him something, but he waved her off.

Back at the truck, he told me what had happened.

"This lady," he said, "had the world's kindest face. Did you see her?"

"Yeah. She did have a kind face."

"She asked what we were doing and I told her. Well, she looked at me. I'm standing there, I haven't changed my shirt since Panama, I'm sick, I can't talk. She figures I need money. She tries to give me a five-dollar bill. It was all crumpled up in her hand."

Garry was very shaky and his eyes glistened.

"Jesus," he said.

The small act of kindness had hit him like a blow and he was still reeling from it.

"I thanked her," he said. "I told her I didn't need any money and showed her pictures of my kids. It was all I could think of to do."

He ran his hand through his hair and said, "The basket case shows pictures of his family."

Garry looked north, into Nicaragua.

"Goddamn it," he said.

Nicaragua

October 14, 1987

Garry's antipathy toward Nicaragua and Nicaraguans was puzzling. Our reconnaissance trip to Managua had been difficult, to be sure. The city, a graceless lowland steambath that is all of fifty feet above sea level, was a mosaic of empty lots and rubble piles interspersed, now and again, by habitations and office buildings. It was hard to get around. Managua had been decimated in the earthquake of 1972 and had never been rebuilt, though ruling General Anastasio Somoza and his family profited hugely from relief efforts.

In Managua, trees and grasses grew out of piles of debris and rubbish, and the concept of numbered addresses had little meaning. Letters to people in Managua are labeled with reference to various landmarks, like this:

In the old Little Rocks section
Below the hospital
One block south
One block west

The telephones generally didn't work. Sometimes, I dialed twenty or thirty times over the space of an hour to get another party in Managua itself. A single page of telex cost an outrageous $36, U.S.

We stayed at the Intercontinental, one of the centers of social life in Managua. There were sometimes Sandinista officials in the bar. It did not seem to be a bar in a war-torn country where drinking and coupling and laughing are matters of some serious import. In the Intercontinental bar, there was a sense of serious import, and nothing else. No one laughed, ever. It seemed the most joyless place on the face of the earth.

Inflation was running at 1,200 percent. Nicaragua's money was useless outside the country and not much good inside. The government needed valid currency to purchase foreign goods, so anyone visiting the country was required to cough up $60, U.S., upon entry. This bought 240,000 córdobas, which you got in hundreds. You could always tell the American citizens who had just flown in. They had huge Cordoba bulges in their pockets and they wore skulking looks of guilt.

They had, doubtless, just read a little pamphlet in English that every American was handed sooner rather than later. It was a history of U.S. involvement in Nicaragua. The United States marines had occupied the country and propped up a corrupt government, on and off, from 1912 to 1933. In the last five years of the occupation, General Cesar Augusto Sandino had fought the Americans, who were in the process of installing General Anastasio Somoza, father of the earthquake profiteer, as supreme commander of the Nicaraguan National Guard.

Sandino was captured by the guard and killed in 1934. The Somoza family, supported by the United States, used the national guard as a personal army. By 1978, the family owned over half the land in the country and had a hand in most of the larger businesses.

In 1978–79, there was fighting in the streets. Anastasio Somoza, the second son of the U.S.-installed general of the same name, was ousted by a coalition of groups calling themselves Sandinistas, after Augusto Sandino, who, pictures in the Nicaraguan embassy in Argentina suggest, had been somewhat cross-eyed.

The U.S. had occupied the country and supported the corrupt Somoza regime. So there was plenty to feel guilty about standing there drinking a beer in the Intercontinental bar with a pocketful of cordobas that you couldn't spend because the hotel wouldn't take them. Hotel bills had to be paid in dollars.

I met a Catholic priest visiting from San Francisco. He was, he said, on a fact-finding mission. He wore civilian clothes and was full of compassion for the poor and dispossessed but I thought he lacked the reporter's instinct. The fact finders, I learned, a dozen of them, were ferried around in a government-owned van. They could ask the driver to stop anywhere.

"Some of the houses," the priest told me, "are very poor. And our translator will ask the people in them any question we have. Just anything at all."

I imagined the scene: a man is sitting in his house and a government representative herds twelve grim-faced gringos inside. The man can see them all noting the dirt floor, the shabby bed, the cooking fire. What does he think of the Sandinista government? He tells the government translator that he thinks the Sandinistas are doing fine. He thinks they're swell.

Nicaragua, the priest said, is a largely Catholic country, and there had been some talk in the United States that the Marxist Sandinistas were suppressing freedom of religion. But the priest told me that his translator had pointed out graffiti that read, THERE IS NO CONTRADICTION BETWEEN THE CHURCH AND THE REVOLUTION.

It was not a message that I saw someone scrawling on a wall in a burst of anger or inspiration. Still, I was willing to entertain the concept. There was a stifling solemnity to life in Managua that reminded me of the Catholic grade school I had attended. Managua was like a city run by nuns.

"There will be no laughing in this classroom. No comic books. Puberty is strictly forbidden. We will keep our thoughts pure and our minds on God."

Instead of God, however, people in Nicaragua were forever being told to keep their minds on the New Man, the proud and free Nicaraguan who would grow out of the revolution.

All over Nicaragua, reading material was strictly censored. The opposition newspaper had been shut down but someone had climbed to the second story of the closed building and hung out a large black cardboard skeleton. It was labeled THE NEW MAN.

The only books available, anywhere, were inspirational tracts about Karl Marx and the New Man. Even at the Intercontinental, the revolving bookrack had nothing but thin paperback volumes with black covers printed on bad stock. They had titles like *Fidel Castro Presents Three Ways You Can Improve Your Village.*

I finally did find something apolitical to read. It was a full-color brochure, in English, that I found on a table in the lobby of the Nicaraguan Institute of Tourism, Intourismo.

> You can visit Nicaragua at any time of the year and will always find an excellent weather. . . . At the central highlands of Nicaragua . . . temperature is cool the whole year long, with a dry atmosphere and during the rainy season between October and November turns out to be one of the most delicious climates in the country.

There's a lot of this sort of thing in the brochure. Weather is an inoffensive proposition. Garry and I were killing time, waiting for an interview with someone from Intourismo. Finally, after some hours, we talked with a zaftig, fashionable young woman named Chistita Caldera. It had to be a hard job, working for the Institute of Tourism in a country at war, and Chistita, who was called Chepy, could barely endure my bad Spanish. She broke into English in the middle of one of my excruciating sentences.

"They don't pay me to translate."

I continued to explain the project in Tarzan Spanish and memorized phrases: nonpolitical . . . mission of peace . . . unity of the Americas . . . Pan-American Highway, a ribbon of hope *World Records* . . . worldwide attention.

And—these sentences specially polished for the interview—"what a shame if we were stopped in Nicaragua." It would be in all the papers all over the world and could even—*¡caramba!*—*negatively affect the tourism industry in the country.*

Chepy listened, and, as she did, her face brightened by degrees. She began speaking English which they didn't pay her for but which was easier for both of us.

"Ahh," she said. "This is good. This is not what I had thought. Not at all."

What had she thought?

Nothing. Nothing. How could she help us?

We asked her if there was a way of smoothing things over at the southern border. Chepy said she would think about it. If it could be arranged, she would come herself to meet us.

Chepy was, in fact, there at the border. She was wearing jeans, a flowered blouse, and an appropriately Latin amount of lipstick. She eased us through the formalities in only three hours and we didn't even have to buy córdobas or demonstrate that we had been taking the malaria pills that Rich Cox had brought to the end of the earth for us.

Garry had not completely shaken off the fever—his bad case of jitters—but he needed to drive through Nicaragua. It seemed to be a matter of principle. Driving would also relieve him of the necessity to talk. He was, he told me privately, afraid of what he might say.

Chepy said that it had been tough for her to get a car from the government, to get the gasoline, to get a photographer who could drive the car back while she rode with us. In the end, the Sandinista government had agreed to assist us in clearing customs because they "are interested in attracting tourists to the country." Chepy said that there were plenty of "internationals" in Nicaragua, people from the United States or

Germany or Sweden who come to see what the revolution had wrought. They came out of curiosity or idealism. They were very sincere and they lived cheaply, in solidarity with the people. Which is not what the Institute of Tourism had in mind.

Officially, the government said it was "interested in classical tourism, not sociopolitical tourism." The Institute of Tourism, for instance, had turned deposed dictator Anastasio Somoza's seaside estate into the Olaf Palme Convention Center. The government hopes the golf course, casino, and private airstrips will be attractive to conventioning dentists.

The photographer took our picture for the Institute of Tourism newsletter. He took our picture because we were real apolitical visitors and a potential inspiration to dentists worldwide.

Chepy told us that she had thought Garry and I were internationals when she first met us in Managua. She had expected us to express solidarity with the revolution and do nothing whatever to foster the cause of classical tourism or in any way help her attract dentists to Nicaragua.

It had taken her half an hour of my bad Spanish before she realized that we were Institute of Tourism kinda guys.

The road was exceptionally bad and there were huge potholes all over. It was like the road into Ecuador from Peru and it was a bad road for all the same reasons. There would be no high-speed invasion over this cratered pavement.

Chepy, sitting in the back of the cab, said she wanted to interview us for the Intourismo newsletter. How did I like Nicaraguans and Nicaragua? We were fifteen miles into the country, driving along the shore of Lake Nicaragua. On the far shore was a huge volcano looming over the blue-gray waters of the lake. It was a perfectly shaped cone, rounded and green and inordinately sensual.

I said that Nicaragua was beautiful, as anyone could see, and all Nicaraguans were imbued with the spirit of friendship. Nicaragua was the friendliest, most beautiful . . .

Chepy cut me off.

"I would like you to comment on the political situation."

"We are apolitical visitors," I said. "That's the point."

"But you must say something about the political situation."

Garry muttered under his breath and shot me a murderous look. I was going to have to take this one. Chepy didn't want to hear what Garry had to say.

I thought about it for a while. Telling the whole truth was out of the question. I thought the Sandinistas were heavy-handed ideologues who had succeeded in squeezing every ounce of joy out of the country.

On the other hand, the contra insurgents were terrorists, funded by my own government. I had seen pictures of women and children who had suffered at the hands of the contras. The pictures were taken by my friend Paul Dix, who lives in my hometown in Montana. He had spent two years in Nicaragua, working for the quasireligious organization Witness for Peace. He was interested in documenting the effects of the conflict on civilians. He would document atrocities on both sides, he said.

Paul tried to get out to the scene of the fighting as soon as it was reported. More often than not he found a house burned to the ground, most of a large family dead, and one or two survivors wandering around in a daze. The contras often targeted health-care workers and teachers.

Paul thought the Sandinista leaders had some poetry in their souls and didn't find life in Managua completely oppressive. He would admit that, under the Sandinistas, Nicaragua wasn't exactly an ideal society. There were some things that irritated him.

"But so what?" he had argued. "What if the whole country is a totalitarian dungeon? Does that give us the right to pay a bunch of terrorists to basically go around and cut the throats of four or five people a night?"

Paul often talked at length with the children who had survived various attacks. He gave them crayons and asked them to draw pictures of what had happened.

One of the pictures I saw showed a bright red house. A stick man standing outside, a contra, was throwing a little round ball through a window into the red house. The little round ball was meant to represent a grenade. Because this was a child's drawing, the contra was smiling. Small children don't know how to draw a face that isn't smiling.

In another drawing, there was a bodyless smiling circle on a stick stuck into the ground. The girl who drew the picture said that contras had decapitated her nineteen-year-old brother and put his head on a fence pole. The head was drawn like a bright, round, happy face.

And now Chepy wanted me to talk about politics, for the record. I had had half an hour of sleep in thirty hours and didn't want to have to think at all. I said that I hoped the Arias peace plan would be fully implemented.

"You are against the interference of foreign governments in Central American affairs?"

"Yes." I sensed that this was what Chepy needed to hear me say, for the sake of her job. It had, for me, the benefit of being my actual opinion.

"Would you write this down so I can translate exactly?"

And so I wrote that down and drew a happy face under the place where I signed my name.

Later, Chepy showed us a picture of her daughter, a blond six-year-old cutie dressed in a clown suit for her birthday party. Chepy and her husband were separated, she said, and she had to raise her daughter alone. He didn't support the child at all.

She had thought about going to the U.S.—one of her sisters was attending college in Seattle—but she imagined that she'd end up being a waitress. "And here," she said, "I work in"—Chepy made an expansive gesture that encompassed the filthy cramped cab of the truck—"international relations."

We dropped her at her home in Masaya and exchanged addresses. Chepy said that her home address would be the best place to reach her. "I don't know what will happen," she said. She might have been referring to the political situation or to her personal life. It seemed best not to inquire more closely.

Garry tried to give her $100 but Chepy said she couldn't take it. "Yes you can," Garry said, "you have a daughter."

"Then," Chepy said, "I will spend it all on her."

The roads in the interior were good and fast. There was little traffic because gasoline was rationed, but we did see several large Bulgarian-made trucks full of people being ferried somewhere for some reason. The people wore civilian clothes and were jammed tightly into the back of these trucks. They weren't shouting or singing or laughing. They didn't look like they were on their way to concentration camps, either. They looked like everyone in Managua: people who weren't having a good time at all.

We were never stopped, not once.

The road to the border with Honduras rose into a series of rounded green hills. The trees were more sparse than in the lowland, but the heat was less oppressive. It was not the great weight upon the land that it had been in Managua. We had found, as the tourist brochure promised, "an excellent weather." When I looked down from the summit of one of the higher mountains, I could see groves of trees separated by meadows of thigh-high grasses. The ridges were closely spaced. It was beautiful country where, I thought, small groups of armed men could maneuver for months and never be detected.

A brisk wind had sprung up and was blowing the petals of some bright red flowers across the road. There were brick houses along the highway, and all of them had flowers growing in the yard. We passed a school. Dozens of children were walking back toward the houses, carrying books and laughing.

We saw several billboards that looked like advertisements for a *Rambo* movie, but the words below the noble-looking armed men and woman read, DEFEND YOUR LAND, DEFEND YOUR CITY, DEFEAT THE ENEMY.

Not far down a slope near the road, there was a pond fringed with green algae that was so bright the color seemed bogus, a kind of artificial Day-Glo green set against the lighter green of the grass and the darker, more brooding cast of the forecast.

The hills were steeper near the border and there were rocky cliffs. A man in patched jeans, a yellow T-shirt, and sandals was pushing a homemade wheelbarrow full of wood. He had an automatic rifle slung over his back.

And then we were at the border, only four hours after we had entered the country. The customs building was located in a small settlement with an indoor market where the produce looked better than anything I had seen in Managua. A group of boys, ranging in age from about ten to eighteen, surrounded the truck and clamored for our attention. They would take us to the right offices, in the right order, and we would clear customs in a flash. We were given to understand that we needed their help, which, they assured us, would be very inexpensive.

Some of the boys looked too young to hire for this purpose, some looked devious. One, an older boy, was a tall gawky fellow with a loony, toothless smile who appeared to be happily insane. We chose the oldest of the border hustlers. This responsible individual promptly turned our papers over to the toothless loon, who gave out with a mighty shout and ran off down the street. He waved our documents over his head and whooped and laughed and staggered as he ran.

All of the other boys were laughing.

"We gave your papers," one of these evil ten-year-olds said, "to the craziest person in all of Nicaragua."

"What did that kid just tell you?" Garry asked.

"He said they gave our papers to a lunatic."

The fever flush bloomed in Garry's face. He took off at a dead run and caught the boy with our documents at the entrance to a building. Inside, I was amazed to discover that there were, in fact, customs offices. The officers seemed to know the boy with our papers, and when he didn't get things right, they gently corrected him and sometimes actually guided him by the arm to the next stamping station.

Garry worked on the act—smile, laugh, hand out lapel pins—but he was flat and unconvincing. We suffered through a pit search and were cleared for immigration.

The officers instructed us to drive a few miles and check in at the immigration trailer on the left side of the road. We gave our guide a five-dollar bill and he ran back down the road, waving it over his head, whooping and laughing, as was his way.

"Shitheads," Garry said.

"I don't know," I said. "Maybe they were giving the kid a chance. Couple of strange-looking gringos. Let the crazy kid have a little fun. Maybe he wasn't crazy. He could have been retarded."

"Those papers," Garry said, "are the key to this whole thing." He was very angry. "They were playing around with us."

"I don't think so."

"Nicaraguans," Garry said. He made the word sound like a curse.

The border was a war zone and the old immigration building didn't look so good. There were bullet holes in the adobe. The roof, what there was of it, consisted of twisted girders. It had apparently taken a direct mortar hit.

So the government was checking passports out of an old airstream trailer home. Soldiers drove it down to the relative safety of town every night. A wooden set of stairs led up to a window in the trailer. There was a thin cloth over the window and we understood that we were to hand our passports through, one at a time. You couldn't see inside. It was like a confessional in a Catholic church. There was no way to know precisely how much disgust the information presented has generated. There could be a big penance to pay.

I don't know what they did with my documents, but I stood on the top stair, alone in the sun, for a full ten minutes. Then a brown hand reached out. I took my passport and saw that I was stamped for exit. No words were exchanged.

When Garry took his passport back, his hands were shaking in fatigue or fury or some combination of more complex emotions.

While Garry drove to the Honduras border station, which was a mile away, over a rocky summit, I quickly hid the letter from the Nicaraguan Institute of Tourism and put the letter from the Honduras Institute of Tourism in its place.

• • •

In Honduras, there was the usual scatter of boys, twenty or twenty-five of them, offering, at top volume, to guide us through customs. I looked out at the customs hustlers, the bustle, the black marketeers sitting on benches, the soft-drink vendors, and I felt myself slide into a bleak depression. Here it was: the border rat race, again. This was the seventh set of formalities we had gone through since starting from Panama thirty hours ago.

Garry did it all, laughing with officials and bargaining with the boys. He had completely shaken off the strange fever that had deviled him for most of the day. It took two hours to clear the vehicle.

Garry had been at the wheel almost continuously since Panama City: twenty-six out of thirty hours. It was Nicaragua that had somehow driven him, kept him awake, and sent the fever flush rushing to his face.

And now that we were out of the country, the tension was gone. Garry sat back in the passenger seat and sang, to the tune of "We're in the Money," a little song of his own. The only lyric was "We're in Honduras, we're in Honduras . . ."

I wanted to know what was going on with Garry and Nicaragua. Perhaps he didn't want to talk about it, and I came at him from an angle. I advanced a theory that the Sandinista government, in its attempt to build the New Man, had appropriated some of the least appealing aspects of classical Catholicism, like the squirming agony of confessional. Guilt. Single-minded pursuit of a higher goal. Restricted reading matter . . .

Garry wasn't as willing to generalize about the country on the basis of a curtain over a window in a trailer. He thought there might be a simpler explanation: "Maybe the Elephant Man got a job in Nicaragua."

The comment was encouraging. Eight hours before, my friend's conversation had to do with an imagined case of malaria.

"Tell me about Nicaragua," I said.

"We made it."

"Something else."

"It was always the biggest obstacle on this . . ."

"There's something else."

Garry paused.

"I lost it there once," he said finally. It was a story he didn't like to tell. "The only time in my life I ever just really lost it."

Back in 1977, Garry had been traveling in Latin America with his girlfriend, a French Canadian named Solange. They were hitchhiking back to Canada. At the southern border of Nicaragua they were detained at customs. Garry was put into a small room. A man who seemed to be the commanding officer came in, and, without a word, took off his cheap digital watch and put it in Garry's shirt pocket. When the man started to walk out of the room, Garry jumped up and gave the watch back.

"The guy was playing around with me," Garry said. "You know. He was showing me he could do anything he wanted to me. A bully kind of deal."

"Yeah, but that was Somoza time."

"You don't understand," Garry said. "It's not politics I'm talking about. I'm talking about losing it."

I thought about the times stress and fatigue gang up on a person; about the swirling mindstorm of dread and anxiety that is panic. It is a kind of insanity, accompanied by profuse sweating, a racing pulse, and the inability to function. And what is more frightening than any outside stimulus is the idea that you are no longer in control of your own life. You think: I can never come back. Not now.

It happens to everyone at some time or another; it happens in business, or in personal relationships. It happens for good reason; or for no reason at all. The context isn't important. When people say they are losing it, they mean they are losing their minds.

Ken Langley, Garry's partner on the around-the-world trip, knew he was "losing it" when he asked to be restrained, tied up, because he couldn't stop seeing himself opening the airplane door and happily stepping to his death.

Garry said: "This customs guy tried to put his watch back in my pocket—I don't know what he was doing or why—and I wouldn't let him. So they wouldn't let us into the country. We had to go back to Costa Rica. The only place to sleep was in that town where we got diesel this morning. What's it, about forty miles from the border?"

A bus came by and Garry flagged it down. The driver would take them to the town for $10. "It was robbery," Garry said, "but we paid it. So we get on the bus and all the women are sitting in front, all the men are in the back. The men started calling out to Solange. She spoke fluent Spanish and didn't like being called what they were calling her. She also had a fiery French-Canadian temper and she said a few things that made the women laugh. The men just shut up and stared at me.

"This all happened in a few seconds. I still hadn't found a seat. The only place for me was in the very back. So I squeezed in there. The guy next to me leans over. I can feel his breath on my neck. He says, in English, 'Twenty bucks or you bleed.'"

"So what did you do?"

"I gave him twenty bucks."

I thought about it for a minute.

"So," I said, "when we came up on that southern border . . ."

"Where it all happened ten years ago . . ."

"You started feeling it again."

"Yeah," Garry said. "And that's probably why I thought I had malaria. I mean, that sounds crazy to me now. And then when they gave our papers to that poor crazy kid, I thought it was starting all over. I thought they were going to start that bully stuff, playing around with us."

"You kind of barked at those kids at the Costa Rican border. I thought there was something wrong then."

"It started before that," Garry said. "I felt it in Panama, but it got worse. And then I'm sitting at the gas station, talking about malaria. I figured you knew I was starting to blow up. But you were calm. You reached out and felt my forehead. I thought, there's another person here. It's going to be all right. I'm going to come through it.

"And then the Costa Rican lady tried to give me five bucks. I looked down at this wadded-up bill in her hand and I felt tears come into my eyes. She saw it. I know she did. And she thought I really needed the money. I don't know . . ."

We hadn't been stopped by police once in Nicaragua. There were no guns and no threats of ambush. The war was on hold until the various parties decided what they wanted to do about the Arias peace plan. It had been a fast, easy drive. And, for Garry Sowerby, it had been terrifying.

"It was never about politics," Garry said. "It wasn't about Nicaragua or Nicaraguans. All that back there: it was about me."

A. J.—as in Foyt
by William Neely

William Neely has written biographies of racing superstars Richard Petty and Cale Yarborough and legendary racing sponsor Jim Gilmore. This 1974 Playboy *article profiled one of American racing's most dominant drivers and personalities.*

H e was standing atop the pit wall, hands on hips, looking out through slitted eyes at the Frenchmen—people he distrusts because they serve fish with the heads and tails still on them. And if that isn't enough, they all talk this goddamn funny language. Close beyond the first tight circle of Frenchmen was a looser stand of European journalists, all of them poised, waiting for some of those clean, cutting, kiss-my-ass quotes they had heard about. And beyond them all, parked on the edge of the track, sat the car.

The car was Ford's Mark IV, rear-engined, low-slung and roofed over, strictly low-mileage; 2580 pounds, exactly 499 horsepower in its 427-cubic-inch engine. It sat there with its tail up and its nose down like a good race car should and on the hood, roof and doors it wore NO. 1. There was no special significance to the NO. 1—but there *was* real meaning behind the red color. That was there to piss off Enzo Ferrari.

Now he reached into his back pocket and pulled out his wallet: the standard leather fold-over model. It was so full of money that it would barely fold over. "Here, hold onna this," he told a friend. The Frenchmen all sighed. The journalists all sighed; some of them jotted down in their notebooks, "Much Indy money." Then he turned to a crew official. "I know it's famous and all that stuff. I mean: I know this here is the scariest track in Europe and all *that*. But what I mean is: This here"—and he waved one hand out at the track—"this here is just a country road that twists around a whole lot and runs through a bunch of trees, right?"

Several heads nodded.

And A. J. Foyt shrugged inside his driving suit. "Well, then," he said, and he smiled.

He has bone-white teeth, something of a natural dental wonder. He is probably so full of calcium that you couldn't break him with repeated blows of a tire iron. This hard-gloss, Kelvinator-door smile has been known to paralyze full-grown women at tight range.

It was France in June 1967 and a couple of weeks earlier Foyt had won the Indianapolis 500 for the third time. He was the darling of the racing world, a status he had carved out over 12 years of the meanest hornyhanded driving anyone had ever seen. And now he was set to drive the 24 hours of Le Mans with Dan Gurney as copilot—over a 8.475-mile course that savages the best men in the world.

Just outside town, along old RN158, the main drag from Alençon to Tours, the road widens up quite a bit and becomes a dead straightaway for about three and one half miles. Once every year they chase all the hay shakers off there, the horse-drawn wagons and old Citroëns and older men pedaling bicycles loaded up with bundles of tied twigs—and it becomes the Mulsanne Straight, then and now the fastest stretch of road ever incorporated into a closed circuit.

There are trees up close along both sides and down toward the end of the straight you have to be hitting 200 or 210 miles an hour or you might as well park it. And as if you haven't got enough to do just hanging on, they've got this row of signs off to one side that tell you something—if you could read the things at that blind speed. Well, the signs are counting down kilometers, because at the end of the straight, just after this little 200-mile-an-hour soft right-hand dog-leg, they've got this 35-mile-an-hour corner where you've got to suck everything up tight. Suddenly you're going in the other direction. Back off a bit and hit the brakes; really mash down, then drag it down to first gear and breathe the brakes. Then hammer her back up to somewhere around 180 mph; gear down to 40 mph for a right-hander, gear down again for that slow left-right; punch it back to 160. Stand on it some more and crank it around the White House Corner and you had better plan to be hitting 180 and climbing as you go past the pits or everybody will think you're a fucking *tourist*. Over the hill and into the esses, where, usually, you are suddenly right up to your ass in little Alfas buzzing along in their own little race. You do all this 350 times in 24 hours, driving through night and day, and half the time it is raining down at one end of the track and sunny at the other—and most of the time they've got this cross wind that huffs up and blows you over one whole lane.

Foyt had it wired from the start. The Le Mans track really is just a little old country road, like he said. Anyone who would pump it full of special mystique and read extra romantic nuance into it just doesn't understand what it is that makes Foyt so special. Foyt recognizes a road and a car for what they really are and what they can do. And he bites people who don't do the same.

They won it, of course, and for the record, they covered 3249.6 miles in 24 hours at an *average* speed of 135.48 miles an hour, shattering the track record by the biggest margin in the history of the event. (They also averaged five and a half miles per gallon of gas and burned 20 quarts of oil.) On the victory stand, after spraying everybody—including chairman Henry Ford II and his new bouffant wife—with champagne, Foyt allowed as how "I tole you; damn, I *tole* you guys, that this here road isn't any different than a whole lot I have drove on."

They loved him in Europe; they still do. Foyt marched through Le Mans chin out and shoulders up in a stance that is peculiar to stock-car racers, and everybody else looked somehow fey by comparison. He also said exactly what he meant—in the land of the devious quote.

European Journalist: First you win ze Indy. And now, ze historic 24 hours of Le Mans. These two victories will make you famous, no?

A. J. Foyt: Famous? Lissen: I'll tell you what made me famous. You see this here right foot? Well, that there *foot* is what made me famous.

At lunch a few days before the race, sitting on a sun-washed terrace at one of the world's better restaurants, Foyt had growled softly at the waiter: "Gahdamn," he had said. "You expect me to eat this here fish? Lookee here, the little old sumbitch is *staring* at me." And while the fish was being whisked away for proper Texas trimming, Foyt had grinned at his companions. "This here is a trick country," he said.

It was a clean, hot day and the companionship was good—fellow race drivers, really the only humans with whom Foyt feels at large ease. Denis Hulme was there, the big, affable New Zealander who had just been named rookie of the year at Indy, and whom everybody calls The Bear. Roger McCluskey was there, a small, very tough survivor of the same sort of racing that had created Foyt: everything from midgets to stockers to Indy cars.

This was the summer before the microskirt had really moved over to the U. S. and among the diners on the terrace was a scattering of bare thighs, belonging to these golden, willowy girls who were looking on at the drivers, clearly interested.

"I wonder if it's true about French ladies; you know, where they don't wear any pants," one of the drivers said.

Everybody looked around. "Man," said another, "if you don't find out in a place like this here, you'll never know."

At the table next to Foyt, one of the girls leaned over.

"You are the racing drivers for Le Mans, no?" she said.

Foyt flashed her the smile and she practically pitched forward into her quiche Lorraine.

"Uh-huh," he said. Then he paused. "Well, all of us here except this one." He pointed to McCluskey. "He's really a monkey."

She nodded brightly, accepting that. "I see the monkey," she said.

McCluskey looked at her and shrugged. "Yeah," he said. "Well, hell, ma'am, I can see yours, too."

• • •

Anthony Joseph Foyt, Jr., now 39 years old, was born in Houston, Texas, of sound stock and raised up to be steady of kidney, a kid with the good sense to leave school before they got to John Greenleaf Whittier or, worse yet, social studies—the sort of thing that can screw up a brain for fair. "I couldn't study any longer," he says now. "I could already take a car apart and put it back together better 'n it was . . ." and he concluded the sentence with a sort of shrug indicating that anybody who needs more schooling than that will probably grow up to be some sort of bum, anyway. It is a matter of record that the exact last time he ever took any advice from anybody was in 1946. He was 11 at the time.

The senior A. J. remembers it well. "It was right after the war and I owned and campaigned two midget race cars those days. So I took one of them to Dallas for a race and Miz Foyt went along with me. We left one of the cars at home—and we left A. J. home, too.

"Well, when we got back—I guess it was about 5:30 in the morning or so—we found the whole yard tore up. I mean everything was gone. The grass was all chewed to bits and there were tire gouges all over the place. The swing set we had in the yard had been knocked over; the place was one mess. I knew right away that A. J. had got some of his buddies to push him and that they had got that midget fired up; it didn't have a self-starter. And then—after I stood there and looked at the messed-up yard, I went into the garage and saw the car. And I knew what had happened; he had caught the thing on fire and had burned up the engine. It was sitting there with the paint all scorched.

"I went right into the house and into his bedroom; I was thinking of whapping him. He was laying there playing he was asleep, but I could tell he wasn't really. My wife said, 'Well, don't say anything to him right now when you're still so mad.' So I didn't shake him up. But I knew right then, standing there in the kid's bedroom, that he would have to race, that there wasn't going to be any other way."

Next day, Dad dispensed the advice: "All right, you want to race, you can race. Only thing you got to promise me is always to drive something good. And one more thing: Stay the hell off the grass."

The rest is history, suitably laced with legend. Foyt drove his dad's midget cars at first, developing a sort of personalized balls-out, catch-me-come-kiss-me style that became part of his trademark. The other part consisted of those teeth and a jaw line that might have been done by Gutzon Borglum, plus real-silk shirts and crisp fresh white pants for every race. The pants probably did it: He acquired the nickname Fancy Pants and promptly kicked the hell out of anyone who said it in the wrong tone of voice—and by the time he was ready for bigger cars, it was clear that he was going to be either a champion driver or the damnedest middleweight ever to come out of Houston.

First time up at Indy, A. J. Fancy Pants talked himself into the Dean Van Lines Special, a hot car of the day—hanging in there in 16th place. Three years later, he won the race, $117,975, and he has been getting richer ever since. "You know," a sponsor once mused, "for a guy who didn't get any schooling, Foyt sure knows how to read a contract."

Through the years, the United States Auto Club has watched A. J.'s career with special pride, mixed with a sort of bemused dread. Foyt is enough to make any organization proud and he is always good copy, a credit to the game and all that bullshit, but he also has a keenly honed sense of swift justice. In a 1963 episode, at a badass, no-account sprint-car race in Williams Grove, Pennsylvania, Foyt felt that fellow racer Johnny White was cutting him off at the turns. This sort of maneuver was a source of considerable irritation to Foyt and the moment the race was over, he vaulted out of his car and sprinted over to White.

According to one U.S.A.C. official, A. J. opened the conversation by slugging White, who reported the incident, and Foyt was suspended from racing.

At the appeal, Foyt brought McCluskey along as a character witness and, in his best courtroom manner, explained what happened: "I didn't either slug him," Foyt said. "Oh, I had him around the *head* pretty good and I was *holding* him, all right. But I didn't hit him." And McCluskey provided the clincher.

"A. J. didn't hit White," he testified. "If he had of, he would have tore his head off."

Case dismissed; driver reinstated.

The reputation grew, shot through, in no special order, with all sorts of highlights:

• Not too many years ago, at a midget race in Terre Haute, Foyt failed to qualify because of car troubles and a deteriorating track. The winner's purse was only $600, and any man would have been well out of it, but Foyt was ticked off. So he walked down the line, found the right driver and paid him $100 to let him have the 24th, and last, starting position. By mid-race, Foyt was in first place, and he won, as they say, by a mile.

• In March of 1964, Foyt showed up for the 12 hours of Sebring, a sports-car race that draws both tough and elegant gentlemen from the road-racing world. The Le Mans–type start sort of threw him; Foyt is a driver, not a sprinter. As a result, he got a late start.

The field roared away, and just as the smartasses in the crowd were pointing out that one should never—but never—leave one's proper niche in the world, the cars came around again.

And there was Foyt: He had passed 51 cars on the first lap. He rolled by the stands and gave them his kiss-my-ass shrug.

And now he is on top. By count, Foyt has won more races and more championships than any other driver alive: in midgets, sprint cars, dirt cars, stock cars, Indy cars, sports cars and God knows.

A few years ago at Indianapolis, they told the story around the pits about the race driver who lost it in the second turn and skidded all the way to the pearly gates. Saint Peter walked up and put his arm around the race driver's shoulder. "Listen, son," he said, "you're in heaven. Don't look so unhappy."

"Hell—I mean, er—excuse me, shucks, I was right smack in the middle of my best season. I had that championship all locked up. And now I can't race anymore."

" 'Course you can," said Saint Peter. "This *is* heaven, ain't it?" And so Saint Peter took him down and showed him a solid-gold track that was so unbelievably beautiful that the driver just stood there and quivered.

"What about race cars?" he asked.

"Race cars," Saint Peter said. "Race cars. Just take your pick." And he waved an arm toward the pit area.

The race driver casually strolled over to a gold-and-white rear-engined Offy and scraped at the finish with a dirty fingernail. Just as he thought: 14-kt.-gold and mother-of-pearl.

"Try it, son," Saint Peter said.

"I don't know. I mean, man, this here is a weird scene," he said. All the while, he was easing himself into the cockpit. He buckled up and slipped on his helmet. The car roared to full power—a throaty, solid sound he knew well—and he wheeled it onto the track. First lap, he broke the track record. Then, suddenly, he was in traffic. There were race cars everywhere and he was blowing them off like he had never been able to do down there at Daytona or Indy. Not even in this best season of his. Why, he could put that rascal up high in the corners or down low. Anywhere. And it stuck right in there.

After six or seven sizzling laps of weaving through traffic, along came this car and it passed him, the driver giving him the finger. And right there on the driver's helmet were the initials A. J. F. He wheeled the car in and coasted to a stop. Saint Peter strode up.

"What's the matter, son? You were turning some pretty fast laps."

"I didn't know Foyt was dead," he said.

"Oh, that's not Foyt. That's God. He just *thinks* He's Foyt."

It was weeks before anyone told Foyt the story. The man who did it was Parnelli Jones, who is carved right out of concrete; if Foyt had punched him, the resulting fight would have torn the track up for miles around.

"Very funny," Foyt said and stomped off.

A visitor talked with A. J. in a motel outside Daytona last year. Foyt was tired after a hard day on the track. He'd blown an engine and now he watched television as Evel Knievel jumped a bunch of Mack trucks.

"You know, he's all right, Evel," Foyt said. "He's been out to my farm and I kind of like him."

It is the highest compliment A. J. gives anybody.

He eased his burly frame onto the bed and patted down his hair to cover the forehead that is becoming more and more apparent these days (A. J. had tried a hairpiece at Atlanta a couple of years ago but shelved it after Bobby Allison met him in the pits and said, "Where's your daddy, sonny? I wanna talk to him about his race car.").

"You know," he mused, looking up at the ceiling, "a lot of people worry about getting to be 40. Not me. Hell, I'll be 40 next January and my reflexes are as good as ever. A man's reflexes don't change. Only his eyes. And lemme tell you, when your eyes go, you're through.

"I mean, did you see that goddamn thing the A.P. wrote about me a couple of weeks ago? Said I was gonna retire after this season. Shit. My eyesight is 20/15 and that's what counts." And he turned back to the television.

"You think he'll ever jump that Snake River Canyon? I do. He's crazy enough to do it. He is."

And he rubbed his scarred hands over his eyes. The hands tell a lot. The knuckles of a fighter and fingers of a mechanic. But that was $2,500,000 ago.

As if on cue, he speaks of those early days (perhaps the A.P. story did get to him):

"You know, there were times when people actually booed me for breaking Tommy Hinnershitz' record on those Pennsylvania dirt tracks. That's when I was running the sprinter.

"Tommy was so popular that the fans couldn't stand watching him get old and seeing a smartassed young kid from Houston taking his records away. But I think his eyes went on him.

"Why, I used to watch Tommy run that track, and it was a sight to behold. We were running knobby tires then. You know, them big old skinny things with knobs for tread, and they were rough. You had to run a lot harder with those tires on the dirt tracks then. I mean, you ran in hard and deep in the corners. Voom!" Foyt uses racing sounds as punctuation, semicolons and all. "And once you committed yourself, it was too late to back off. You had to run in straight and just throw the car sideways. Blam! And hope to hell those old tires didn't get a bite then. Because if they did, it would throw the whole goddamn car out of the park," Foyt said. "Blooey!

"It was so rough that a lot of people got fractured elbows and broken arms, just from trying to hang on to that wheel. I got two busted elbows. Man, when a race was over, it looked like everybody had been in a hatchet fight.

"And ol' Tommy would run in so hard that he'd get the car up on its right wheels so far you could see the whole undercarriage. He could have sold billboard space on the bottom of the car.

"Ah, hell," he said. "Those were the days."

"I still tell anybody to go to hell if I feel like it," Foyt says. "I mean, some people think that old crash at Riverside slowed me down, but look at my record. I won Indy again after that and Le Mans and the Daytona 500 and a hell of a lot of other races. Is that slowing down?"

The Riverside crash, however, makes him stop and think. It has been nine years since it happened, and it was the only time he was ever seriously hurt (this does not count routine breaks, bruises, burns and lumps, including being run over by one's own race car). At Riverside, Foyt was running in a NASCAR stock-car race on the road course and had been one of the front runners most of the afternoon.

About two thirds of the way through the race, the twisting course had taken its toll on the 4000-pound stocker: The brakes were completely gone and a quick pit stop determined that they couldn't be repaired. At this point, a lot of racers would have parked it behind the pit wall and gone for a Coors. Foyt roared out of the pits and ducked in behind Junior Johnson, one of NASCAR's best and a man A. J. knew he could trust. One does not follow just anybody closely when one has no brakes. A. J. knew that Junior was not apt to make a mistake.

It worked for about ten laps and, true, Junior did not make a mistake. But the car in *front* of Johnson did and Junior had to hit his brakes—having no idea that Foyt didn't have any to hit. They were just entering the sweeping turn nine at about 140 mph. A. J. had a fraction of a second to weigh the situation. He could hit Junior full-bore in the rear or turn right. He turned right and the car leaped over the embankment. The nose dug in and the force catapulted the car 50 feet into the air; it slammed down on its top with a sickening crash.

Foyt was unconscious when they got to him. It wasn't until they got him to the hospital that a discerning doctor discovered that Foyt had a broken back. "A. J. Foyt will never race again," they pronounced; the sort of refrain that race drivers could set to music.

It took Foyt roughly two weeks to convince the doctors that he would be just as well off at home in bed. From there it took him another week to convince his wife, Lucy, that he would be better off in the Arizona sun, watching an Indy car race from a nice, easy wheelchair.

Two weeks later, he was watching a race from a nice, easy race car. He winced a lot as he got in and out of the car and everybody knew that he assuredly hurt like hell during the races, but he was back racing.

Now they say he's mellowing.

"I don't feel that I have to prove myself. If I decide I want to win, I go out and win. If I don't, I just don't care," he says.

But can one believe that the best race driver around doesn't care about winning? He drives as hard today as he ever has. And he isn't shy about declaring his intention to pass another car. I mean, if he waves you over, you ought really to give him room.

And he knows the quick route around every track in the country. "I know the tracks pretty good now," he says. "But I can never tell exactly how I'm going to drive a track until the time comes. When I get ahead, I just follow the groove. If I get behind, I just work my way back up front the best way I know how. My hands get tired in a 500-miler from hanging on to the wheel. Sometimes on the straights I open my hands and push down on the wheel with my palms to rest my fingers. If things are going real well, I might drive with one hand. But it's no Hollywood effect. My hands just get tired."

Foyt *has* been known to ham it up, though. A few years ago at Daytona, he had his Ford running so far out in front of the pack that he could have coasted the remaining five or six laps. He had led the race for so long that the covey of Ford executives in the paddock area had already made reservations for the victory dinner that night. His pit crew was lounging on stacks of tires examining their fingernails. That's when Foyt came out of the fourth turn, backed off the accelerator and ducked into the pits for an unscheduled stop. The Ford execs froze. The pit-crew members fell all over themselves getting to the pit wall. They stood in horror as Foyt poked his head through the window.

"You all want me for anything?" he asked. Then he flashed the white smile, dumped it back into gear and roared out of the pits, still comfortably in first place. He won, of course.

So here he is at Daytona, Super Tex at 39, who says he won't quit, no matter what the Associated Press says. The Associated Press can kiss his ass.

He is standing by his pit, looking out at the world through the slitted eyes—ready to talk only to those he really cares to talk to. A driver comes into view.

This is Paul Newman. Mr. Blue Eyes, the face that American millions adore; there are folks all over Daytona, men and women alike, who would give their right front fenders to stand alongside a pit wall and chat with Paul Newman.

True, Newman has credentials; he is a race driver himself, though undistinguished, in a sport that regularly attracts movie stars. Steve McQueen races; James Garner is a buff; so is one Smothers brother—and who really gives a damn which one it is?

They chat until Foyt figures he has had enough. He turns to the growing circle of fans. "Lissen, you guys, I gotta go," he says. And then he turns to Newman:

"So long, Steve," he says.

from A Boot Full of Right Arms
by Evan Green

Australian journalist Evan Green got hooked on rally racing while preparing to cover the 1954 Around Australia race. He later teamed up with former wrestling champion "Gelignite" Jack Murray to enter a Triumph 2.5 in the 1970 World Cup Rally, a race through Europe and Latin America. They were joined by British journalist Hamish Cardno (Jack nicknamed him "Habeas Corpus").

Our first disaster took place on the first corner of the first special stage. It was in Yugoslavia.

Rally cars with disc brakes normally use competition grade brake pads. These are harder and more resistant to fade (loss of efficiency when hot) than the normal material. During their manufacturing process they absorb oil. This has to be eliminated before they will work efficiently, and the way to do it is to work them so hard that they fade. Completely.

You do this before starting a serious stage. You keep working the brakes until the discs grow from red to white hot. Braking efficiency fades away. The oil in the pads is drawn to the surface and burnt off.

Once the brakes cool, they're fine. You can cane them without further loss of efficiency.

Hamish Cardno did this fading for Car 92 on the way to Titograd, start of the initial special stage. I was trying to sleep in the back. Paddy Hopkirk passed us and Hamish clung to his tail as the two Triumphs swept down the mountains to the town.

The smell of burning brake linings filled the cabin until there was no question of all the oil having been eliminated. A Leyland mechanic was waiting at Titograd and I asked him to check the brakes before we set off on the stage. 'I don't know how much is left,' I joked.

The three of us relieved ourselves behind a nearby building among some trees.

'Plenty of pad left,' the mechanic said on our return.

Jack and I strapped ourselves in and fitted the crash helmets. They were compulsory wear on all special stages. Hamish was waiting at the control table, to have our route book stamped.

We were also supposed to collect pace notes for the section. Team manager Peter Browning had arranged for a non-competing crew to travel over the stage a few days earlier and prepare the notes.

These give you a corner-by-corner description of the road. Distances and degree of difficulty are given. Your navigator reads them to you.

'One hundred metres fast left' he will say and you know the left hander looming up can be taken quickly. It's a great aid to rapid travel, as long as your man is on the right page.

Unknown to me, there was no copy of the pace notes left for us. Hamish ran to the car, and said: 'Go.' He spoke softly and his voice was hard to hear through the crash hat. But there was no mistaking the message. I went. Running hard on most cylinders, No 92 misfired its way on to the stage.

Hamish and I had never driven together with pace notes, of course. Still unaware that he had none, I awaited his first instruction. Despite the misfire, the Triumph managed 4000 rpm in overdrive top. That was 160 km/h.

Groups of people were lining the road. The surface was bitumen. I would have preferred dirt. I'm better on loose surfaces than sealed roads. I'm also a nervous starter and a gravel road lets you work off suppressed energy quickly and soon get the feel of the car.

We neared a crest and still Hamish said nothing. Silence normally means flat out, so I kept going. As we neared the crest, I could see a right-hand bend ahead. A flick of the overdrive knob and the car was back in fourth. I waited for Hamish's advice.

He spoke, very softly, and I thought he said 'Go fast'. So I stayed in fourth.

What I now think he said was: 'Oh Christ.'

As the corner rushed into view, I noted a row of white-painted stones on the outside of the bend, a row of trees further on, and a group of cheering children. They greeted us enthusiastically because, obviously, we were about to turn on the most spectacular demonstration of the day.

My left foot hit the brake pedal. It went straight to the floor. Had it been dirt, I would have put the car sideways and had a go. On bitumen that would have been impossible. We'd have rolled or slammed into the trees.

Happenings seem to slow down when disaster is imminent. I remember noticing the white stones were far enough apart for the Triumph to slip through. Beyond them was a drop to a fence and beyond that a ploughed field.

Still doing around 130 km/h, we left the road. The car sailed over the fence. It landed on all four wheels and soon lost speed in the ploughed soil. I spun into a U-turn to head for an open gate I'd noticed as we crossed the fence. We almost bogged in the deep furrows.

Jack, who had been lying on the back seat, sat up as we regained the road.

'Like, what happened?' he said.

The children on the corner were still waving. 'No brakes,' I said, and apologized to Hamish. It was his first time with us and it was a rough introduction.

The heat from fading the brakes had cooked an oil seal on one of the back drums and hydraulic fluid was leaking. We had to cover the 72 km to Kotor without brakes. The last seven miles were all down hill, through 19 hairpin bends.

We arrived nine minutes late, to be fourteenth. I don't think Hamish was relishing the prospect of the journey through the Andes.

We took a wrong turn on the next special stage, were blocked by three bogged trucks and then had a stroke of good fortune. We discovered what had been causing the misfire.

A valve guide had broken. It was a freakish sort of mishap, due almost certainly to a flaw in the metal of this small, cylindrical part. Where it was cracked—so that the guide was in two pieces—chafing was sending small fragments of metal down the valve and into the combustion chamber. These particles were fouling the injector. Number six cylinder was affected.

To stop the valve working, we removed the pushrods. Then, to prevent raw petrol being squirted into the cylinder, and diluting the engine oil, we disconnected the petrol line and ran it into a plastic tube which we trailed out the side of the engine bay.

Running on five cylinders, and with every sixth measure of petrol being blown in the wind, we continued. Controls were a hazard. One of us had to jump out, and banish any onlookers smoking cigarettes.

The Triumph ran better on five cylinders. We joined the leading few cars in clean-sheeting the San Remo special stage in Italy. We felt better. But alas, our misfortunes had only begun.

We changed tyres near the French border, going from mud and snow pattern radials to SP sports, for the bitumen sections ahead. Work was carried out by a service crew who were desperately short of time. We'd been delayed modifying the engine and the mechanics were due to leave to catch an aircraft for Spain. They worked while we went to get food, to last us for the next day.

I can only assume one wheel wasn't fully tightened. One hundred and fifty kilometres later, it came off.

It was a ghastly moment, like the sudden accumulation of all your nightmares.

We were in high mountains, travelling on a winding road beyond the village of Le Broc. Jack was sleeping in the back. Hamish was map reading and we were nearing the start of a special stage. It was late at night.

The road climbed to a ridge, turned hard left, and then began to wind down a mountain in a series of hairpins.

The front rumbled once, as I accelerated hard along the short straight. Then there came a crack like a rifle firing. I thought the steering had broken, for the wheel went dead in my hand.

Hamish saw the left front wheel leave the car. There was no time to say anything.

The car began to dip to the left. Then, almost instantaneously, it changed course as the sole front wheel slewed right under the influence of the Triumph's nose settling on one side. We shot off the road.

Our six lights left the bitumen and arced through the dark night. They swept across slim trunks and the leafy tops of trees stationed down the side of the mountain.

The car—white, neatly signwritten, and representing an investment of something like $50,000 as its share of the factory's total commitment to the event—plunged towards its almost certain destruction. It began to barrel roll.

Well, that's the end of South America, I thought.

We grazed one large tree trunk. It lost its bark, we lost an outside mirror and the back door handle. The door swung open. Luckily, Jack was strapped in.

Two trees rushed towards us. They were tall, but slender. And being on the hillside, they were lightly rooted.

We hit them flush in the middle of the bonnet. The metal crumpled, as it should, to absorb energy. The trees snapped, and were partly uprooted. The Triumph began to climb the trunks and the trunks began to topple.

Very gently, the car and its supporting timber came to rest in a bed of nettles. We were partly on our side.

Hamish and I hit hands as we went for the master switch, to disconnect the battery. We had no desire for the high pressure fuel pump to continue spraying petrol over whatever wreckage lay under the mangled bonnet.

Without the battery, the lights went out. Timber was still crashing around us. A quick check established that no one was hurt.

Jack undid his belt and almost fell out the open door.

'Don't get out,' Hamish warned. 'There's a big drop down there.'

Jack explored the void with his leg and suffered the only injury of the incident. He was stung by a nettle.

The first car on the scene was a Rolls Royce. It was a competing vehicle that had dropped well back in the field, and it came gliding around the bend just as I was scrambling to the edge of the road.

We had discovered, to our astonishment, that the Triumph was mechanically intact. An inspection by torchlight had revealed no damage to the motor or front suspension.

The nose and bonnet had suffered massive distortion; the side was buckled where we had grazed the first tree; the front wheel was missing, with the studs sheared.

We had a spare hub and could fix the matter of the missing wheel. The motor could run—we had tried it briefly, down the mountainside. Our problem was to get the car out of the trees and on the road.

So I had just regained the road when the Rolls arrived. The driver braked, bringing the car to a halt next to me. He did it smoothly.

'I say, are you all right?' he asked.

I assured him we were, and explained what had happened.

'Jolly bad luck,' he said. 'Would you like a cup of tea?'

I wasn't sure I'd heard him correctly and hesitated. He repeated the offer. 'We have a thermos,' he explained. It sounded like lines from Noel Coward, *circa* 1934. Not Le Broc, in the depths of 1970.

I declined. Since we had established that the car was drivable, time had become a worry. We had to get back on the road and reach the next control within two hours. Otherwise, we would be eliminated from the rally.

'We need a tow truck,' I said. Hamish and Jack were scrambling up the bank, to see who had arrived.

'We don't have much time,' I added. 'If you could enquire at the next control I'd be grateful. It's about 15 km away.'

He looked offended. 'I know where it is,' he said, and then proceeded to display an absolute knowledge of the local geography. He ran through a list of nearby towns, and their lack of garage facilities.

'The nearest tow truck is based at Nice, and that's 100 km away,' he said. 'I doubt whether you'll be in luck, but we'll try.'

Jack had joined me.

'They mightn't speak English at this next place,' Jack said.

'That will be all right,' the Rolls driver said. I suspect he spoke better French than the locals. He was a middle-aged man, very Rolls-Royce in appearance. He was travelling in the rally with his two adult sons.

A voice murmured from the rear of the car: 'We should be going. We don't have much time.'

The driver lifted his hand, to silence the son.

'I'll try to get you a tow truck. I'm not hopeful.' He paused. 'You've had jolly bad luck. Are you sure you wouldn't like a cup of tea?'

We assured him our sole need was a tow truck. He departed, at a modest rate of acceleration.

We followed the car's lights descending the lacets, imagining that our last link with the World Cup Rally was disappearing down the mountainside.

Three quarters of an hour later, the tow truck arrived.

It had come that day from Nice, having been retained by a Peugeot team in case one of their cars had need of its services. That team didn't; we did. The tow truck crew came to our aid with great enthusiasm. They also brought our lost wheel. They had found it lying on the road at the bottom of the valley.

Like a goldfish being lifted from a bowl, our Triumph was plucked, tail first, from the trees.

It took more than half an hour to replace the hub, from which the wheel studs were missing—they'd snapped as the wheel let go—and a few more minutes to belt out the mudguards, so that both front wheels had clearance to turn.

The spot lights had disappeared in the impact, but the four headlamps were untouched, although wildly out of adjustment. They were perfect for possum hunting, less suited to rally driving. But they would do. Our sole aim was to get moving and reach the control before it closed.

The Frenchmen with the tow truck had been joined by a small crowd who had driven back from the control, to witness our rescue. To their cheers and horn blasts, we finally coaxed the Triumph into life and moved down the road. Our four lights criss-crossed in the tree-tops and the right wheel grated in its guard as we turned the first hairpin.

One of the spectators followed us in his BMW, to help if we had further trouble, or at least see the action if we went over the edge again. We outpaced him, for we were desperately short of time.

We reached the control with three minutes to spare.

Our benefactor in the Rolls was less fortunate than we, when he had trouble in South America. He was the last rally car on the road when he tackled a muddy section in the southern part of Brazil. The big car slid into an embankment, severely denting the elegant mudguard, and breaking part of the front suspension. No one was following to fetch a tow truck for him.

Eventually, a small truck came, travelling slowly on the slippery road. The Englishman spoke fluent Portuguese. He was one of those men who display uncommon talents with impeccable reservation. He explained his problem to the truck driver.

'There is no truck anywhere near here Senor,' the local explained. 'But there is a town 27 km down the road where there is a garage. They must be able to help.'

So the driver went in the small truck to the town. There he spoke to the garage owner. He would be delighted to help someone in the World Cup Rally. There was a man in the town with a large truck, big enough to carry the Rolls-Royce. He would borrow it.

He did, and in the large vehicle, the party returned to the stranded car and the driver's sons.

The problem was to get the Rolls on to the back of the truck. No problem to the garage man. The bank that had damaged the car would now be made to act as a loading ramp.

The Rolls, on three wheels, was part-driven, part-shoved from the road to the top of the embankment. With a shovel, the earth was trimmed to the height of the truck's load platform. The truck was reversed against the bank, and the Rolls pushed on to its platform.

The car's brakes had been affected by the damage to the front suspension and when it slid on to the truck, it kept sliding. The result: a hefty whack against the truck's cab. The blow didn't seem to offend the

Brazilians. They were remarkably keen to help—as they were about to demonstrate.

They carried the Rolls to the garage. There they were faced with another problem. They couldn't get the car off the truck. So they worked on it, where it rested.

The Englishman explained that he was no longer in a hurry. He had lost so much time that he could not possibly reach the next control before it closed, excluding him from the event. This was not understood. Anyone in the Great Race must be in a hurry.

The garage owner had four mechanics. They were enthusiastic, industrious and ingenious. Working without rest, they removed the damaged components and, using those on the other side of the car as a pattern, machined a new front end for the Rolls. They also panel-beat the damaged guard back into its original shape.

The work took 28 hours.

Once the car was rebuilt, they took the truck to the nearest embankment, and reversed the Rolls on to the grass.

The Englishman was stunned by the service. 'You have been too kind,' he said, and asked for the bill.

The garage man told him the repairs would cost the equivalent of £10.

'That is too little,' he protested.

'No, no Senor,' the man said. 'That is all the money I need.' And he explained how the bill was composed. Six pounds was needed to pay for materials (to make part of the front end of a Rolls Royce!). Four pounds would go to his four mechanics, for their 28 hours of non-stop work.

'But there is nothing for you,' the car owner said.

'Ah Senor, from you I require something very special.'

The Englishman braced himself.

'From you, I require your permission to paint a sign on the front of my garage.'

'A sign?'

'Yes Senor,' and with his hand, he gestured towards the appropriate space on the front of his building. 'Up there, I would like to paint "Here we repair Rolls Royces"!'

• • •

Our crash had buckled the rear door. It was above the exhaust pipe outlet. As a result, our journey across France and into Spain was a sickening progress, with exhaust gas and petrol fumes penetrating the cabin.

Hamish and I stayed in the front for some time with the result that Jack, in the back, soaked in a dangerous amount of both gas and fumes.

Passing through Pamplona, in Spain, Jack suddenly became ill. It was about nine o'clock at night. Hamish was driving. I had just gone to sleep when Jack began shouting for me to let him out. The damaged door was wired in place, having lost its handle in the crash, while the other door had no internal handle, the inside having been equipped as a tool rack.

'Let me out, I'm crook,' he cried. Jack is a supremely fit man and it was a shock to find him this way.

Dopey from sleep—or lack of it—I stepped outside and was almost run down. I hadn't realized we were in a big city. Hamish had stopped in a busy part, opposite a high-class restaurant. A doorman, dressed in elaborate uniform, with cap and epaulettes, was studying our battered and muddy car.

I opened Jack's door.

'Gees, I've got to have a crap,' he said, with desperation. 'Where can I go?'

He had difficulty in standing upright, so severe were his stomach cramps. Without waiting for a suggestion he staggered across the road, oblivious of the traffic, towards the restaurant.

The doorman retreated from the strange visitor. Jack tried to explain that he wanted to use the toilet. He mimed the need. The doorman looked horrified.

Jack fainted.

I ran to where he lay. Before I reached him, he had risen and fallen again. The doorman, suddenly compassionate, came near.

Jack was on his side, doubled up. He didn't move. His eyes were open, but showed no sign of life. I touched him. Every muscle in his body seemed rigid. His skin felt like leather over stone.

I thought he was dead. Then I noticed his nose had been cut, and blood was still trickling from the wound.

His eyes flickered. He took a deep breath and tried to move.

'I think I've cacked the nest,' he said.

We took him to a nearby first aid post. Jack showered, washing his soiled clothing. 'I haven't done that for years,' he said. He laughed, and then fell over again.

The attendant spoke no English, and neither Hamish nor I had a grasp of Spanish but all of us could muster a little French.

'You should take him to a hospital,' the man said. We agreed, and he telephoned, to advise the hospital that an unusual patient was on his way.

To save weight, we had carried no spare clothes, so we dressed Jack in my rally jacket and a sleeping bag which he held at waist level. We were then escorted to Pamplona Hospital.

Two nursing nuns, in elaborate white outfits were waiting at the hospital entrance. They came forward to help Jack.

He was still bleeding from the nose. And he was stumbling, as he tried to walk in the sleeping bag.

The nuns held out their hands to support Jack's arms. He reached for them, and dropped the sleeping bag. That surprised them.

They regained their composure, before Hamish and I could untangle the bag from Jack's ankles. They slipped a sheet around him, persuaded him to lie on a trolley and took him away.

Now the rules of the rally insisted that all members of a crew travel in a car, or else the entry was disqualified. To continue, therefore, we needed Jack. If he was too ill to carry on, then we were prepared to accept the disappointment of retirement. But if he could be repaired quickly we would like him back—and soon. Again, we were running short of time.

It dawned on us that the nurses probably assumed that Jack was an accident victim. The blood on his face and the damaged car would force such a conclusion.

We searched for a doctor. We could find no one who spoke English, or even French. Our team mate had disappeared into the hospital system. No one knew where he was. Or what we wanted.

More than half an hour passed before someone fetched a girl who spoke English. We explained our problem. She returned with a doctor.

They were putting Jack to bed for the night, he explained, and planned x-raying his head in the morning.

We described what had happened. He smiled with understanding when we told him of the rally requirement for a complete crew. He had Jack wheeled in to a room for immediate examination.

We could hear Jack coming down the corridor, still on a trolley. He was obviously unhappy about his incarceration. Jack is fluent in two languages, English and Profane, and he was exhibiting great virtuosity in the latter.

'He sounds all right,' the doctor said, through the translator.

'What are you pair of poofters doing,' Jack said when he saw us. 'Aren't we in a rally or something?'

He stood up, and fell over. The doctor looked concerned.

The two nurses helped him into a chair in a corner of the room. He was mumbling what sounded like a nursery rhyme.

The nuns stood beside him. When he tried to stand, each of them reached out to restrain him.

Jack wrestled for many years, and the movement must have triggered some well-practised reaction. He seized each of the nuns by the wrist, drew them to him, and then flicked them clear.

Like a pair of upturned penguins, they slid on their backs across the room. Legs in the air, they passed one on either side of the doctor.

Jack fell off the chair and lay on the floor. The doctor rammed a needle in his exposed tail.

Within 20 minutes we were on our way—all three of us. The doctor had given Jack medicine to ease the stomach pain and we had bundled him into the back seat of the car. He slept for the remainder of the night.

Hamish and I took turns at the wheel. Our driving shifts became shorter. By dawn, we were down to 20 minutes at a time, which is disastrous. Neither of us was getting the sleep he needed. We crossed into Portugal.

Occasionally Jack would wake and cry out: 'Everything OK?' and then lapse into a drugged sleep.

When we changed places, Hamish and I would circle the car, partly to check the tyres and the general condition of the much-battered Triumph, and partly to stir the incoming driver into wakefulness.

After one such lap, I found Jack behind the wheel. He had stepped out of the sleeping bag and slid into the driver's seat.

'Come on Jack, it's not your turn yet,' I said. I could still remember him lying on the footpath back at Pamplona, and recalled the doctor's advice: 'Make sure he rests for a day or so. He is suffering severely from stomach cramps and is in great pain. I would rather keep him here, but in view of the circumstances you can take him with you.'

So again I asked Jack to get in the back.

'Am I supposed to be in this team or not?' he exploded. 'How long is it since I've driven? Last week?'

He was half joking, half serious.

'Talk sense and have some sleep,' he added. 'Habeas Corpus looks as though he could earn a living haunting houses and you look like you've gone 15 rounds with Cassius Clay.'

'Come on Jack, I'm all right.'

'You know the big roan bull at the Royal Show?' he said, beginning one of his more Rabelaisian stories. He sounded normal. And he had no intention of moving.

'Come on Jack,' Hamish said.

'We're wasting time,' Jack said.

I climbed in the back. Just as a precaution, I lay on the floor, and covered myself with a pair of pillows. I was asleep in minutes.

Jack drove for three hours. He stopped once when a front tyre punctured. I awoke to hear him cursing the local drivers, all of whom blew their horns as they went by.

'What the hell's wrong with them,' he muttered, getting back in the car, and still wearing only the rally jacket.

Car 92 arrived at Lisbon control with just three minutes to spare. We were glad to have reached the end of Europe.

• • •

Our car engine, having digested quantities of metal from the broken valve guide, finally expired in Southern Argentina.

We had our moments, before retiring.

Near Sao Paulo we were detained as suspects in a hit-run accident. Someone had been killed on the highway from Rio de Janeiro. Our car was badly dented at the front. Why? asked the man in a white suit, backed by a chorus line of soldiers bearing arms.

We were doing well, fumbling with the Portuguese words for tree, mountain and France when Gelignite Jack took over. He went to the front of the car and performed the great Murray mime act. He meant to represent a tree but gave a perfect imitation of a pedestrian being spreadeagled. We were arrested.

Much talking, and one request for a rally jacket followed before we were on our way.

A VW hit us in Porto Allegre. The policeman who had signalled each of us into the intersection ran away. Some soldiers came. So did a crowd, who showed interest in lynching the Volkswagen driver. His car was wrecked, but ours had so many scars by now that it was hard to find the impact point.

We had to wait to fill out a report.

Eventually an officer came. He was friendly, but had difficulty with the form.

Almost inevitably, we were befriended by someone who spoke English.

'May I help you,' he said, and, without waiting for an answer, suggested our best course of action was to run over the officer. This would save time and avoid the loss of more points in the Great Race.

I accepted his offer of help, but decided against following his advice.

He shrugged, and took over proceedings. 'This man,' he said, indicating the beaming officer, 'has trouble with writing.'

I presented all my travel documents. Our friend chose those which interested him most. He wrote down my name as Green Evan, noted my address as Australia and copied out my motor sport licence number.

I suggested my international driving licence would be more appropriate.

'The other is more impressive,' he said.

He halted, however, when it came to 'make of vehicle'.

'What is it?' he asked. 'I have not seen such an automobile.'

'A Triumph,' I said.

'He would not know that,' he said, and searched the body for some other name.

One of our stickers read 'Shell.'

'That will do,' he said. 'That's a word he will know.' So he wrote down that we were driving a Shell.

The officer was supremely contented. We shook hands and drove away. The crowd, hundreds thick by now, roared approval, then turned towards the man in the VW . . .

Our engine was running badly, and we were scheduled to have it partly rebuilt south of Buenos Aires. Unfortunately, the plans were upset by an outbreak of hostilities between Britain and Russia. Or their rally representatives.

The Leyland survey team had selected a garage as the factory service point and hired the workshops for the night. The mechanics laid out their tools, spare parts, wheels and tyres across both service bays. Then they waited for the cars to arrive.

Autoexport, the Soviet export agency, had entered a team of Moskvitch sedans, and mechanics were travelling the course to service them. They decided the Leyland garage would be an ideal service point. They would use one of the service bays.

The Russians, who remained by themselves for most of the event, spoke no English and the Leyland mechanics couldn't get beyond 'yes' and 'no' in Russian.

The Russians began laying out their spares.

When verbal opposition failed, the Englishmen tried to move the Moskvitch parts. They needed the space for their four works Triumphs, plus a host of private 1800s.

The Russians responded by bringing up one of their vans and driving it over the row of Leyland spare parts. The first boxes contained spare headlamps.

So it was on. Like rival fans at a soccer match, they set to.

I'm not sure who won. Both sides seemed to enjoy the tussle.

The Russians retreated when the Triumphs began to arrive. Faced with overwhelming odds and the lack of a single Moskvitch to provide a cause for prolonging the conflict, they retreated to neutral ground.

We missed our engine rebuild. A thousand miles later, in Patagonia, the long suffering, ill fated but remarkably dogged Triumph finally decided it had had enough. It put a piston through a cylinder wall.

We were out of the event, after trying so hard.

And on the cold, grassy plains of Patagonia, near a village whose name means The Quicksands, I resolved to try again, when next one of these motoring marathons was held.

from The Sweet Hereafter
by Russell Banks

Novelist Russell Banks (born 1940) has said that most of his characters "only learn anything as adults as a result of a terrible calamity." This passage from his 1991 novel is narrated by a school bus driver who is married to a stroke victim named Abbott.

B y the time I reached the bottom of Bartlett Hill Road, where it enters Route 73 by the old mill, I had half my load, over twenty kids, on board. They had walked to their places on Bartlett Hill Road from the smaller roads and lanes that run off it, bright little knots of three and four children gathered by a cluster of mailboxes to wait there for me—like berries waiting to be plucked, I sometimes thought as I made my descent, clearing the hillside of its children. I always enjoyed watching the older children, the seventh and eighth graders, play their music on their Walkmans and portable radios and dance around each other, flirting and jostling for position in their numerous and mysterious pecking orders, impossible for me or any adult to understand, while the younger boys and girls soberly studied and evaluated the older kids' moves for their own later use. I liked the way the older boys slicked their hair back in precise dips and waves, and the way the girls dolled themselves up with lipstick and eyeliner, as if they weren't already as beautiful as they would ever be again.

When they climbed onto the bus, they had to shut their radios off. It was one of the three rules I laid down every year the first day of school. Rule one: No tape players or radios playing inside the bus. Headsets, Walkmans, were permissible, of course, but I could not abide half a dozen tiny radio speakers squawking three kinds of rock 'n' roll behind me. Not with all the other noises those kids made. Rule number two: No fighting. Anyone fights, he by God walks. And no matter who starts it, both parties walk. Girls the same as boys. They could argue and holler at one another all they wanted, but let one of them strike another, and both of them were on the road in seconds. I usually had to enforce this rule no more than once a year, and after that the kids enforced it themselves. Or if they did hit each other, they did it silently, since the victim knew that he or she would have to walk too. I was well aware that I couldn't ever stop them altogether from striking each other, but at least I could make them conscious of it, which is a start. Rule number three: No throwing things. Not food, not paper airplanes, not hats or mittens—nothing. That rule was basically so I could drive without sudden undue distraction. For safety's sake.

I'm a fairly large woman, taller and heavier than even the biggest eighth-grade boy (although Bear Otto was soon going to be bigger than I am), and my voice is sharp, so it was not especially difficult, with only these few rules, to maintain order and establish tranquillity. Also, I made no attempt to teach them manners, no moves to curb or restrain their language—I figured they heard enough of that from their teachers and parents—and I think this kept them loose enough that they did not feel particularly restricted. Besides, I have always liked listening to the way kids talk when they're not trying to please or deceive an adult. I just perched up there in the driver's seat and drove, letting them forget all about me, while I listened to their jumble of words, songs, and shouts and cries, and it was almost as if I were not present, or were invisible, or as if I were a child again myself, a child blessed or cursed (I'm not sure which) with foresight, with the ability to see the closing off that adulthood would bring, the pleasures, the shame, the secrets, the fearfulness. The eventual silence; that too.

At Route 73 by the old mill, I banged a left and headed north along the Ausable River, picking up the valley kids. There was always a fair amount of vehicular traffic on 73 at this hour, mostly local people driving to work, which never presented a problem, but sometimes there were downstate skiers up early on their way to a long weekend at Lake Placid and Whiteface. Them I had to watch out for, especially today, this being a Friday—they were generally young urban-type drivers and were not used to coming up suddenly on a school bus stopped at the side of the road to pick up children, and the flashing red lights on the bus didn't seem to register somehow, as if they thought all they had to do was slow down a little and then pass me by. They thought they were up in the mountains and no people lived here. To let them know, I kept a notebook and pen next to my seat, and whenever one of those turkeys blew past me in his Porsche or BMW, I took his number and later phoned it in to Wyatt Pitney at state police headquarters in Marlowe. Wyatt usually managed to get their attention.

Anyhow, this morning I was stopped across from the Bide-a-Wile Motel, which is owned and operated by Risa and Wendell Walker, and Risa was walking their little boy, Sean, across Route 73, as is customary. Sean had some kind of learning disability—he was close to ten but seemed more like a very nervous, frightened five or six, an unusually runtish boy and delicate, with a sickly pale complexion and huge dark eyes. He was a strange little fellow, but you couldn't help liking him and feeling protective toward him. Apparently, although he was way behind all the other kids his age in school and was too fragile and nervous to play at sports, he was expert at playing video games and much admired for it by the other children. A wizard, they say, with fabulous eye-hand coordination, and when sitting in front of a video game, he was supposed to be capable of scary concentration. It was probably the only time he felt competent and was not lonely.

It had started to snow, light windblown flecks falling like bits of wood ash. Risa had her down parka over her nightgown and bathrobe and was wearing slippers, and she held Sean by the hand and carefully walked him from the motel office, where they had an apartment in back, to the road, which, although it's only two lanes, is actually a state highway along there, the main truck route connecting Placid and the Saranac region to the Northway.

There were no cars or trucks in sight as Risa brought her son across to the bus. He was Risa's and Wendell's only child and the frail object of all their attention. Wendell was a pleasantly withdrawn sort of man who seemed to have given up on life, but Risa, I knew, still had dreams. In warm weather, she'd be out there roofing the motel or repainting the signs, while Wendell stayed inside and watched baseball on TV. They had a lot of financial problems—the motel had about a dozen units and was old and in shabby condition; they had bought it in a foreclosure sale eight or ten years before, and I don't think they'd put up the No Vacancy sign once in that time. (Sam Dent is one of those towns that's on the way to somewhere else, and people get this far, they usually keep going.) Also, I think that the Walkers' marriage was shaky. Judging from what happened to them after the accident, it was probably just that motel and their love for the boy, Sean, that had bound them.

I flung open the door, and the child, because he was so small, stepped up with difficulty, and when he got to the landing he turned and did an unusual thing. Like a scared baby who wanted his mother to lift him up and hug him, he held his arms out to Risa and said, "I want to stay with you."

Risa had large dark circles under her eyes, as if she hadn't slept well, or at all, for that matter, and her hair was tangled and matted, and for a second I wondered if she had a drinking problem. "Go on now," she said to the boy in a weary voice. "Go on."

The kids sitting near the door were watching Sean, surprised and puzzled by his behavior, maybe embarrassed by it, since he was doing what so many of them would sometimes like to do but did not dare, certainly not in public like this. One of the eighth-grade girls, Nichole Burnell, who was sitting next to the door and has a wonderful maternal streak, squinched over a few inches and patted the seat next to her and said, "C'mon, Sean, sit next to me."

With his large eyes fixed on Risa's face, the boy edged sideways toward Nichole and finally sat, but still he watched his mother, as if he was frightened. Not for himself but for her. "Is he okay?" I asked Risa. Normally he just marched on board and found himself a seat and stared out the window for the whole trip. A very private boy enjoying his thoughts and fancies, thinking maybe about his video games.

"I don't know. He's fine, I mean. Not sick or anything. It's just one of those mornings, I guess. We all have them, Dolores, don't we?" She made a wistful smile.

"By Jesus, I sure do!" I said, trying to cheer the woman up, although in fact I almost never had those mornings myself, so long as I had the school bus to drive. It's almost impossible to say how important and pleasurable that job was to me. Though I liked being at home with Abbott and had the post office and mail carrier job to get me through the summers, I could hardly wait till school started again in September and I could get back out there in the early morning light and start up my bus and commence to gather the children of the town and carry them to school. I have what you call a sanguine personality. That's what Abbott calls it.

"Are *you* okay, Risa?" I asked.

She looked at me and sighed. Woman to woman. "You want to buy a good used motel?" she said. She looked across the road at the row of empty units. Not a car in the lot, except their Wagoneer. It's the Holiday Inns and the Marriotts that keep folks like the Walkers from making a living.

"Winter's been tough, eh?"

"No more than usual, I guess. The usual just gets harder and harder, though."

"I guess it does," I said. A big Grand Union sixteen-wheeler had come up behind me and stopped. "But I got enough problems of my own, honey," I said. "Last thing I need is a motel." We were talking finances, not husbands—or at least I was. I suspected she was talking husband, however. "I got to get moving," I said, "before the snow blows."

"Yes. It will snow some today. Six to eight inches by nightfall."

I thought about the chains again. Sean was still watching his mother with that strange grief-stricken expression on his small, bony face, and she waved limply at him, like she was dismissing him, and stepped away. Shutting the door with one hand, I released the brake with the other, waited a second for Risa to cross in front of the bus, and pulled slowly out. I heard the air brakes of the sixteen-wheeler hiss as the driver chunked into gear and, checking the side mirror, saw him move into line behind me.'

Then suddenly Sean shrieked, *"Mommy!"* and he was all over me, scrambling across my lap to the window, and I glimpsed Risa off to my left, leaping out of the way of a red Saab that seemed to have bolted out of nowhere. It had come around the bend in front of me and the truck and hadn't slowed a bit as I drew back onto the road, and the driver must have felt squeezed and had accelerated and had just missed clipping Risa as she crossed to the other side. I hit the brakes, and thank God the driver of the truck behind me did too, managing to pull up an inch or two from my rear.

"Sean! Sit the hell down!" I yelled. "She's okay! Now sit down," I said, and he obeyed.

I slid my window open and called to Risa. "You get his number?" All I'd caught was that the car was a tomato-red Saab with a ski rack on top.

She was shaken, standing there white-faced in the motel lot with her arms wrapped around herself. She shook her head no, turned away, and walked slowly back to the office. I drew a couple of deep breaths and checked Sean, who was seated now but still craning and peering wide-eyed after his mother. Nichole had him on her lap, with her arms around his narrow shoulders.

"There's a lot of damn fool idiots out there, Sean," I said. "I guess you got a right to worry." I smiled at him, but he only glared back at me, as if I was to blame.

Again, I put the bus into first gear and started moving cautiously down the road, with the Grand Union truck rumbling along behind. I said, "I'm sorry, Sean. I'm really sorry." That was all I could think of to say.

There were half a dozen more stops along the valley, and then I turned right onto Staples Mill Road and made my way uphill to the ridge, where you get a terrific view east and south toward Limekiln and Avalanche mountains. It's mostly state forest up there, not many houses, and the few you see are old, built back before the Adirondack Park was created.

The snow was falling lightly now, hard dry flakes floating on the breeze. There was enough daylight that I could have shut off my headlights, but I didn't, even though they weren't helping me see the road any better. In fact, it was the time of day when headlights make no difference, on or off, but they let the bus itself be seen sooner and more clearly by oncoming cars. Not that there was any traffic up on Staples Mill Road, especially this early. But when you drive a school bus you have to think of these things. You have to anticipate the worst.

Obviously, you can't control everything, but you are obliged to take care of the few things you can. I'm an optimist, basically, who acts like a pessimist. On principle. Just in case.

Abbott says, "Biggest . . . difference . . . between . . . people . . . is . . . quality . . . of . . . attention." And since a person's quality of attention is one of the few things about her that a human *can* control, then she damn well better do it, say I. Put that together with the Golden Rule in a nutshell, and you've got my philosophy of life. Abbott's too. And you don't need religion for it.

Oh, like most people, we go to church—First Methodist—but irregularly and mostly for social reasons, so as not to stand out too much in the community. But we're not religious persons, Abbott and I. Although, since the accident, there have been numerous times when I have wished that I was. Religion being the main way the unexplainable gets explained. God's will and all.

The first house you come to up there on the ridge is Billy Ansel's old cut-stone colonial. I always liked stopping at Billy's. For one thing, he used me as an alarm clock, not leaving for work himself until I arrived to pick up his children, Jessica and Mason, nine-year-old twins. I liked it when the parents were aware of my arrival, and he was always looking out the kitchen window when I pulled up, waiting for his kids to climb into the bus. Then as I pulled away I'd see the house lights go out, and a mile or two down the road, I'd look into my side mirror, and there he'd be, coming along behind in his pickup, on his way into town to open up his Sunoco station.

Normally he followed me the whole distance over the ridge to the Marlowe road, then south all the way into town, keeping a slow and distant sort of company with the bus, never bothering to pass on the straightaways, until finally, just before I got to the school, he turned off at the garage. Once I asked him why he didn't pass me by, so he wouldn't have to stop and wait every time I pulled over to make a pickup. He just laughed. "Well," he said, "then I'd get to work before eight, wouldn't I, and I'd have to stand around the garage waiting for the help to show up. There's no point to that," he said.

Truth is, I don't think he wanted to move through that big empty house alone, once his kids were gone to school, and I believe it particularly pleased and comforted him, as he drove into town, to catch glimpses of his son and daughter in the school bus, waving back at him. Their mother, Lydia, a fairy princess of a woman, died of cancer some four years ago, and Billy took over raising the children by himself— although believe me, there are plenty of young women who would have been happy to help him out, as he is one fine-looking man. Smart and charming. And a successful businessman too. Even I found him sexy, and normally I don't give a younger man a second look.

But it was more than sexy; there was always something noble about Billy Ansel. In high school, he was the boy other boys imitated and followed, quarterback and captain of the football team, president of his senior class, et cetera. After graduation, like a lot of boys from Sam Dent back then, he went into the service. The Marines. In Vietnam, he was field commissioned as a lieutenant, and when he came back to Sam Dent in the mid-seventies, he married his high school sweetheart, Lydia Storrow, and borrowed a lot of money from the bank and bought Creppitt's old Sunoco station, where he had worked summers, and turned it into a regular automotive repair shop, with three bays and all kinds of electronic troubleshooting equipment. Lydia, who had gone to Plattsburgh State and knew accounting, kept the books, and Billy ran the garage. The stone house up on Staples Mill they bought a few years later, when the twins were born, and then renovated top to bottom, which it sorely needed. They were an ideal couple. An ideal family.

Billy Ansel, though, was always a man with a mission. Nothing discouraged him or made him bitter. When he came back to Sam Dent, right away he joined the VFW post in Placid, and soon he became an officer and went to work making the boys who had served in Vietnam respectable there, at a time when, most places, people still thought of them as drug addicts and murderers. He got them out marching proudly with the other vets every Fourth of July and Veterans Day. In fact, until recently, to work for him at the garage, you yourself had to be a Vietnam vet. He hired young men from all over the region, surly boys with long hair and hurt looks on their faces. At different times he even had a couple of black men working for him—very unusual in Sam Dent. His men were loyal to him and treated him like he was their lieutenant and they were still back in Vietnam. It was strange and in a way thrilling to watch a lost boy get rehabilitated like that. After a year or two, the fellow would have learned a trade, more or less, and he'd brighten up, and soon he'd be gone, replaced a week later by another sad-faced angry young man.

All the way across the back ridge on Staples Mill Road, Billy followed the bus. Whenever I slowed to pick up a waiting child, I'd look into the side mirror, and there he'd be, grinning through his beard at the kids in the back seat, who liked to turn and make V-for-victory signs at him. Especially Bear Otto, who regarded Billy Ansel as a hero, and of course the twins, who, because of Bear's protection, were allowed by the older boys to sit in the back seat of the bus. Bear dreamed of going into the Marines himself someday and working afterwards in Billy's garage. "Can't go to no Vietnam no more," he once told me. "But there's always someplace where they need the U.S. Marines, right?" I nodded and hoped he was wrong. I have a son in the military, after all. But I understood Bear Otto's desire to become a noble man, a man like Billy Ansel, and I respected that, naturally. I just wished the boy had more ways of imagining the thing than by becoming a good soldier. But that's boys, I guess.

Out there on the far side of Irish Hill, just before Staples Mill Road ties onto the old Marlowe road and makes a beeline for Sam Dent, three miles away, there's a stretch of tableland called Wilmot Flats. Supposedly, in ancient times it was the bottom of a glacial river or lake, but now it's mostly poor sandy soil and scrub brush and jack pine, with no open views of the mountains or valleys, at least not from the road. The town dump takes up half the Flats, with the other half parceled into odd lots with trailers on them and a couple of hand-built houses that are little more than shanties, tarpaper-covered clusters of tiny rooms heated by kerosene and wood. The folks who live in them are mostly named Atwater, with a few Bilodeaus thrown in. Every winter there's a bad fire up on the Flats, and at town meeting for a spell everyone talks about instituting regulations to govern the ways houses are heated, as if the state legislature hadn't already tried to regulate them from down in Albany. But nothing ever comes of it—there's too many of us who heat with kerosene or wood to change things. They're dangerous, of course, but what isn't?

Anyhow, I was making my stops up along the Flats, picking up the last of my load—nine kids up there, except when there's a virus going around—boys and girls of various ages who are the poorest children in town, generally. Their parents are young, little more than teenaged kids themselves, and half of them are cousins or actual siblings. There's inter-marriage up there and all sorts of mingling that it's better not to know about, and between that and alcohol and ignorance, the children have little chance of doing more with their lives than imitating their parents' lives. With them, says Abbott, you have to sympathize. Regardless of what you think of their parents and the rest of the adults up there. It's like all those poor children are born banished and spend their lives trying to get back to where they belong. And only a few of them manage it. The occasional plucky one, who happens also to be lucky and gifted with intelligence, good looks, and charm, he might get back, before he dies, to his native town. But the rest stay banished, permanently exiled, if not up there on Wilmot Flats, then someplace just like it.

That's when I saw the dog. The actual dog, I mean—not the one I thought I saw on the Marlowe road a few minutes later. It's probably irrelevant, but I offer it as a possible explanation for my seeing what I thought was a dog later, since both were the same dull red color. The dog on Wilmot Flats was a garbage hound, one of those wandering strays you see hanging around the dump. They are often sick and vicious and are known to chase deer, so the boys in town shoot them whenever they come across one in the woods. Over the years I've come up on four or five of their rotting corpses in the woods behind our house, and it always gives me a painful chill and then a protracted sad feeling. I don't like the dogs one bit, but I hate to see them dead.

As I was saying, I had picked up the kids on the Flats and was passing by the open chain-link entrance to the dump, when this raggedy old mutt shot out the gate and ran across the road in front of me, and it scared the bejesus out of me, although I could not for the life of me tell you why, as he was ordinary-looking and there was no danger of my hitting him.

My mind must have been locked onto something contrasted—my sons Reginald and William, probably, since I felt that morning particularly estranged from them, and you tend to embrace with thought what you're forbidden to embrace in fact. For when that dog entered my field of vision, it somehow astonished and then frightened me. The dog was skinny and torn-looking, a yellow-eyed young male with a long pointed head and large ears laid flat against his skull as he darted across the road, leapt over the snowbank, and disappeared into the darkness of the scrub pine woods there.

Although the snow was blowing in feathery waves by then, the road was still dry and black, easy to see, and I gripped the wheel and drove straight on, as if nothing had happened. For nothing *had* happened! Yet I wanted intensely to pull the bus over and stop, to sit there for a moment and try to gather my fragmented thoughts and calm my clanging nerves.

I glanced into the side mirror at Billy Ansel's face smiling through the windshield of his pickup, an innocent and diligent man waving to children at play, and I felt a wave of pity for him come over me, although I did not know what I pitied him for. I turned back from the mirror and stared straight ahead at the road and clamped my hands onto the steering wheel and drove on toward the intersection at the Marlowe road, where I slowed, and when I saw that there was no traffic coming or even going, I turned right and headed down the long slope toward town.

The road was recently rebuilt and is wide and straight, with a passing lane and narrow shoulders and a bed of gravel and guardrails, before it drops off a ways on the right-hand side, to Jones Brook, which is mostly boulders up there and not much water. Eventually, as the brook descends it fills and by the time it joins the Ausable River down in the valley it's a significant fast-running stream. There's an old town sandpit down there dug into the ancient lakebed, and a closed-off road in from the Flats, near the dump. On the left-hand side, the land is wooded and rises slowly toward Knob Lock Mountain and Giant in the southeast.

Coming down from the Flats on the Marlowe road toward town, the greatest danger was that I would be going too slow and a lumber truck or some idiot in a car would come barreling along at seventy-five or eighty, which you can easily do up there, once you've made the crest from the other side, and would come up on me fast and not be able to slow or pass and would run smack into me, or, more likely, first would hit Billy Ansel's pickup truck lollygagging along behind and then the bus. As a result, since I didn't have any more stops to make once I'd gathered the kids from the Flats, I tended to drive that stretch of road at a pretty good clip. Nothing reckless, you understand. Nothing illegal. Fifty, fifty-five is all. Also, if I happened to be running a few minutes late, that was the only time when I could make up for it.

After passing through the gloom and closed-in feeling of Wilmot Flats, when you turn onto the Marlowe road and start the drive toward town, you tend to feel uplifted, released. Or I should say, I always did. The road is straight and there is more sky than land for the first time, and the valley opens up below you and on your right, like Montana or Wyoming—a large snow-covered bowl with a range of distant mountains surrounding it, and beyond the mountains there are still more mountains shouldering toward the sky, as if the surface of the planet were the same everywhere as here. This was always the most pleasurable part of my journey—with the bus in high gear and running smooth, enough pale daylight now, despite the thin gauzy snow falling, to see the entire landscape stretched out before me, and the busload of children peaceful behind me as they contentedly conversed with one another or silently prepared themselves for the next segment of their long day.

And, yes, it was then that I saw the dog, the second dog, the one I maybe only thought I saw. It emerged from the blowing snow on the right side of the road, popped up from the ditch there, or so it seemed, and crossed to the center of the road, where it appeared to stop, as if unsure whether to continue or go back. No, I am almost sure now that it was an optical illusion or a mirage, a sort of afterimage, maybe, of the dog that I had seen on the Flats and that had frightened and moved me so. But at the time I could not tell the difference.

And as I have always done when I've had two bad choices and nothing else available to me, I arranged it so that if I erred I'd come out on the side of the angels. Which is to say, I acted as though it was a real dog I saw or a small deer or possibly even a lost child from the Flats, barely a half mile away.

For the rest of my life I will remember that red-brown blur, like a stain of dried blood, standing against the road with a thin screen of blown snow suspended between it and me, the full weight of the vehicle and the thirty-four children in it bearing down on me like a wall of water. And I will remember the formal clarity of my mind, beyond thinking or choosing now, for I had made my choice, as I wrenched the steering wheel to the right and slapped my foot against the brake pedal, and I wasn't the driver anymore, so I hunched my shoulders and ducked my head, as if the bus were a huge wave about to break over me. There was Bear Otto, and the Lamston kids, and the Walkers, the Hamiltons, and the Prescotts and the teenaged boys and girls from Bartlett Hill, and Risa and Wendell Walker's sad little boy, Sean, and sweet Nichole Burnell, and all the kids from the valley, and the children from Wilmot Flats, and Billy Ansel's twins, Jessica and Mason—the children of my town—their wide-eyed faces and fragile bodies swirling and tumbling in a tangled mass as the bus went over and the sky tipped and veered away and the ground lurched brutally forward.

from The Dog of the South
by Charles Portis

In Charles Portis' (born 1933) third novel Ray Midge's wife Norma runs off with her first husband—taking Ray's credit cards and Ford Turino and leaving behind a musty 1963 Buick Special. Ray follows the couple's credit card receipts to Mexico; there he encounters Dr. Symes, an elderly man who lives in a decrepit school bus ("the Dog of the South") and wants to go to British Honduras. Ray offers the doctor a ride, and they hit the road.

asked him if he was going to British Honduras on vacation and he said, "Vacation! Do you think I'm the kind of man who takes vacations?"

"What are you going down there for?"

"My mother's there. I need to see her."

His mother! I couldn't believe it. "Is she sick?" I said.

"I don't know. I need to see her on some business."

"How old is she?"

"She's so old she's walking sideways. I hate to see it too. That's a bad sign. When these old folks start creeping around and shuffling their feet, church is about out."

He wanted to see her about some land she owned in Louisiana near the town of Ferriday. It was an island in the Mississippi River called Jean's Island.

"It's not doing her any good," he said. "She's just turned it over to the birds and snakes. She pays taxes on it every year and there's not one penny of income. There's no gain at all except for the appreciated value. She won't give it to me and she won't let me use it. She's my mother and I think the world of her but she's hard to do business with."

"It's not cultivated land?"

"No, it's just rough timber. The potential is enormous. The black-walnut trees alone are worth fifty thousand dollars for furniture veneer. The stumps could then be cut up and made into pistol grips. How does fifty thousand dollars sound to you?"

"It sounds pretty good."

"Some of those trees are whoppers. Double trunks."

"Maybe you could get a timber lease."

"I'd take a lease if I could get it. What I want is a deed. I don't mean a quitclaim either, I mean a warranty deed with a seal on it. So you understand what I'm telling you?"

"Yes."

"Did you say *timber* lease?"

"Yes."

"That's what I thought you said. Why would you want to cut the timber?"

"That was your idea. The walnut trees."

"I was only trying to suggest to you the value of the place. I'm not going to cut those trees. Are you crazy? Cut the trees and the whole thing would wash away and then where would you be? Do you want my opinion? I say leave the trees and make a private hunting preserve out of the place. I'm not talking about squirrels and ducks either. I mean stock the place with some real brutes. Wart hogs and Cape buffalo. I don't say it would be cheap but these hunters have plenty of money and they don't mind spending it."

"That's not a bad idea."

"I've got a hundred ideas better than that but Mama won't answer my letters. What about a Christian boys' ranch? It's an ideal setting. You'd think that would appeal to her, wouldn't you? Well, you'd be wrong. How about a theme park? Jefferson Davis Land. It's not far from the old Davis plantation. Listen to this. I would dress up like Davis in a frock coat and greet the tourists as they stepped off the ferry. I would glower at them like old Davis with his cloudy eye and the children would cry and clutch their mothers' hands and then— here's the payoff—they would see the twinkle in my clear eye. I'd have Lee too, and Jackson and Albert Sidney Johnston, walking around the midway. Hire some people with beards, you know, to do that. I wouldn't have Braxton Bragg or Joseph E. Johnston. Every afternoon at three Lee would take off his gray coat and wrestle an alligator in a mud hole. Prize drawings. A lot of T-shirts and maybe a few black-and-white portables. If you don't like that, how about a stock-car track? Year-round racing with hardly any rules. Deadly curves right on the water. The Symes 500 on Christmas Day. Get a promotional tie-in with the Sugar Bowl. How about an industrial park? How about a high-rise condominium with a roof garden? How about a baseball clinic? How about a monkey island? I don't say it would be cheap. Nobody's going to pay to see one or two monkeys these days. People want to see a lot of monkeys. I've got plenty of ideas but first I have to get my hands on the island. Can you see what I'm driving at? It's the hottest piece of real estate in Louisiana, bar none."

"Are you a student of the Civil War, Dr. Symes?"

"No, but my father was."

"What was that about Bragg? You said you wouldn't have Bragg walking around in your park."

"My father had no time for Bragg or Joseph E. Johnston. He always said Bragg lost the war. What do you know about these revolving restaurants, Speed?"

"I don't know anything about them but I can tell you that Braxton Bragg didn't lose the war by himself."

"I'm talking about these restaurants up on top of buildings that turn around and around while the people are in there eating."

"I know what you're talking about but I've never been in one. Look here, you can't just go around saying Braxton Bragg lost the war."

"My father said he lost it at Chickamauga."

"I know what Bragg did at Chickamauga, or rather what he didn't do. I can't accept Joseph E. Johnston's excuses either for not going to help Pemberton but I don't go around saying he lost the war."

"Well, my father believed it. Pollard was his man. A fellow named Pollard, he said, wrote the only fair account of the thing."

"I've read Pollard. He calls Lincoln the Illinois ape."

"Pollard was his man. I don't read that old-timey stuff myself. That's water over the dam. I've never wasted my time with that trash. What's your personal opinion of these revolving restaurants?"

"I think they're all right."

"Leon Vurro's wife said I should have a fifty-story tower right in the middle of the park with a revolving restaurant on top. What do you think?"

"I think it would be all right."

"That's your opinion. I happen to have my own. Let's cost it out. Let's look a little closer. All right, your sap tourists and honeymooners are up there eating and they say, 'Let's see, are we looking into Louisiana now or Mississippi, which?' I say what the hell difference would it make? One side of the river looks just like the other. You think it would be cheap? All that machinery? Gears and chains breaking every day? You'd have to hire two or three union bastards full time just to keep it working. What about your light bill? A thousand dollars a month? Two thousand? You'd have to charge eighteen dollars for a steak to come out on a deal like that. And just so some sap and his family can see three hundred and sixty degrees of the same damned cotton fields. I don't like it myself. Do you have the faintest notion of what it would cost to erect a fifty-story tower? No, you don't, and neither does Bella Vurro. And you probably don't care. I'm the poor son of a bitch who will have to shoulder the debt."

"Look here. Dr. Symes, I know that Bragg should have been relieved earlier. Everybody knows that today. Joe Johnston too, but that's a long way from saying they lost the war."

"What line of work are you in, Speed?"

"I'm back in college now. I'm trying to pick up some education hours so I can get a teaching certificate."

"What you are then is a thirty-year-old schoolboy."

"I'm twenty-six."

"Well, I don't guess you're bothering anybody."

"The Civil War used to be my field."

"A big waste of time."

"I didn't think so. I studied for two years at Ole Miss under Dr. Buddy Casey. He's a fine man and a fine scholar."

"You might as well loiter for two years. You might as well play Parcheesi for two years."

"That's a foolish remark."

"You think so?"

"It's dumb."

"All right, listen to me. Are you a reader? Do you read a lot of books?"

"I read quite a bit."

"And you come from a family of readers, right?"

"No, that's not right. That's completely wrong. My father doesn't own six books. He reads the paper about twice a week. He reads fishing magazines and he reads the construction bids. He works. He doesn't have time to read."

"But you're a big reader yourself."

"I have more than four hundred volumes of military history in my apartment. All told, I have sixty-six lineal feet of books."

"All right, now listen to me. Throw that trash out the window. Every bit of it."

He reached into his grip and brought out a little book with yellow paper covers. The cellophane that had once been bonded to the covers was cracked and peeling. He flourished the book. "Throw all that dead stuff out the window and put this on your shelf. Put it by your bed."

What a statement! Books, heavy ones, flying out the windows of the Rhino apartment! I couldn't take my eyes from the road for very long but I glanced at the cover. The title was *With Wings as Eagles* and the author was John Selmer Dix, M.A.

Dr. Symes turned through the pages. "Dix wrote this book forty years ago and it's still just as fresh as the morning dew. Well, why shouldn't it be? The truth never dies. Now this is a first edition. That's important. This is the one you want. Remember the yellow cover. They've changed up things in these later editions. Just a word here and there but it adds up. I don't know who's behind it. They'll have Marvin watching television instead of listening to dance music on the radio. Stuff like that. This is the one you want. This is straight Dix. This is the book you want on your night table right beside your glass of water, *With Wings as Eagles* in the yellow cover. Dix was the greatest man of our time. He was truly a master of the arts, and of some of the sciences too. He was the greatest writer who ever lived."

"They say Shakespeare was the greatest writer who ever lived."

"Dix puts William Shakespeare in the shithouse."

"I've never heard of him. Where is he from?"

"He was from all over. He's dead now. He's buried in Ardmore, Oklahoma. He got his mail in Fort Worth, Texas."

"Did he live in Fort Worth?"

"He lived all over. Do you know the old Elks Club in Shreveport?"

"No."

"Not the new one. I'm not talking about the new lodge."

"I don't know anything about Shreveport."

"Well, it doesn't matter. It's one of my great regrets that I never got to meet Dix. He died broke in a railroad hotel in Tulsa. The last thing he saw from his window is anyone's guess. They never found his trunk, you know. He had a big tin trunk that was all tied up with wire and ropes and belts and straps, and he took it with him everywhere. They never found it. Nobody knows what happened to it. Nobody even knows what was in the trunk."

"Well, his clothes, don't you think?"

"No, he didn't have any clothes to speak of. No *change* of clothes. His famous slippers of course."

"His correspondence maybe."

"He burned all letters unread. I don't want to hear any more of your guesses. Do you think you're going to hit on the answer right off? Smarter people than you have been studying this problem for years."

"Books then."

"No, no, no. Dix never read anything but the daily papers. He *wrote* books, he didn't have to read them. No, he traveled light except for the trunk. He did his clearest thinking while moving. He did all his best work on a bus. Do you know that express bus that leaves Dallas every day at noon for Los Angeles? That's the one he liked. He rode back and forth on it for an entire year when he was working on *Wings*. He saw the seasons change on that bus. He knew all the drivers. He had a board that he put on his lap so he could spread his stuff out, you see, and work right there in his seat by the window."

"I don't see how you could ride a bus for a year."

"He was completely exhausted at the end of that year and he never fully recovered his health. His tin trunk had a thousand dents in it by that time and the hinges and latches were little better than a joke. That's when he began tying it up with ropes and belts. His mouth was bleeding from scurvy, from mucosal lesions and suppurating ulcers, his gums gone all spongy. He was a broken man all right but by God the work got done. He wrecked his health so that we might have *Wings as Eagles*."

The doctor went on and on. He said that all other writing, compared to Dix's work, was just "foul grunting." I could understand how a man might say such things about the Bible or the Koran, some holy book, but this Dix book, from what I could see of it, was nothing more than an inspirational work for salesmen. Still, I didn't want to judge it too quickly. There might be some useful tips in those pages, some Dix thoughts that would throw a new light on things. I was still on the alert for chance messages.

I asked the doctor what his mother was doing in British Honduras.

"Preaching," he said. "Teaching hygiene to pickaninnies."

"She's not retired?"

"She'll never retire."

"How does she happen to be in British Honduras?"

"She first went down there with some church folks to take clothes to hurricane victims. After my father died in 1950, she went back to help run a mission. Then she just stayed on. The church bosses tried to run her off two or three times but they couldn't get her out because she owned the building. She just started her own church. She says God told her to stay on the job down there. She's deathly afraid of hurricanes but she stays on anyway."

"Do you think God really told her to do that?"

"Well, I don't know. That's the only thing that would keep me down there. Mama claims she likes it. She and Melba both. She lives in the church with her pal Melba. There's a pair for you."

"Have you ever been down there?"

"Just once."

"What's it like?"

"Hot. A bunch of niggers."

"It seems a long way off from everything."

"After you get there it doesn't. It's the same old stuff."

"What does your mother do, go back and forth to Louisiana?"

"No, she doesn't go back at all."

"And you haven't seen her but once since she's been there?"

"It's a hard trip. You see the trouble I'm having. This is my last shot."

"You could fly down in a few hours."

"I've never been interested in aviation."

"I'm going down there after a stolen car."

"Say you are."

He kept twisting about in the seat to look at the cars approaching us from behind. He examined them all as they passed us and once he said to me, "Can you see that man's arms?"

"What man?"

"Driving that station wagon."

"I can see his hands."

"No, his arms. Ski has tattoos on his forearms. Flowers and stars and spiders."

"I can't see his arms. Who is Ski?"

He wouldn't answer me and he had no curiosity at all about my business. I told him about Norma and Dupree. He said nothing, but I could sense his contempt. I was not only a schoolboy but a cuckold too. And broke to boot.

He nodded and dozed whenever I was doing the talking. His heavy crested head would droop over and topple him forward and the angle-head flashlight on his belt would poke him in the belly and wake him. Then he would sit up and do it over again. I could see a tangle of gray hair in his long left ear. I wondered at what age that business started, the hair-in-the-ear business. I was getting on myself. The doctor had taken me for thirty. I felt in my ears and found nothing, but I knew the stuff would be sprouting there soon, perhaps in a matter of hours. I was gaining weight too. In the last few months I had begun to see my own cheeks, little pink horizons.

I was hypnotized by the road. I was leaning forward and I let the speed gradually creep up and I bypassed Mexico City with hardly a thought for Winfield Scott and the heights of Chapultepec. To pass it like that! Mexico City! On the long empty stretches I tried to imagine that I was stationary and that the brown earth was being rolled beneath me by the Buick tires. It was a shaky illusion at best and it broke down entirely when I met another car.

A front tire went flat in a suburb of Puebla and I drove on it for about half a mile. The spare was flat too, and it took the rest of the afternoon to get everything fixed. The casing I had driven on had two breaks in the sidewall. I didn't see how it could be repaired but the Mexican tire man put two boots and an inner tube in the thing and it stood up fine. He was quite a man, doing all this filthy work in the street in front of his mud house without a mechanical tire breaker or an impact wrench or any other kind of special tool.

We found a bakery and bought some rolls and left Puebla in the night. Dr. Symes took a blood-pressure cuff from his grip. He put it on his arm and pumped it up and I had to drive with one hand and hold the flashlight with the other so he could take the reading. He grunted but he didn't say whether it pleased him or not. He crawled over into the back seat and cleared things out of his way and said he was going to take a nap. He threw something out the window and I realized later it must have been my Zachary Taylor book.

"You might keep your eye peeled for a tan station wagon," he said.

"I don't know what kind it is but it's a nice car. Texas plates. Dealer plates. Ski will be driving. He's a pale man with no chin. Tattoos on his forearms. He wears a little straw hat with one of those things in the hat-band. I can't think of the word."

"Feather."

"No, I can think of feather. This is harder to think of. A brass thing."

"Who is this Ski?"

"Ted Brunowski. He's an old friend of mine. They call him Ski. You know how they call people Ski and Chief and Tex in the army."

"I've never been in the service."

"Did you have asthma?"

"No."

"What are you taking for it?"

"I don't have asthma."

"Have you tried the Chihuahua dogs in your bedroom at night? They say it works. I'm an orthodox physician but I'm also for whatever works. You might try it anyway."

"I have never had asthma."

"The slacker's friend. That's what they called it during the war. I certified many a one at a hundred and fifty bucks a throw."

"What do you want to see this fellow for?"

"It's a tan station wagon. He's a pale man in a straw hat and he has no more chin than a bird. Look for dealer plates. Ski has never been a car dealer but he always has dealer plates. He's not a Mason either but when he shakes your hand he does something with his thumb. He knows how to give the Masonic sign of distress too. He would never show me how to do it. Do you understand what I'm telling you?"

"I understand what you've said so far. Do you want to talk to him or what?"

"Just let me know if you see him."

"Is there some possibility of trouble?"

"There's every possibility."

"You didn't say anything about this."

"Get Ski out of sorts and he'll crack your bones. He'll smack you right in the snout, the foremost part of the body. He'll knock you white-eyed on the least provocation. He'll teach you a lesson you won't soon forget."

"You should have said something about this."

"He kicked a merchant seaman to death down on the ship channel. He was trying to get a line on the Blackie Steadman mob, just trying to do his job, you see, and the chap didn't want to help him."

"You should have told me about all this."

"Blackie was hiring these merchant seamen to do his killings for him. He would hire one of those boys to do the job on the night before he shipped out and by the time the body was found the killer would be in some place like Poland. But Ski got wise to their game."

"What does he want you for?"

"He made short work of that sailor. Ski's all business. He's tough. He's stout. I'm not talking about these puffy muscles from the gymnasium either, I'm talking about hard thick arms like bodark posts. You'd do better to leave him alone."

All this time the doctor was squirming around in the back trying to arrange himself comfortably on the seat. He made the car rock. I was afraid he would bump the door latch and fall out of the car. He hummed and snuffled. He sang one verse of "My Happiness" over and over again and then, with a church quaver, "He's the Lily of the Valley, the bright and morning star."

I tuned him out. After a while he slept. I roared through the dark mountains, descending mostly, and I thought I would never reach the bottom. I checked the mirror over and over again and I examined every vehicle that passed us. There weren't many. The doctor had given me a tough job and now he was sleeping.

The guidebook advised against driving at night in Mexico but I figured that stuff was written for fools. I was leaning forward again and going at a headlong pace like an ant running home with something. The guidebook was right. It was a nightmare. Trucks with no taillights! Cows and donkeys and bicyclists in the middle of the road! A stalled bus on the crest of a hill! A pile of rocks coming up fast! An overturned truck and ten thousand oranges rolling down the road! I was trying to deal with all this and watch for Ski at the same time and I was furious at Dr. Symes for sleeping through it. I no longer cared whether he fell out or not.

Finally I woke him, although the worst was over by that time.

"What is it?" he said.

"I'm not looking for that station wagon anymore. I've got my hands full up here."

"What?"

"It's driving me crazy. I can't tell what color these cars are."

"What are you talking about?"

"I'm talking about Ski!"

"I wouldn't worry about Ski. Leon Vurro is the man he's looking for. Where did you know Ski?"

"I don't know Ski."

"Do you want me to drive for a while?"

"No, I don't."

"Where are we?"

"I don't know exactly. Out of the mountains anyway. We're near Veracruz somewhere."

I kept thinking I would pull over at some point and sleep until daylight but I couldn't find a place that looked just right. The Pemex stations were too noisy and busy. The doctor had me stop once on the highway so he could put some drops in his red eye. This was a slow and messy business. He flung his elbows out like a skeet shooter. I held the army flashlight for him. He said the drops were cold. While I was at it, I checked the transmission fluid and there were a lot of little blue flashes playing around the engine where the spark-plug cables were cracked and arcing.

He napped again and then he started talking to me about Houston, which he pronounced "Yooston." I like to keep things straight and his movements had me confused. I had thought at first that he came to Mexico direct from Louisiana. Then it was California. Now it was Houston. Ski was from Houston and it was from that same city that the doctor had departed in haste for Mexico, or "Old Mexico" as he called it.

"Who is this Ski anyway?"

"He's an old friend of mine. I thought I told you that."

"Is he a crook?"

"He's a real-estate smarty. He makes money while he's sleeping. He used to be a policeman. He says he made more unassisted arrests than any other officer in the colorful history of Harris County. I can't vouch for that but I know he made plenty. I've known him for years. I used to play poker with him at the Rice Hotel. I gave distemper shots to his puppies. I removed a benign wart from his shoulder that was as big as a Stuart pecan. It looked like a little man's head, or a baby's head, like it might talk, or cry. I never charged him a dime. Ski has forgotten all that."

"Why did you tell me he was looking for you?"

"He almost caught me at Alvin. It was nip and tuck. Do you know the County Line Lounge between Arcadia and Alvin?"

"No."

"The Uncle Sam Muffler Shop?"

"No."

"Shoe City?"

"No."

"Well, it was right in there where I lost him. That traffic circle is where he tore his britches. I never saw him after that. He has no chin, you know."

"You told me that."

"Captain Hughes of the Rangers used to say that if they ever hanged old Ski they would have to put the rope under his nose."

"Why was he after you?"

"Leon Vurro is the man he really wants."

The highways of Mexico, I thought, must be teeming with American investigators. The doctor and I, neither of us very sinister, had met by chance and we were both being more or less pursued. What about all the others? I had seen some strange birds down here from the States. Creeps! Nuts! Crooks! Fruits! Liars! California dopers!

I tried not to show much interest in his story after the way he had dozed while I was telling mine. It didn't matter, because he paid no attention to other people anyway. He spoke conversational English to all the Mexicans along the way and never seemed to notice that they couldn't understand a word he said.

The story was hard to follow. He and a man named Leon Vurro had put out a tip sheet in Houston called the *Bayou Blue Sheet.* They booked a few bets too, and they handled a few layoff bets from smaller bookies, with Ski as a silent partner. They worked the national time zones to their advantage in some way that I couldn't understand. Ski had many other interests. He had political connections. No deal was too big or too small for him. He managed to get a contract to publish a directory called *Stouthearted Men*, which was to be a collection of photographs and capsule biographies of all the county supervisors in Texas. Or maybe it was the county clerks. Anyway, Ski and the county officers put up an initial sum of $6,500 for operating expenses. Dr. Symes and Leon Vurro gathered the materials for the book and did some work on the dummy makeup. They also sold advertisements for it. Then Leon Vurro disappeared with the money. That, at any rate, was the doctor's account.

"Leon's an ordinary son of a bitch," he said, "but I didn't think he was an out-and-out crook. He said he was tired. Tired! He was sleeping sixteen hours a day and going to the picture show every afternoon. I was the one who was tired, and hot too, but we could have finished that thing in another two weeks. Sooner than that if Leon had kept his wife out of it. She had to stick her nose into everything. She got the pictures all mixed up. She claimed she had been a trapeze artist with Sells-Floto. Told fortunes is more like it. Reader and Advisor is more like it. A bullwhip act is more like it. She looked like a gypsy to me. With that fat ass she would have broke the trapeze ropes. Gone through the net like a shot. We had to work fast, you see, because the pictures were turning green and curling up. I don't know how they got wet. There's a lot of mildew in Houston. You can bet I got tired of looking at those things. I wish you could have seen those faces, Speed. Prune Face and BB Eyes are not in it with those boys."

"You must think I'm a dope," I said. "You never intended to publish that book."

"No, it was a straight deal. Do you know the Moon Publishing Company?"

"No."

"They have offices in Palestine, Texas, and Muldrow, Oklahoma."

"I've never heard of it."

"It's a well-known outfit. They do job printing and they put out calendars and cookbooks and flying-saucer books and children's books, books on boating safety, all kinds of stuff. *A Boy's Life of Lyndon B. Johnson.* That's a Moon book. It was a straight enough deal."

"How much money did Leon Vurro get?"

"I don't know. Whatever was there, he cleaned it out. It's a shame too. We could have finished that thing in two weeks. We were already through the M's and that was halfway. More, really, because there wouldn't be many X's and Z's. You never know. Maybe Leon was right. You have to know when to lay 'em down. It was a weekend deal, you see. There's a lot of mischief on weekends and not just check-kiting either. Leon cleared out the account on Friday afternoon. I was in San Antonio trying to sell ads for that fool book. The word got out fast on Leon but it didn't get to me. It didn't reach the Alamo City. I got back in my room in Houston on Sunday night. I was staying at Jim's Modern Cabins out on Galveston Road. My cabin was dark and the window was open. You had to leave your windows open. Jim doesn't have air conditioning except in his own office. He's got a big window unit in his office that will rattle the walls. I walked by my front window and I could smell Ski's fruity breath. He has diabetes, you see. These young doctors tell everybody they have diabetes but Ski really has it. I knew he was waiting inside that cabin in the dark and I didn't know why. I left with hardly any delay and then it was nip and tuck in south Houston. I made it on down to Corpus and traded my car for that hippie bus at the first car lot that opened up. I knew I didn't have any business driving a car forty feet long but that was the only unit on the lot the fellow would trade even for. I thought it might make a nice little home on the road. Your top gospel singers all have private buses."

"Why would Ski be after you if Leon Vurro got the money?"

"Leon's wife was behind all that. Bella set that up. I never said she was dumb."

"How do you know all that stuff if you left town so fast? That part is not clear to me."

"You get a feel for these things."

"I don't see how you could get a feel for all the circumstances."

"I should never have tied up with Leon. People like that can do nothing but drag you down. He didn't know the first thing about meeting the public and he was never dressed properly. They'll bury that son of a bitch in his zipper jacket."

"How did you know, for instance, that Leon had cleaned out the bank account?"

"I always tried to help Leon and you see the thanks I got. I hired him to drive for me right after his rat died. He was with Murrell Brothers Shows at that time, exhibiting a fifty-pound rat from the sewers of Paris, France. Of course it didn't really weigh fifty pounds and it wasn't your true rat and it wasn't from Paris, France, either. It was some kind of animal from South America. Anyway, the thing died and I hired Leon to drive for me. I was selling birthstone rings and vibrating jowl straps from door to door and he would let me out at one end of the block and wait on me at the other end. He could handle that all right. That was just about his speed. I made a serious mistake when I promoted Leon to a higher level of responsibility."

I pressed the doctor with searching questions about the Houston blowout but I couldn't get any straight answers and so I gave it up.

The sun came up out of the sea, or I should say the Bay of Campeche. The warm air seemed heavy and I had the fanciful notion that it was pressing against us and holding us back. I say "seemed" because I know as well as any professional pilot that warm air is less dense than cool air. I had forgotten about the baloney and cheese in the ice chest.

We ate the marshmallows and rolls, and after the rolls got hard I threw them out to goats along the way.

In the town of Coatzacoalcos I double-parked on a narrow street in front of an auto supply store and bought two quarts of transmission fluid and a small can of solvent. This solvent was a patent medicine from the States that was supposed to cure sticking valves and noisy valve lifters. Dr. Symes was worried about the clicking noise. He wouldn't shut up about it.

Down the way I found a shady grove of palm trees just off the road. I got out my plastic funnel and red fluid and topped up the transmission. Then I read all the print on the solvent can. There were warnings about breathing the stuff and lengthy instructions as to its use. At the very bottom there was a hedging note in red that had caught my eye too late: "May take two cans." I poured half of it through the carburetor at a fast idle and emptied the rest into the crankcase. The clicking went on as before.

Dr. Symes said, "I can still hear it. I think you've made it worse. I think it's louder than it was."

"It hasn't had time to work yet."

"How long does it take?"

"It says about five minutes. It says it may take two cans."

"How many cans did you get?"

"One."

"Why didn't you get two?"

"I didn't know that at the time."

He took the empty can from me and studied it. He found the red note and pointed it out to me. "It says, 'May take two cans.' "

"I know what it says now."

"You should have known a car like this would need two cans."

"How was I to know that? I didn't have time to read all that stuff."

"We'll never get there!"

"Yes, we will."

"Never! We'll never make it! Look how little it is!" The size of the can was funny to him. He went into a laughing fit and then a coughing fit, which in turn triggered a sneezing fit.

"Half of the cars on the road are making this noise," I said. "It's not serious. The engine's not going to stop."

"One can! One can of this shit wouldn't fix a lawn mower and you expect it to fix a Buick! Fifty cans would be more like it! You chump! You said you'd take me to Mama and you don't even know where we are! You don't know your ass from first base! I never can get where I want to go because I'm always stuck with chumps like you! Rolling along! Oh, yes! Rolling along! Rolling on home to Mama!"

He sang these last words to a little tune.

I knew where we were all right. It was the doctor himself who had funny notions about geography. He thought we were driving along the Pacific Ocean, and he had the idea that a momentary lapse at the wheel, one wrong turn, would always lead to monstrous circular error, taking us back where we started. Maybe it had happened to him a lot.

We drove straight through without stopping anywhere to sleep. The road was closed on the direct route across southern Campeche and so we had to take the longer coastal road, which meant waiting for ferries and crossing on them in the night. It also meant that we had to go north up into Yucatán and then south again through Quintana Roo to the border town of Chetumal.

What these ferries crossed were the mouths of rivers along the Gulf, two rivers and a lagoon, I believe, or maybe the other way around, a long stretch of delta at any rate. Dr. Symes remained in the car and I strode the decks and took the air, although there was nothing to see in the darkness, nothing but the bow waves, curling and glassy. There was fog too, and once again I was denied the spectacle of the southern heavens.

I had told the doctor that the engine wasn't going to stop and then in the midday heat of Yucatán it did stop. He might have thrown one of his fits if we had not been in a village with people standing around watching us. He sulked instead. I thought the fuel filter was clogged, the little sintered bronze device in the side of the carburetor. I borrowed two pairs of pliers and got it out and rapped it and blew through it. That didn't help. A Mexican truck driver diagnosed the trouble as vapor lock. He draped a wet rag over the fuel pump to cool it down, to condense the vapor in the gas line. I had never seen that trick before but it worked and we were soon off again.

The road was flat and straight in this country and there was very little traffic. Visibility was good too. I decided to let the doctor drive for a bit while I took a short nap. We swapped seats. He was a better driver than I had any reason to expect. I've seen many worse. The steering slack didn't throw him at all. Still he had his own style and there was to be no sleeping with him at the wheel. He would hold the accelerator down for about four seconds and then let up on it. Then he would press it down again and let up on it again. That was the way he drove. I was rocking back and forth like one of those toy birds that drinks water from a glass.

I tried to read the Dix book. I couldn't seem to penetrate the man's message. The pages were brittle and the type was heavy and black and hard to read. There were tips on how to turn disadvantages into advantages and how to take insults and rebuffs in stride. The good salesman must make *one more call*, Dix said, before stopping for the day. That might be the big one! He said you must save your money but you must not be afraid to spend it either, and at the same time you must give no thought to money. A lot of his stuff was formulated in this way. You must do this and that, two contrary things, and you must also be careful to do neither. Dynamic tension! Avoid excessive blinking and wild eye movement, Dix said, when talking to prospects. Restrain your hands. Watch for openings, for the tiniest breaches. These were good enough tips in their way but I had been led to expect balls of fire. I became impatient with the thing. The doctor had deposited bits of gray snot on every page and these boogers were dried and crystallized.

"This car seems to be going sideways," he said to me.

The car wasn't going sideways and I didn't bother to answer him.

A little later he said, "This engine seems to be sucking air."

I let that go too. He began to talk about his youth, about his days as a medical student at Wooten Institute in New Orleans. I couldn't follow all that stuff and I tuned him out as best I could. He ended the long account by saying that Dr. Wooten "invented clamps."

"Medical clamps?" I idly inquired.

"No, just clamps. He invented the clamp."

"I don't understand that. What kind of clamp are you talking about?"

"Clamps! Clamps! That you hold two things together with! Can't you understand plain English?"

"Are you saying this man made the first clamp?"

"He got a patent on it. He invented the clamp."

"No, he didn't."

"Then who did?"

"I don't know."

"You don't know. And you don't know Smitty Wooten either but you want to tell me he didn't invent the clamp."

"He may have invented some special kind of clamp but he didn't invent *the clamp*. The principle of the clamp was probably known to the Sumerians. You can't go around saying this fellow from Louisiana invented the clamp."

"He was the finest diagnostician of our time. I suppose you deny that too."

"That's something else."

"No, go ahead. Attack him all you please. He's dead now and can't defend himself. Call him a liar and a bum. It's great sport for people who sit on the sidelines of life. They do the same thing with Dix. People who aren't fit to utter his name."

I didn't want to provoke another frenzy while he was driving, so I let the matter drop. There was very little traffic, as I say, in that desolate green scrubland, and no rivers and creeks at all, but he managed to find a narrow bridge and meet a cattle truck on it. As soon as the truck hove into view, a good half-mile away, the doctor began to make delicate speed adjustments so as to assure an encounter in the exact center of the bridge. We clipped a mirror off the truck and when we were well clear of the scene I took the wheel again.

Then one of the motor mounts snapped. The decayed rubber finally gave way. Strength of materials! With this support gone the least acceleration would throw the engine over to the right from the torque, and the fan blades would clatter against the shroud. I straightened out two coat hangers and fastened one end of the stiff wires to the exhaust manifold on the left side, and anchored the other ends to the frame member. This steadied the engine somewhat and kept it from jumping over so far. I thought it was a clever piece of work, even though I had burned my fingers on the manifold.

For a little car it had a lot of secrets. Another tire went flat near Chetumal, the left rear, and I almost twisted the lug bolts off before I figured out that they had left-hand threads. Far from being clever, I was slow and stupid! Of all the odd-sized tires on the car this one was the smallest, and when I got it off I saw molded in the rubber these words: "Property of U-Haul Co. Not to be sold." A trailer tire!

Dr. Symes waited in the shade of some bushes. My blistered fingers hurt and I was angry at myself and I was hot and dirty and thirsty. I asked him to bring me the water jug. He didn't answer and I spoke to him again, sharply. He just stared at me with his mouth open. His face was gray and he was breathing hard. One eye was closed, the red one. The old man was sick! No laughing fits here!

I took the grip and the water jug to him. He drank some chalky-looking medicine and almost gagged on it. He said he was dizzy. He didn't want to move for a few minutes. I drank the last of the tepid water in the jug and lay back in the shade. The sand was coarse and warm. I said I would take him to a doctor in Chetumal. He said, "No, it's just a spell. It'll pass. I'll be all right in a minute. It's not far to Mama's place, is it?"

"No, it's not far now."

He took off his long belt and this seemed to give him some relief. Then he took off his bow tie. He unchained the giant wallet from his clothes and handed it to me, along with his flashlight, and told me to see that his mother got these things, a Mrs. Nell Symes. I didn't like the sound of that. We sat there for a long time and said nothing.

The booted tire thumped all the way in to Chetumal, and then to the border crossing, which was a river just outside of town. The officer there on the Mexican end of the bridge paid no attention to my faulty papers but he didn't like the doctor, didn't want to touch him or brush up against him, this hollow-eyed old gringo with his mouth open, and he was determined not to let him leave Mexico without his bus. Dr. Symes's tourist card was clearly stamped *"Entro con Automóvil,"* as was mine, and if one enters Mexico with an *automóvil* then one must also leave with it.

I explained that the doctor's bus had broken down through no fault of his own and that he intended to return for it after a brief visit with his ailing mother in Belize. The officer said that anyone might tell such a story, which was true enough. The law was the law. Produce the bus. Dr. Symes offered the man a hundred pesos and the man studied the brown note for an instant and then shook his head; this was a serious matter and money could not settle it, certainly not a hundred pesos.

I took the doctor aside and suggested that he give the man five hundred pesos. He said, "No, that's too much."

"What are you going to do then?"

"I don't know, but I'm not giving that son of a bitch forty dollars."

I saw a red bus cross the bridge with only a brief inspection at each end. I told the doctor I would take him back to Chetumal. He could wait there until dark and catch a red bus to Belize. Then, very likely, there would be a different officer here at this post. The doctor would probably not be noticed and the bus ride would not be a long one. It was only another eighty miles or so to Belize.

He was wobbly and vague. He had heat staggers. I couldn't get any sense out of him. He had diarrhea too, and he was drinking paregoric from a little bottle. We drove back to Chetumal, the tire bumping.

He said, "Are you going to dump me, Speed?"

"You won't let me take you to a doctor."

"I never thought you would just throw me out."

"I'm not throwing you out. Listen to what I'm saying. You can take a bus across the border tonight. I'll see that you get on it. I'll follow the bus."

"I thought we had a deal."

"I don't know what you expect me to do. I can't force these people to let you out of the country."

"You said you'd take me to Belize. I thought it was a straight deal."

"I'm doing the best I can. You forget I have my own business to see to."

"That's hard, Speed. That's strong. I don't know you but I know that's not worthy of you."

"What you need is a doctor."

"I'll be all right if I can just get something cool to drink."

I parked on the waterfront in Chetumal and got him out of the car and walked him over to a dockside refreshment stand. We sat on folding metal chairs under a palm-thatched cabana rig. He looked like a dead man. When the waitress came over, he rallied a little and tried to smile. He said, "Little lady, I want the biggest Co'-Cola you are permitted to serve." She was a pretty Indian girl with sharp black eyes. He tried to wink, and said, "They're getting these little girls out of Hollywood now." A man at the next table was eating a whole fresh pineapple with a knife. I ordered a pineapple for myself and a Coca *grande* for the doctor.

There was a rising wind. Small boats were chugging about in the bay. Vultures walked boldly along the dock like domestic turkeys. The doctor drank three Cokes and asked for his wallet back. I gave it to him.

"What happened to my flashlight?"

"It's in the car."

He saw something shiny and leaned over and scratched at it, trying to pick it up.

I said, "That's a nailhead."

"I knew it wasn't a dime. I just wanted to see what it was."

"I've got to get the spare fixed and I need to see about the bus. I want you to wait right here and don't go wandering off."

"I'm not riding any bus."

"What are you going to do then?"

"I'm not going off a cliff in a Mexican bus."

His old carcass was very dear to him.

We sat in silence for a while. I went to the car and got my Esso map of British Honduras. It was a beautiful blue map with hardly any roads to clutter it up. Just down the bay from here was a coastal village in British Honduras called Corozal. Why couldn't the border be bypassed by water? There were plenty of boats available. It wouldn't be much of a trip—a matter of a few miles.

I proposed this plan to the doctor and showed him how things lay on the map. To keep it from blowing away, I had to anchor the corners with bottles. Over and over again I explained the scheme to him but he couldn't take it in. "Do what, Speed?" he would say. He was fading again.

Most of the boats were now coming in. I walked along the dock and talked to the owners, trying to explain and sell the plan to them in my feeble Spanish. I got nowhere. They wanted no part of it. There was too much wind and the water was too rough and it would soon be dark. Maybe tomorrow, they said, or the next day. I put the map back in the car and returned to the table. Dr. Symes was drinking yet another Coke. The girl wanted her money and he was trying to match her for it, double or nothing. He had a ready line of patter for all cashiers, the idea being to confuse them so that they might make an error in his favor.

"It's no use," I said. "The wind is too high. It's too dangerous. It was a bad plan anyway. You'll have to ride the red bus and that's all there is to it."

"The wind?" he said.

Newspapers were being whipped against our legs and the tablecloth was snapping and donkeys were leaning against buildings and the heavy traffic light that hung over the intersection was standing about thirty degrees off vertical, and into the teeth of this gale he asked me that question.

"A bus. I'm going to put you on a bus. It's the only way."

"Not a bus, no."

"Do you want to see your mother or do you want to stay here?"

"Mama?"

"She's waiting for you just down the road. You can be there in no time. The bus is safe, I tell you. This is flat country. There are no mountains between here and Belize, not one. It's a coastal plain. I'll see that you get there. I'll drive right along behind the bus."

"Send me over the mountains in a bus, is that it? That's your answer for everything. Did you make sure it has no brakes? I don't even know the name of this town. I wanted to go to Belize and you land us in this place instead. Why do we keep hanging around here anyway?"

"You can be in Belize in just a few hours if you'll listen to me and do what I say. Do you understand what I'm telling you?"

In my desperation I had fallen into the doctor's habits of speech. He must have spent half his life shouting that hopeless question. I thought of hiring an ambulance. Surely the border guards would not interfere with a mercy dash. But wouldn't it be very expensive?

Someone pinched me on the fleshy part of my upper arm and I jumped. An Indian boy about seventeen years old was standing behind me. "Corozal?" he said. He took me over to the slip where his wooden boat was tied up, a slender homemade craft with an old-fashioned four-cycle outboard engine on the stern. It was about a six-horse engine, with a high profile. I asked about life preservers. *No hay*, he said. I indicated that the water was rough and getting rougher all the time. He shrugged it off as inconsequential. We quickly reached an agreement.

The doctor was too weak and confused to resist. I took his wallet again for safekeeping and we loaded him into the boat. I gave the boy a ten-dollar bill and promised him a twenty—a balloon payment to encourage compliance—upon delivery of the old man in Corozal. The boy jerked the rope many times before the engine started. Then he pushed off and I, with great misgivings, watched them leave, the little boat battering sluggishly through the whitecaps. The sun was going down. The doctor had lied to me about his funds. That wallet was packed with twenties and fifties.

I drove back to the border crossing and had no trouble getting out of Mexico. At the other end of the bridge I had to deal with a British Honduras officer. He was a dapper Negro in shorts and high stockings and Sam Browne belt. I had shed my coat long ago but I was still wearing my tie. I was filthy and I needed a shave.

He asked my occupation. I said I was a businessman. He pointed out that my spare tire was flat. I thanked him. Was I a doctor? What was I doing with a doctor's bag? What was the silverware for? I had no very good answers for him. He poked into everything, even the ice chest. The ice had melted days ago and the cheese and baloney were spoiled. The water was brown from the rusting rims of the beer cans. At the bottom of this mess my Colt Cobra was washing about in the plastic bag. I had forgotten all about it. The old man had made me neglect my business! The officer wiped the pistol dry with a handkerchief and stuck it in his hip pocket. He shook his finger at me but said nothing. He was keeping it for himself.

He asked if I planned to sell the Buick and I said no. He wrote his name and address for me on the back of a card advertising the Fair Play Hotel in Belize and said he would be happy to handle the sale. I took the card and told him I would keep it in mind. He said I didn't look like much of a businessman to him. I described my Torino and asked about Norma and Dupree and the dog—and was I knocked for a loop when this bird said he remembered them. He remembered the car and the pretty girl and yes, the red dog, and the fellow with the glasses who was driving; he remembered him very well.

"Played that 'Sweet Lorraine' on the mouth harp."

"No, that wouldn't be him. That wouldn't be Dupree."

"Yes, and 'Twilight Time' too."

I couldn't believe my ears. Was it possible that some identical people had passed through here with a chow dog in a blue Torino? An antimatter Dupree playing tunes on a mouth organ! A young Meigs! The doctor had told me that I could expect the same old stuff down here but this didn't sound like the same old stuff to me.

I asked about the road to Belize. Was it paved? Should I chance it with no spare tire? He said it was an excellent road, much better than anything I had seen in Mexico. And not only that, but I would now be able to get some good gasoline for a change. The Mexican petrol was inferior stuff, he said, and it smelled funny. Here it had the proper smell.

There was a T-head pier in Corozal and I stood at the end of it and waited anxiously in the dark. The wind had dropped off somewhat. Now it was cool. I supposed there was some colorful local name for it, for this particular kind of wind. I was just fifteen degrees or so above the equator and I was at sea level and yet I was chilly. A cool snap like this on the Louisiana island and the doctor would have a thousand coughing chimps on his hands. I could make out a few stars through the drifting clouds but not the Southern Cross.

I began to worry more and more about that little boat in open water at night. It wasn't the open sea but it was a big bay, big enough for trouble. Why had I suggested this? It would all be my fault, the sea disaster. Criminal folly! The boat would be swamped and the doctor, a nuisance to the end, would flail away in the water and take the Indian boy down with him.

A Spanish-looking man joined me at the edge of the pier. He was barefooted, his trouser legs rolled up, and he was pushing a bicycle. He parked the bike and looked out at the water, his hands in his pockets, a brooding figure. I didn't want to intrude on his thoughts but when the wind blew his bike over I thought it would then be all right to speak, the clatter having broken his reverie. I said, "*Mucho viento.*" He nodded and picked up his bike and left. Much wind. What a remark! No wonder everybody took foreigners for dopes.

I heard the engine popping and then I saw the boat low in the water. Choppy waves were breaking against it. The boy was angry because the doctor had vomited marshmallows and Coke in his boat. The old man was wet and only semiconscious. We laid him out on the pier and let him drain for a minute. It was like trying to lug a wet mattress. I gave the boy an extra ten dollars for his trouble. He helped me get the doctor into the car and then he fearlessly took to the dark water again.

Part of the road to Belize was broken pavement and the rest was washboard gravel. Great flat slabs of concrete had been wrenched out of place as though from an earthquake. What a road! Time after time the Buick's weak coil springs bottomed out, and I mean dead bottom. When we came bounding back up on the return phase, I feared that something would tear loose, some suspension component. I worried about the tires too. The gravel part was only a little better. I tried to find a speed at which we could skim along on the crests of the corrugations but with no luck. We skittered all over the roadbed. The doctor groaned in the back seat. I too was beginning to fade. My head throbbed and I took some more of the bitter orange pills.

It was late when we reached Belize and I didn't feel like asking directions and floundering around in a strange place. It wasn't a big town but the streets were narrow and dark and irregular. I found a taxicab at a Shell station and I asked the Negro driver if he knew a Mrs. Nell Symes, who had a church here. It took him a while to puzzle it out. Did I mean "Meemaw?" Well, I didn't know, but I hired him to go to Meemaw's anyway and I trailed along behind in the Buick.

The church was a converted dwelling house, a white frame structure of two stories. Some of the windows had fixed wooden louvers and some had shutters that folded back. The roof was galvanized sheet iron. It was just the kind of old house that needed the Midgestone treatment.

A wooden sign beside the door said:

> *Unity Tabernacle*
> *"Whosoever will"*

The house was dark and I rapped on the door for a long time before I roused anyone. I heard them coming down the stairs very slowly. The door opened and two old ladies looked out at me. One was in a flannel bathrobe and the other one was wearing a red sweater. The one in the sweater had wisps of pink hair on her scalp. It was a bright chemical pink like that of a dyed Easter chick. I could see at once that the other one was Dr. Symes's mother. She had the same raccoon eyes. She used an aluminum walking stick but she didn't appear to be much more decrepit than the doctor himself.

"Mrs. Symes?"

"Yes?"

"I have your son out here in the car."

"What's that you say?"

"Dr. Symes. He's out here in the car."

"Reo. My word."

"He's sick."

"Who are you?"

"My name is Ray Midge. He rode down from Mexico with me."

"Are you with the postal authorities?"

"No, ma'am."

"We weren't even thinking about Reo, were we, Melba?"

The other lady said, "*I* sure wasn't. I was thinking about a snack."

Mrs. Symes turned back to me. "Has he got some old floozie with him?"

"No, ma'am, he's by himself."

"You say he's in the car?"

"Yes."

"Why is he staying in the car? Why doesn't he get out of the car?"

"He's sick."

"Go see if it's really him, Melba."

Melba came out to the car. I opened a door so the dome light would come on. She studied the rumpled figure in the back seat. "It's Reo all right," she said. "He's asleep. He's lost weight. His clothes are smoking. He's wearing those same old white pants he had on last time. I didn't know pants lasted that long."

Mrs. Symes said, "He may have several pair, all identical. Some men do that with socks."

Many Miles Per Hour

by William Saroyan

William Saroyan (1908–1981) grew up in pre-Depression California, in what he later described as "the most amazing and comical poverty in the world." Saroyan in 1934 earned fame by writing a new story every day for a month for Story magazine, and soon became one of America's most successful writers. Many of his stories, including this one, hearken back to his childhood.

W

e used to see him going down the highway fifty miles an hour, and my brother Mike used to look kind of sore and jealous.

There he goes, Mike used to say. Where in hell do you think he's going?

Nowhere, I guess, I used to say.

He's in a pretty big hurry for a man who's going nowhere.

I guess he's just turning her loose to see how fast she'll go.

She goes fast enough, Mike used to say. Where the hell can he go from here? Fowler, that's where. That good-for-nothing town.

Or Hanford, I used to say. Or Bakersfield. Don't forget Bakersfield, because it's on the highway. He could make it in three hours.

Two, Mike used to say. He could make it in an hour and three quarters.

Mike was twelve and I was ten, and in those days, 1918, a coupé was a funny-looking affair, an apple box on four wheels. It wasn't easy to get any kind of a car to go fifty miles an hour, let alone a Ford coupé but we figured this man had fixed up the motor of his car. We figured he had made a racer out of his little yellow coupé.

We used to see the automobile every day, going down the highway toward Fowler, and an hour or so later we used to see it coming back. On the way down, the car would be travelling like a bat out of hell, rattling and shaking and bouncing, and the man in the car would be smoking a cigarette and smiling to himself, like somebody a little crazy. But on the way back, it would be going no more than ten miles an hour, and the man at the wheel would be calm and sort of slumped down, kind of tired.

He was a fellow you couldn't tell anything about. You couldn't tell how old he was, or what nationality, or anything else. He certainly wasn't more than forty, although he might be less than thirty; and he certainly wasn't Italian, Greek, Armenian, Russian, Chinese, Japanese, German, or any of the other nationalities we knew.

I figure he's an American, Mike used to say. I figure he's a salesman of some kind. He hurries down the highway to some little town and sells something, and comes back, taking it easy.

Maybe, I used to say.

But I didn't think so. I figured he was more likely to be a guy who *liked* to drive down the highway in a big hurry, just for the devil of it.

Those were the years of automobile races: Dario Resta, Jimmie Murphy, Jimmie Chevrolet, and a lot of other boys who finally got killed in racetrack accidents. Those were the days when everybody in America was getting acquainted with the idea of speed. My brother Mike often thought of getting some money somewhere and buying a second-hand car and fixing it up and making it go very fast. Sixty miles an hour maybe. He thought that would be something to do. It was the money, though, that he didn't have.

When I buy my hack, Mike used to say, you're going to see some real speed.

You ain't going to buy no hack, I used to say. What you going to buy a hack with?

I'll get money some way, Mike used to say.

The highway passed in front of our house on Railroad Avenue, just a half-mile south of Rosenberg's Dried Fruit Packing House. Rosenberg's was four brothers who bought figs, dried peaches, apricots, nectarines, and raisins, and put them up in nice cartons and sent them all over the country, and even to foreign countries in Europe. Every summer they hired a lot of people from our part of town, and the women packed the stuff, and the men did harder work, with hand trucks. Mike went down for a job, but one of the brothers told him to wait another year till he got a little huskier.

That was better than nothing, and Mike couldn't wait to get huskier. He used to look at the pulp-paper magazines for the advertisements of guys like Lionel Strongfort and Earl Liederman, them giants of physical culture, them big guys who could lift a sack of flour over their heads with one arm, and a lot of other things. Mike used to wonder how them big guys got that way, and he used to go down to Cosmos Playground and practice chinning himself on the crossbars, and he used to do a lot of running to develop the muscles of his legs. Mike got to be pretty solid, but not much huskier than he had been. When the hot weather came Mike stopped training. It was too hot to bother.

We started sitting on the steps of our front porch, watching the cars go by. In front of the highway were the railroad tracks, and we could look north and south for miles because it was all level land. We could see a locomotive coming south from town, and we could sit on the steps of our front porch and watch it come closer and closer, and hear it too, and then we could look south and watch it disappear. We did that all one summer during school vacation.

There goes locomotive S. P. 797, Mike used to say.

Yes, sir.

There goes Santa Fe 485321, I used to say. What do you figure is in that boxcar, Mike?

Raisins, Mike used to say. Rosenberg's raisins, or figs, or dried peaches, or apricots. Boy, I'll be glad when next summer rolls around, so I can go to work at Rosenberg's and buy me that hack.

Boy, I used to say.

Just thinking of working at Rosenberg's used to do something to Mike. He used to jump up and start shadowboxing, puffing like a professional fighter, pulling up his tights every once in a while, and grunting.

Boy.

Boy, what he was going to do at Rosenberg's.

It was hell for Mike not to have a job at Rosenberg's, making money, so he could buy his old hack and fix the motor and make it go sixty miles an hour. He used to talk about the old hack all day, sitting on the steps of the porch and watching the cars and trains go by. When the yellow Ford coupé showed up, Mike used to get a little sore, because it was fast. It made him jealous to think of that fellow in the fast car, going down the highway fifty miles an hour.

When I get my hack, Mike used to say, I'll show that guy what real speed is.

We used to walk to town every once in a while. Actually it was at least once every day, but the days were so long every day seemed like a week and it would seem like we hadn't been to town for a week, although we had been there the day before. We used to walk to town, and around town, and then back home again. There was nowhere to go and nothing to do, but we used to get a kick out of walking by the garages and used-car lots on Broadway, especially Mike.

One day we saw the yellow Ford coupé in Ben Mallock's garage on Broadway, and Mike grabbed me by the arm.

There it is, Joe, he said. There's that racer. Let's go in.

We went in and stood by the car. There was no one around, and it was very quiet.

Then the man who owned the car stuck his head out from underneath the car. He looked like the happiest man in the world.

Hello, Mike said.

Howdy, boys, said the man who owned the yellow coupé.

Something wrong? said Mike.

Nothing serious, said the man. Just keeping the old boat in shape.

You don't know us, said Mike. We live in that white house on Railroad Avenue, near Walnut. We see you going down the highway every day.

Oh, yes, said the man. I thought I'd seen you boys somewhere.

My brother Mike, I said, says you're a salesman.

He's wrong, said the man.

I waited for him to tell us *what* he was, if he wasn't a salesman, but he didn't say anything.

I'm going to buy a car myself next year, said Mike. I figure I'll get me a fast Chevrolet.

He did a little shadowboxing, just thinking about the car, and then he got self-conscious, and the man busted out laughing.

Great idea, he said. Great idea.

He crawled out from under the car and lit a cigarette.

I figure you go about fifty miles an hour, said Mike.

Fifty-two to be exact, said the man. I hope to make sixty one of these days.

I could see Mike liked the fellow very much, and I knew I liked him. He was younger than we had imagined. He was probably no more than twenty-five, but he acted no older than a boy of fifteen or sixteen. We thought he was great.

Mike said, What's your name?

Mike could ask a question like that without sounding silly.

Bill, said the man. Bill Wallace. Everybody calls me Speed Wallace.

My name's Mike Flor, said Mike. I'm pleased to meet you. This is my brother Joe.

Mike and the man shook hands. Mike began to shadowbox again.

How would you boys like a little ride? Speed Wallace said.

Oh boy, said Mike.

We jumped into the yellow coupé, and Speed drove out of the garage, down Broadway, and across the railroad tracks in front of Rosenberg's where the highway began. On the highway he opened up to show us a little speed. We passed our house in no time and pretty soon we were tearing down the highway forty miles an hour, then forty-five, then fifty, and pretty soon the speedometer said fifty-one, fifty-two, fifty-three, and the car was rattling like anything.

By the time we were going fifty-six miles an hour we were in Fowler and the man slowed the car down, then stopped. It was very hot.

How about a cold drink? he said.

We got out of the car and walked into a store. Mike drank a bottle of strawberry, and so did I, and then the man said to have another. I said no, but Mike drank another.

The man drank four bottles of strawberry.

Then we got into the car and he drove back very slowly, not more than ten miles an hour, talking all the time about the car, and how fine it was to be able to go down a highway fifty miles an hour.

Do you make money? Mike said.

Not a nickel, Speed said. But one of these days I'm going to build myself a racer and get into the County Fair races, and make some money.

Boy, said Mike.

He let us off at our house, and we talked about the ride for three hours straight.

It was swell. Speed Wallace was a great guy.

In September the County Fair opened. There was a dirt track out there, a mile around. We read advertising cards on fences that said there would be automobile races out there this year.

One day we noticed that the yellow Ford coupé hadn't gone down the highway a whole week.

Mike jumped up all of a sudden when he realized it.

That guy's in the races at the Fair, he said. Come on, let's go.

And we started running down Railroad Avenue.

It was nine in the morning and the races wouldn't begin till around two-thirty, but we ran just the same.

We had to get to the Fairgrounds early so we could sneak in. It took us an hour and a half to walk and run to the Fairgrounds, and then it took us two hours more to sneak in. We were caught twice, but finally we got in.

We climbed into the grandstand and everything looked okey-dokey. There were two racing cars on the track, one black, and the other green.

After a while the black one started going around the track. When it got around to where we were sitting we both jumped up because the guy at the wheel was the man who owned the yellow coupé. We felt swell. Boy, he went fast and made a lot of noise. And plenty of dust too, going around the corners.

The races didn't start at two-thirty, they started at three. The grandstands were full of excited people. Seven racing cars got in line. Each was cranked, and the noise they made was very loud and very exciting. Then the race started and Mike started acting like a crazy man, talking to himself, shadowboxing, and jumping around.

It was the first race, a short one, twenty miles, and Speed Wallace came in fourth.

The next race was forty miles, and Speed Wallace came in second.

The third and last race was seventy-five miles, seventy-five times around the track, and the thirtieth time around Speed Wallace got out in front, just a little way, but out in front just the same: then something went wrong, the inside front wheel of Speed Wallace's racing car busted off and the car turned a furious somersault, away up into the air. Everybody saw Speed Wallace fly out of the car. Everybody saw the car smash him against the wooden fence.

Mike started running down the grandstand, to get closer. I ran after him and I could hear him swearing.

The race didn't stop, but a lot of mechanics got Speed Wallace's wrecked car out of the way, and carried Speed Wallace to an ambulance. While the other cars were going around the track for the seventieth time a man got up and told the people Speed Wallace had been instantly killed.

Holy Christ.

That fellow, Mike said, he got killed. That fellow who used to go down the highway in that yellow Ford coupé, he got killed, Joe. That fellow who gave us a ride to Fowler and bought us drinks.

When it got dark, walking home, Mike started to cry. Just a little. I could tell he was crying from the way his voice sounded. He wasn't really crying.

You remember that swell guy, Joe, he said. He was the one who got killed.

We started sitting on the steps of our front porch again, watching the cars go by, but it was sad. We knew the fellow in the yellow Ford coupé wouldn't go down the highway again. Every once in a while Mike would jump up and start shadowboxing, only it wasn't the way it used to be. He wasn't happy anymore, he was sore, and it looked like he was trying to knock hell out of something in the world that caused such a lousy thing like that to happen to a guy like Speed Wallace.

Driver

by Frederick Barthelme

Writer Daniel Akst has called Frederick Barthelme (born 1943) "the bard of suburban disconnectedness." Bathelme has said that his characters mistrust language, and instead "show what they think and feel through actions and reactions, through choices, through oblique bits of dialogue."

Rita says the living-room lights keep her awake when she goes to bed before I do, which is most of the time. The light comes down the hall and under the bedroom door, she says, and in the dark it's like a laser. So on Sunday, after she'd gone to bed, I started to read *Money* in semidarkness, tilting the pages to get the light from a book lamp clipped onto the magazine. That didn't work, so I gave it up and watched a TV program about lowriders in San Diego. They put special suspensions in their cars so they can bounce them up and down. That's not all they do, but it's sort of the center of things for them. I'd seen the cars before, seen pictures of them jumping—a wonderful thing, just on its own merits. I watched the whole show. It lasted half an hour, and ended with a parade of these wobbling, hopping, jerking cars creeping down a tree-lined California street with a tinkly Mexican love song in the background, and when it was done I had tears in my eyes because I wasn't driving one of the cars. I muted the sound, sat in the dark, and imagined flirting with a pretty Latin girl in a short, tight, shiny dress with a red belt slung waist to hip, her cleavage perfect and brown, on a hot summer night with a breeze, on a glittering street, with the smell of gasoline and Armor-All in the air, oak leaves rattling over the thump of the car engine, and me slouched at the wheel of a violet Mercury, ready to pop the front end for a smile.

In the morning I left a note attached to the refrigerator with the tiny TV dinner magnet, telling Rita what time I'd be home from the office, then got in the Celica and headed for the freeway. I'd been in traffic for half an hour, most of it behind a bald, architect-looking guy in a BMW 2002, when I saw a sign for Kleindienst Highway Auto Sales. This was a hand-painted sign, one quarter billboard size, in a vacant lot alongside the freeway—a rendering of a customized 1949 Ford. I got off at the next exit and went back up the feeder to get to this place, which was a shell-paved lot with a house trailer at the rear, strings of silver and gold decorations above, and a ten-foot Cyclone fence topped with knife wire surrounding it.

A guy jumped out of the trailer the minute I got onto the property. He followed me until I parked, then threw an arm around my shoulders before I had my car door shut. "Howdy," he said. "Phil Kleindienst. Hunting a big beauty, am I right?"

"Just looking," I said.

"We got the classics," he said, making a broad gesture with his free arm. He swung me around toward a Buick four-door. "Mainstream, high-profile, domestic, soon-to-be-sought-after classic road machines for the world of tomorrow."

"That's a big amen," I said.

He liked that. He laughed and walked me around the lot, keeping his hands on me the whole time—on my shoulder, my forearm, my back. He didn't have any cars that weren't huge and American, and he didn't have any custom cars. "Take a gander at this," he said, opening a brown Chrysler sedan. "This baby's autorama clean."

We went up and down the rows together. He was citing virtues, giving me histories, and I was looking for the hot rods. Finally, I said, "What about this sign?"

"What sign?" Phil said.

"Out there on the freeway," I said. I pointed back up to where the sign was. We could just see the back of it.

"Aw, you don't want to mess with that stuff. Lemme show you an Eldorado I got."

He started to move again. I said, "I'm a little late. I guess I'll have to come back another time. Thanks anyway."

"Hold your hanky there," he said. "I got one. I'll show you one. A Lincoln, pretty old."

He took me around beside the trailer to a corner with a banner that said "Bargain Corral" strung over the top. There was one car there, and it could have been in the TV show I'd seen. No price was soaped on the windshield, so I asked.

"Oh, hell," he said. "I don't know. Too much. Let's go back up front, lemme show you some sweethearts." He turned me toward the front of the lot. "How about this Caddy? About a '77, a honey-dripper. Purrs like a pistol."

I stopped him. "You don't want to tell me what you're getting for this one? What's the deal?"

"Whew," he said. "You're too tough. You're kidding me, right?" He waited a minute, looking me over to see whether or not I was kidding him. "You don't want that porker, do you?"

The Lincoln was pale blue with black and green pinstripes, front wheels smaller than the rear, and it was low, maybe two inches off the ground. There was an airbrush illustration on the side, between the front and rear wheel wells—a picture of the Blessed Virgin, in aqua-and-white robes, strolling in an orange grove, behind each tree of which was a wolf, lip curled, saliva shining. The glass in the windshield and in the doors was dark green, and the steering wheel was huge and white. A head-bobbing metal Bambi—I think it was supposed to be Bambi—sat on the shelf behind the back seat, staring out the rear window.

I said, "I'm just curious. What's it worth?"

He let go of me for the first time since I'd arrived, backing away, putting a little distance between us as he studied the car. Finally, he slapped his hands together and said, "I don't even want to give you a price on that there. See, that's my boy Pico's car. Was anyway. Pico got shot up in Nam. He was this kid used to hang around, then worked for me. Built the car himself—did all the custom work, put in the hydraulics, stereo. All that in there's rhino skin. I don't even know where he got that."

"Looks professional," I said.

"Oh, yeah, heck yeah. He was good. He's got D. & H. Reds in there. It's real clean. It's about a thousand percent clean. He's got so much chrome under the hood you could put the hoses in your bathroom, use 'em for mirrors. I don't know why he's got these tiny wheels up front here, I guess that's a cholo thing. . . ." Phil gazed at the Lincoln. He was half-fat, maybe forty, with prickly blond hair, double-knit pants, a short-sleeved white shirt with a spread collar. "Pico cut her himself— know what I'm saying? Build a car like that today cost a fortune." He grinned and held his hands up as if giving me the bottom line. "I figure we're talking six, in the six area."

"What about the Toyota?" I said.

"O.K. Fine. That's all right," he said. "I can work with you on that." He locked an arm around one of mine and gave me a quick pull toward the office. "Let's boot some numbers around."

His trailer smelled like Pine-Sol. Everything was covered in knubby fabrics, earth tones. There was a dining booth, a tiny kitchen, a living space with a six-foot ceiling and a bubble skylight. He had four TVs, all consoles and all turned off, lined up against one wall. When we sat down, he said, "Let's verify our situation here. What's your line?" He was shuffling around, looking through a wood-grained-cardboard file cabinet.

I said, "I'm in sales. Pools, pool accessories, like that. Above ground stuff. Is that what you mean?"

"Naw. I mean how come you want this car? Is this a kick-out-the-jambs thing for you, or what?" He waited a second, then went on.

"O.K., so don't tell me. What's your telephone? I'll check your wife on the deal. You got a wife, don't you?"

"Rita," I said.

"I mean, you tool in Nipponese and want to leave a Flying Burrito Brother, and I don't buy it. What's the better half gonna say? How do I know you got the bucks? How do I know you're in your right mind?"

"I don't know, I do, and I am," I said.

"Ha," he said. "That's good. What's the number? Better gimme the bank, too."

I gave him the numbers. He said, "Great. Get you something in the fridge. I got some Baby Ruths in there, if you got Olympic teeth. Help yourself."

He wiggled out from behind the table, went through a narrow hall to the rear of the trailer, shut a door between that room and the one I was in. There was a Plexiglas panel in the door, so I could see him in there, black telephone receiver to his ear, staring at the ceiling as he talked, swatting his hair with the papers from the file cabinet.

He was only in there a minute. When he came back he said, "The woman's not home, but the bank thinks you're aces." Then he gave me a long look. "Now listen," he said. He reached up under his shirtsleeve to scratch his shoulder. "I'm thinking you don't genuinely want this car. I know I'm supposed to be breaking your leg to sell it, but I figure you got some kind of momentary thing going, some kind of mid life thing—you look like you're about mid life."

I shrugged. "Not yet."

"Yet don't matter," he said. "My brother had his at twenty-seven. By twenty-nine he was putting toast in milk during the local news." Phil brushed something off the table. "Tell you what," he said. "I'll rent it. You take it maybe a day or two, leave yours on a collateral basis, take this guy, drive him a couple of days. Then, you still want it, we come to closure. How's that? I don't want you down my throat next week begging to undo the deal, right?"

I said, "I'll rent it right now."

"Sure you will," he said. "And I don't like it, but now and then, hell—what's it hurt?" He started through the file cabinet again. "I got a form here saves my heinie when you go to Heaven in it."

Phil had to go to his house to get the form. He lived right down the street, and he asked me to mind the store while he went, so I sat on the steps of the trailer and watched the highway. Traffic had thinned out a lot. He was gone forty minutes. When he got back I took the Lincoln.

I stopped at an Exxon station and filled up with gas, then drove to my office. I had just gotten into my assigned parking space when a young associate of mine, Reiner Gautier, pulled up in the drive behind me.

"What, you went overboard on chimichangas?" he said. "What is that? Where'd you get it?"

"Just trying her out," I said.

"You got a built-in Pez dispenser on there?"

I waved the remark away and pretended to search my briefcase, hoping Reiner would move along. Finally, I had to get out. He'd left his car door open and was giving the Lincoln a careful look.

"That's Mary," he said, pointing to the picture on the side of the car. "She's got wolf trouble there, doesn't she?"

I shrugged. "She'll make out."

He looked at the picture another minute, turning his head back and forth. "That says it all, know what I mean? I like it. I go for this cross-cultural stuff." He walked back toward his car, giving my shoulder a pat on the way.

I let him leave, then got back in the Lincoln and pulled out of my space. I went to the shopping center near the office, stopped in the parking lot, and tried out the lifts. I looked out the door and I was better than eighteen inches off the ground. That got the attention of a black woman who was standing outside the ice-cream store, leaning against one of those phone-on-a-pole phone booths.

She said, "That some kind of trick car?" She was a young woman, in her twenties, and good-looking except that she was snaggletoothed. She was holding a clear plastic shopping bag with yellow rosettes on it.

I said, "Yeah. I guess it is."

She looked at me, then at the car, with a kind of amused curiosity, tilting her head back, squinting her eyes as she sized me up. "Well," she finally said. "What else do it do? Do it dance or anything?"

I grinned at her, shaking my head, then put the car in gear and left. At a bar called Splasher's, which I pass every day on my way back from work, I pulled up and went in for a beer. I'd never been in this bar before. It was one in the afternoon and the place was deserted except for a woman with feathery hair who handed me a wet bottle of Budweiser. She was cleaning up. The ceiling was falling in on this place. The walls were black, and the only illumination came from back of the bar and from the beer signs you always see, the kind that sparkle and throw little dots of light. One sign had a waterfall that light rushed over. I took my beer to a window table so I could watch the car through the stick blinds.

The woman played Country Joe and the Fish on the jukebox. I thought that was amazing. I spun my coaster, listening to this music I hadn't heard in twenty years. Between tunes I went to get a bag of beer nuts from a metal rack next to the cash register. The woman watched me search my pocket for change, then nodded when I put two quarters on the bar.

Two kids on trail bikes stopped outside to give the car a look. These kids were about fourteen, with dirty T-shirts and minimal hair. They straddled their bikes and stared in the car windows, and I smiled about it until I saw that the kid on the driver's side was prying off the door mirror. Then I rapped on the glass and went out. "Hey! Get off of that, will you?"

The kid who had been doing the prying gave me an innocent look. "Great car," he said. "We're checking it out. Right, Binnie?"

Binnie was already on the move, standing on the pedals of his bike, rolling away. "Pretty good," he said. "For a dork-mobile."

I said, "Sorry you're leaving."

"Whoa . . ." he said.

The first kid started moving, too. Then he stopped his bike and turned to me. "Hey," he said. "You know that mirror on your side? It's real loose. I can probably fix it up. Ten bucks."

I gave him a nasty look and shook my head, then got in the car. I stopped at a drugstore on the way home, went in to get cigarettes. A college-age guy with blue eyes and pretty brown hair was in back, sitting at a folding table, eating his lunch. It didn't look like takeout food—it looked homemade. He had a dinner plate, a salad plate, a jelly glass with red and green swirls on the side. There was milk in the glass. He asked if he could help me.

"I need a pack of cigarettes," I said.

He came across to the cigarette counter, wiping his mouth with a yellow paper towel. "What kind?"

I said, "True. Menthol."

He looked at his cigarette rack, one end to the other, then turned around and said, "I don't see 'em. You see 'em out there?" He pointed to the front of the counter, where more cigarettes were displayed.

I'd already checked, but I looked again. "None here."

He came out from behind the counter rewiping his mouth. "I don't guess we have 'em. I was sure we did, but I guess I was wrong. I can order you some."

I waited a second or so, looking at the guy, then picked a pack of Kools off the counter. "How about these?"

"We got those," he said.

Rita came to the window when I pulled up in the driveway and honked. It took her a minute, but then she figured out it was me and dropped the curtain. "What's this?" she said, coming out the front door.

I held up a hand and said, "Wait a minute. Stay there. Watch."

She stopped by the gas lamp at the edge of the drive. I jumped the front end of the Lincoln a little, then as far as it would go. Then I raised the rear to full height, then the front. I kept the car up until she was coming for a closer look, then I let it down, left front first, like an elephant getting on its knees in a circus show. That stopped her.

I got out of the car. "How do you like it?"

"Whose is it?" she said.

"Ours." I put an arm around her and did a Phil Kleindienst sweep with my free hand, covering the Lincoln front to back.

"What about the Celica? Where's the Celica?"

I reached in the driver's window and pulled the hood release, so I could show her the chrome on the engine. "Traded it," I said, leading her around to the front. "Guy gave me a whopper deal."

She stopped dead, folding her arms across her chest. "You traded the Toyota?"

"Well, sort of. But this is a killer car. Look at the engine. Everything's chrome. It's worth a zillion."

Rita looked at the sky.

"C'mon," I said. I tugged her arm, leading her to the passenger side, and put her in the car. I went back around, latched the hood, then got in and started the engine. I waited, listening to the idle. "Amazing, isn't it? Can you hear that?"

"The motor? I hear the motor. Is that what you're talking about, that rumbling?"

We toured the neighborhood, then I started to go downtown, but Rita remembered she needed some lemon-pepper marinade, so we stopped at the supermarket. I sat in the car while she went inside. A lot of people walked by wearing shorts, and all of them looked good.

We picked up a family bucket of fried chicken on the way back, ate most of it in the car, then finished up inside. Then we had bananas and ice cream. After that Rita switched on the VCR and put in a tape. "I want you to see this," she said.

It was a PBS documentary about China—about a peasant family. The grandmother ran things and got carried around on the back of a bicycle through this gorgeous countryside of misty, contoured land. Her son didn't know much about communism but felt things were a lot better now, with the Four Modernizations. His wife cooked, his daughters helped in the field, and his son wore a leather motor-cycle jacket when he went out to help with the harvest. At the end they cut to the father, alone in some room, sitting by a big vase with thin branches in it, dusty light slanting in. He talked about the family, his voice ricocheting around the high registers while out-of-sync white translations popped on the bottom of the screen. When he got to his son, what he said was that the boy had been "stunned by the West."

That was it. Rita stopped the sound and we watched the credits go by, then the network logo, then some previews of WGBH shows. She poked me and pointed to the *TV Guide*, which was on the coffee table on my side of the couch. I gave her the guide and then watched her look up listings.

When she finished, she tossed the magazine back on the table. "Well?" she said.

"It's a rent-purchase thing," I said. I showed her the paper I'd signed for Phil Kleindienst. "I can give it back any time."

She laughed and said, "Hey! Not so fast. I may love it. I may want to go for a spin."

We went out about ten o'clock. It was cool, so we slouched down in the seats and left the windows open. We went by an apartment project we used to live in, and then we went over to the other side of town, where there is a lot of heavy industry—chemical plants and refineries.

Rita said, "It rides pretty good, doesn't it?"

"It's stiff when it's down," I said.

"So pump her up," she said. "I wonder what it'd be like to keep."

"People would stare."

"Great," she said. "It's about time."

She looked terrific in the car. She had on a checked shirt open over a white Danskin, her feet were up on the dash, and her short hair was wet and rippled with wind. Her skin was olive and rough, and it was glowing as if she were in front of a fire. When I missed a light next to Pfeiffer Chemicals, a couple of acres of pipes and ladders and vats and winking green lamps, I leaned over to kiss her cheek, but she turned at the last minute and caught me with her lips.

"Why, thank you," she said when I sat back again.

"Yes," I said.

On the way home we stopped at the mall. The stores were closed, but there were kids roller-skating in the parking lot, and a couple of cars parked nose to nose under one of the tall lights. We pulled up next to a palm tree in a planter about fifty yards away from the kids.

Rita said, "It's amazing out here, isn't it? How can this place be so good-looking?"

"Beats me," I said.

She put her head in her hands. "It's awful, but I have a craving for tamales. Really. I'm not making a joke, O.K.?"

One of the kids, a girl in shorts, pointed a finger at us and skated over. "How come it stays up like that?" she said.

"Just magic," I said. But then I opened the door and showed her, letting the car down real easy, then jumping the front a little bit for her.

"You've got her now," Rita whispered.

The girl stood back with her hands on her waist for a second. "Boy," she said.

She was pretty. Her shorts were satin, with little specks of glitter on them, and she had on a tiny undershirt-style top. Some trucks sailed by on the highway. I offered Rita a Kool. She took it and held it under her nose.

"What's your name?" I said to the girl, rolling my cigarette between my fingers.

"Sherri," she said. "With an 'i.' "

I nodded. "You out here a lot?" I wagged my hand toward the other kids, who were sitting on the hoods of their cars watching us.

"Sure," she said. She rocked back and forth on her skates, rolling a little, then stopping herself with her toe. "Make it go up again, O.K.?"

I did that, getting it wrong the first try, so that I had one side up while the other was down. Rita was laughing in a lovely way.

The girl watched, then shook her head. "Boy," she said, smiling and skating two small circles before starting back toward her friends. "You guys are weird."

"Howdy," Rita kept saying all the way home. "Howdy, howdy, howdy. Howdy."

She went to bed at one. I couldn't sleep, so I watched a movie we'd rented a couple days earlier. When that was over I rewound it, paged through an issue of *Spin* that she'd picked up at the grocery store, then watched the end of a horror show on HBO. By then it was after four. I tried to sleep but couldn't, so I got up and went outside. It was almost light enough to see out there. I sat in the Lincoln and thought about how nice it was that Rita could just sleep whenever she wanted to. After a while I started the car and went for a drive. I stopped at an off-brand all-night market and bought some liquid refreshment in a sixteen-ounce nonreturnable foam-sleeved bottle. I wondered if the glass was less good than glass in regular bottles.

The scent of countryside in the morning was in the air. The rear window was smeared with condensation, and the storefronts were that way, too, and it was hard to focus on the stoplights, because of the way they made rings around themselves.

I went downtown, and it was like one of those end-of-the-world movies down there, with somebody's red hamburger wrapper skittering across a deserted intersection. The sky was graying. I made a loop around the mayor's Vietnam memorial, then took the highway running west, out past the city limits. The mist got thicker. Close to the road the trees looked right, but farther away they just dissolved. In the rearview mirror I could make out the empty four-lane highway, but above that it was like looking through a Kleenex.

Finally, I turned around and drove back by my secretary's apartment, saw her car with its windows solidly fogged, then passed the mall again. Some overnight campers had turned up in the lot, and their generators were chugging away. There were two Holiday Ramblers, cream-colored, squarish things, and an Airstream hitched to a once green Chevrolet. I pulled in and stopped. The air was so wet you could feel it when you rubbed your fingers together. The sky showed bits of pink behind a gray cloud that was big above the eastern horizon. A bird sailed by in front of the car, six feet off the blacktop, and landed next to a light pole.

These two dogs came prancing into the lot, side by side, jumping on each other, playfully biting each other's neck. They were having a great time. They stopped not far away and stared at the bird, which was a bobwhite and was walking circles on the pavement. They stared, crouched for a second, then leaped this way and that, backward or to one side, then stared more. It was wonderful the way they were so serious about this bird. These dogs were identical twins, black-and-white, each with an ear that stood up and one that flopped over. I made a noise and their heads snapped around, and they stared at me for a minute. One of them sat down, forepaws stretched out in front, and the other took a couple of steps in my direction, looked for a sign from me, then twisted his head and checked the bird.

The dash clock said it was eight minutes to six. I wanted to drive home real fast and get Rita and bring her back to see everything—the dogs, the brittle light, the fuzzy air—but I figured by the time we got back it'd all be gone.

The lead dog took two more steps toward me, stopped, then stretched and yawned.

I said, "Well. How are you?"

He wagged his tail.

I said, "So. What do you think of the car?"

I guess he could tell from my voice that I was friendly, because then he did a little spasm thing and came toward me, having trouble keeping his back legs behind his front. I opened the car door and, when he came around, patted the seat. He jumped right in. He was frisky. He scrambled all over the place—into the back seat, back into the front—stuck his head out the passenger window, ducked back in and came over to smell the gearshift knob. The other dog was watching all this. I called him, then put the car in gear and rolled up next to him. He didn't move for a minute, just gave me a stare, kind of over his shoulder. I made that kissing noise you use to call dogs, and he got up and came to the door, sniffing. Finally, he climbed in. I shut the car door and headed home. They were bouncing around, and I was telling them the whole way about the girl in the parking lot and about Rita and me, how weird we had been. "We aren't weird now," I told them. "But we were weird. Once. In olden days."

from The Bonfire of the Vanities
by Tom Wolfe

*In this excerpt from his blockbuster 1987 novel,
Tom Wolfe (born 1931) writes about what hap-
pens when a master of the universe drives a
Mercedes into the wrong neighborhood.*

Thumpathumpathumpathumpathumpathumpathumpa—the
noise of the airliners taking off pounded down so hard, he
could feel it. The air was full of jet fumes. The stench cut
straight through to his stomach. Cars kept popping up from
out of the mouth of a ramp and threading their way through the
swarms of people who were roaming about on the roof in the dusk
looking for the elevators or their cars or other people's cars—steal!
steal! steal!—and his would be the leading candidate, wouldn't it?
Sherman stood with one hand resting on the door, wondering if he
dared leave it here. The car was a black Mercedes two-seat sports roadster that had cost $48,000—or $120,000, according to how you
wanted to look at it. In a Master of the Universe tax bracket, with federal, New York State, and New York City taxes to pay, Sherman had to
make $120,000 in order to have $48,000 left to spend on a two-seat
sports roadster. How would he explain it to Judy if the thing were
stolen from up here on the roof of a terminal at Kennedy Airport?

Well—why would he even owe her an explanation? For a solid week he had had dinner at home every night. It must have been the first time he had managed that since he started working for Pierce & Pierce. He had been attentive to Campbell, spending upward of forty-five minutes with her one evening, which was unusual, although he would have been surprised and offended if anybody had ever pointed that out. He had rewired a floor lamp in the library without any undue fuming and sighing. After three days of his model performance, Judy had given up the daybed in the dressing room and come back to the bedroom. True, the Berlin Wall now ran down the center of the bed, and she wouldn't give him an inch of small talk. But she was always civil to him when Campbell was around. That was the most important thing.

Two hours ago when he had called Judy to say he would be working late, she had taken it in stride. Well—he deserved it! He took one last look at the Mercedes and headed for the international arrivals area.

It was down in the bowels of the building, in what must have been designed as a baggage area originally. Strips of fluorescent lights struggled against the gloominess of the space. People were jammed behind a metal fence, waiting for passengers coming in from abroad to emerge from Customs. Suppose there was someone here who knew him and Judy? He surveyed the crowd. Shorts, sneakers, jeans, football jerseys—Christ, who were these people? One by one the travelers were straggling out of Customs. Sweat suits, T-shirts, windbreakers, tube socks, overalls, warm-up jackets, baseball caps, and tank tops; just in from Rome, Milan, Paris, Brussels, Munich, and London; the world travelers; the cosmopolites; Sherman lifted his Yale chin against the tide.

When Maria finally appeared, she wasn't hard to spot. In this mob she looked like something from another galaxy. She was wearing a skirt and a big-shouldered jacket of a royal blue that was fashionable in France, a blue-and-white-striped silk blouse, and electric-blue lizard pumps with white calf caps on the toes. The price of the blouse and the shoes alone would have paid for the clothes on the backs of any twenty women on the floor. She walked with a nose-up sprocket-hipped model-girl gait calculated to provoke maximum envy and resentment. People were staring. Beside her marched a porter with an aluminum dolly cart heaped with luggage, a prodigious amount of it, a matched set, cream-colored leather with chocolate leather trim on the edges. Vulgar, but not as vulgar as Louis Vuitton, thought Sherman. She had only gone to Italy for a week, to find a house on Lake Como for the summer. He couldn't imagine why she had taken so many bags. (Unconsciously he associated such things with a slack upbringing.) He wondered how he was going to get it all in the Mercedes.

He made his way around the fence and strode toward her. He squared his shoulders.

"Hello, babe," he said.

"*Babe?*" said Maria. She added a smile, as if she weren't really annoyed, but obviously she was. It was true that he had never called her babe before. He had wanted to sound confident but casual, like a Master of the Universe meeting his girlfriend in an airport.

He took her arm and fell in step with her and decided to try again. "How was the flight?"

"It was great," said Maria, "if you don't mind being bowed by some Brit for six hours." It was a couple of beats before Sherman realized she was saying *bored*. She gazed into the distance, as if reflecting upon her ordeal.

Up on the roof, the Mercedes had survived the thieving multitudes. The skycap couldn't get much of the luggage into the car's sporty little trunk. He had to stack half of it up on the back seat, which wasn't much more than an upholstered ledge. Terrific, thought Sherman. If I have to stop short, I'll get hit in the base of the skull by matched flying cream-colored vanity cases with chocolate-brown trim.

By the time they got out of the airport and went onto the Van Wyck Expressway toward Manhattan, only the last low dull glow of daylight was visible behind the buildings and the trees of South Ozone Park. It was that hour of dusk when the streetlights and headlights come on but make little difference. A stream of red taillights rolled on ahead of them. Over on the side of the expressway, just past Rockaway Boulevard he saw an enormous two-door sedan, the sort of car they used to make in the 1970s, up against a stone retaining wall. A man . . .

spread-eagled on the highway! . . . No, as they drew closer, he could see it wasn't a man at all. It was the hood of the car. The entire hood had been pulled off and was lying on the pavement. The wheels, seats, and steering wheel were gone . . . This huge derelict machine was now part of the landscape . . . Sherman, Maria, the luggage, and the Mercedes rolled on.

He tried once more. "Well, how was Milan? What's going on at Lake Como?"

"Sherman, who's Christopher Marlowe?" *Shuhmun, who's Christuphuh Muhlowe?*

Christopher Marlowe? "I don't know. Do I know him?"

"The one I'm talking about was a writer."

"You don't mean the playwright?"

"I guess so. Who was he?" Maria continued to look straight ahead. She sounded as if her last friend had died.

"Christopher Marlowe . . . He was a British playwright, about the time of Shakespeare, I think. Maybe a little before Shakespeare. Why?"

"Which was when?" She couldn't have sounded more miserable.

"Let's see. I don't know . . . The sixteenth century—15-something. Why?"

"What did he write?"

"God . . . beats me. Listen, I thought I was doing well just to remember who he was. Why?"

"Yes, but you do know who he was."

"Barely. Why?"

"What about Dr. Faustus?"

"Dr. Faustus?"

"Did he write something about Dr. Faustus?"

"Mmmmmmmm." A tiny flash of memory; but it slipped away. "Could be. Dr. Faustus . . . *The Jew of Malta!* He wrote a play called *The Jew of Malta.* I'm pretty sure of that. *The Jew of Malta.* I don't even know how I remember *The Jew of Malta.* I'm sure I never read it."

"But you do know who he was. That's one of the things you're supposed to know, isn't it?"

And there she had put her finger on it. The only thing that had truly stuck in Sherman's mind about Christopher Marlowe, after nine years at Buckley, four years at St. Paul's, and four years at Yale, was that you were, in fact, supposed to know who Christopher Marlowe was. But he wasn't about to say that.

Instead, he asked: "Who's supposed to?"

"Anybody," Maria mumbled. "Me."

It was getting darker. The Mercedes's spiffy dials and gauges were now lit up like a fighter plane's. They were nearing the Atlantic Avenue overpass. There was another abandoned car by the side of the road. The wheels were gone, the hood was up, and two figures, one holding a flashlight, were jackknifed over the engine well.

Maria continued to look straight ahead as they merged with the traffic on Grand Central Parkway. A galaxy of streaming headlights and taillights filled their field of vision, as if the energy of the city were now transformed into millions of globes of light orbiting in the darkness. Here, inside the Mercedes, with the windows rolled up, the entire stupendous show came gliding by without a sound.

"You know something, Sherman?" You know somethun, Shuhmun? "I hate the Brits. I *hate* 'um."

"You hate Christopher Marlowe?"

"Thank you, smartie," said Maria. "You sound just like the sonofabitch I sat next to."

Now she was looking at Sherman and smiling. It was the kind of smile you bring up bravely through great pain. Her eyes looked as if they might be about to spring tears.

"Which sonofabitch?" he said.

"On the plane. This *Brit.*" Synonymous with worm. "He started talking to me. I was looking at the catalogue from the Refiner Fetting show I saw in Milano"—it annoyed Sherman that she used the Italian, Milano, instead of the English, Milan, especially since he had never heard of Refiner Fetting—"and he starts talking about Refiner Fetting. He had one a those gold Rolexes, those huge things? It's a wonder you can lift your arm?" She had the Southern Girl habit of turning declarative sentences into questions.

"You think he was making a play?"

Maria smiled, this time with pleasure. "Of course he was!"

The smile brought Sherman great relief. The spell was broken. Just why, he didn't know. He didn't realize that there were women who thought about sexual attractiveness the way he thought about the bond market. He only knew that the spell had been broken and that the weight had been lifted. It didn't really matter what she chattered on about now. And she did chatter on. She headed deep into the indignity she had suffered.

"He couldn't wait to tell me he was a movie producer. He was making a movie based on this play, *Doctor Faustus*, by Christopher Marlowe, or just Marlowe, I think that was all he said, just Marlowe, and I don't even know why I said anything, but I thought somebody named Marlowe wrote for the movies. Actually, what I think I was thinking about was, there was this movie with a *character* named Marlowe. Robert Mitchum was in it."

"That's right. It was a Raymond Chandler story."

Maria looked at him with utter blankness. He dropped Raymond Chandler. "So what did you say to him?"

"I said, 'Oh, Christopher Marlowe. Didn't he write a movie?' And you know what this . . . bastard . . . says to me? He says, 'I shouldn't think so. He died in 1593.' *I shouldn't think so.*"

Her eyes were blazing with the recollection. Sherman waited a moment. "That's it?"

"That's *it*? I wanted to strangle him. It was . . . hum*i*liating. *I shouldn't think so.* I couldn't believe the . . . snottiness."

"What did you say to him?"

"Nothing. I turned red. I couldn't say a word."

"And that's what accounts for this mood of yours?"

"Sherman, tell me the honest truth. If you don't know who Christopher Marlowe is, does that make you stupid?"

"Oh, for God's sake, Maria. I can't believe that's what put you in such a mood."

"What mood?"

"This black cloud you landed in."

"You didn't answer me, Sherman. Does that make you stupid?"

"Don't be ridiculous. I could barely think of who he was, and I probably had him in a course or something."

"Well, that's just the point. At least you had him in a course. I didn't have him in any course. That's what makes me feel so—you don't even understand what I'm talking about, do you?"

"I sure don't." He smiled at her, and she smiled back.

By now they were passing La Guardia Airport, which was lit up by hundreds of sodium vapor lights. It didn't look like a great gateway to the sky. It looked like a factory. Sherman swung to the outside and hit the accelerator and sent the Mercedes barreling under the Thirty-first Street overpass and up the ramp onto the Triborough Bridge. The cloud had passed. He was feeling pleased with himself once again. He had jollied her out of it.

Now he had to slow down. All four lanes were heavy with traffic. As the Mercedes ascended the bridge's great arc, he could see the island of Manhattan off to the left. The towers were jammed together so tightly, he could feel the mass and stupendous weight. Just think of the millions, from all over the globe, who yearned to be on that island, in those towers, in those narrow streets! There it was, the Rome, the Paris, the London of the twentieth century, the city of ambition, the dense magnetic rock, the irresistible destination of all those who insist on being *where things are happening*—and he was among the victors! He lived on Park Avenue, the street of dreams! He worked on Wall Street, fifty floors up, for the legendary Pierce & Pierce, overlooking the world! He was at the wheel of a $48,000 roadster with one of the most beautiful women in New York—no Comp. Lit. scholar, perhaps, but gorgeous—beside him! A frisky young animal! He was of that breed whose natural destiny it was . . . to have what they wanted!

He took one hand off the wheel and made a grand gesture toward the mighty island.

"There it is, babe!"

"We're back to babe again?"

"I just feel like calling you babe, babe. New York City. There it is."

"Do you really think I'm the babe type?"

"You're as babe as they come, Maria. Where do you want to have dinner? It's all yours. New York City."

"Sherman! Aren't you supposed to turn there?"

He looked to the right. It was true. He was two lanes to the left of the lanes that led to the off-ramp to Manhattan, and there was no way he could cut across. By now this lane—the next lane—the next lane— every lane—was a train of cars and trucks, bumper to bumper, inching toward a toll plaza a hundred yards ahead. Above the plaza was a huge green sign, lit up by yellow lamps, saying BRONX UPSTATE N.Y. NEW ENGLAND.

"Sherman, I'm sure that's the turnoff to Manhattan."

"You're right, sweetheart, but there's no way I can get over there now."

"Where does this go?"

"The Bronx."

The trains of vehicles inched forward in a cloud of carbon and sulphur particles toward the toll gates.

The Mercedes was so low-slung, Sherman had to reach way up to surrender two dollar bills at the booth. A tired-looking black man stared down at him from the window of a very high perch. Something had made a long gash in the side of the booth. The gully was corroding.

A vague smoky abysmal uneasiness was seeping into Sherman's skull. The Bronx . . . He had been born and raised in New York and took a manly pride in knowing the city. *I know the city.* But in fact his familiarity with the Bronx, over the course of his thirty-eight years, was derived from five or six trips to the Bronx Zoo, two to the Botanical Gardens, and perhaps a dozen trips to Yankee Stadium, the last one in 1977 for a World Series game. He did know that the Bronx had numbered streets, which were a continuation of Manhattan's. What he would do would be—well, he would get on a cross street and take that west until he reached one of the avenues that take you back down into Manhattan. How bad could it be?

The tide of red taillights flowed on ahead of them, and now they bothered him. In the darkness, amid this red swarm, he couldn't get his bearings. His sense of direction was slipping away. He must be heading north still. The down side of the bridge hadn't curved a great deal. But now there were only signs to go by. His entire stock of landmarks was gone, left behind. At the end of the bridge the expressway split into a Y. MAJOR DEEGAN GEO. WASHINGTON BRIDGE . . . BRUCKNER NEW ENGLAND . . . Major Deegan went upstate . . . No! . . . Veer right . . . Suddenly another Y . . . EAST BRONX NEW ENGLAND . . . EAST 138TH BRUCKNER BOULEVARD . . . Choose one, you ninny! . . . Acey-deucey . . . one finger, two fingers . . . He veered right again . . . EAST 138TH . . . a ramp . . . All at once there was no more ramp, no more clean cordoned expressway. He was at ground level. It was as if he had fallen into a junkyard. He seemed to be underneath the expressway. In the blackness he could make out a cyclone fence over on the left . . . something caught in it . . . A woman's head! . . . No, it was a chair with three legs and a burnt seat with the charred stuffing hanging out in great wads, rammed halfway through a cyclone fence . . . Who on earth would jam a chair into the mesh of a cyclone fence? And why?

"Where are we, Sherman?"

He could tell by the tone of her voice that there weren't going to be any more discussions of Christopher Marlowe or where to have dinner.

"We're in the Bronx."

"You know how to get outta here?"

"Sure. If I can just find a cross street . . . Let's see, let's see, let's see . . . 138th Street . . ."

They were traveling north underneath the expressway. But what expressway? Two lanes, both heading north . . . To the left a retaining wall and cyclone fencing and concrete columns supporting the expressway . . . Should head west to find a street back to Manhattan . . . turn left . . . but he can't turn left because of the wall . . . Let's see, let's see . . . 138th Street . . . Where is it? . . . There! The sign—138th Street . . . He keeps to the left, to make the turn . . . A big opening in the wall . . . 138th Street . . . But he can't turn left! To his left are four or five lanes of traffic, down here underneath the expressway, two going north, two going south, and another one beyond them, cars and trucks barreling in both directions—there's no way he can cut across that traffic . . . So he keeps going . . . into the Bronx . . . Another opening in the wall coming up . . . He hugs the left lane . . . Same situation! . . . No way to turn left! . . . He begins to feel trapped here in the gloom beneath the expressway . . . But how bad could it be? . . . Plenty of traffic . . .

"What are we doing, Sherman?"

"I'm trying to turn left, but there's no way you can turn left off of this goddamned road. I'm going to have to turn right somewhere up here and make a U-turn or something and come back across."

Maria had no comment. Sherman glanced at her. She was looking straight ahead, grimly. Off to the right, above some low decrepit buildings, he could see a billboard that said

TOPS IN THE BRONX

MEAT WAREHOUSE

Meat warehouse . . . deep in the Bronx . . . Another opening in the wall up ahead . . . He starts bearing to the right this time—a tremendous horn!—a truck passing him on the right . . . He swerves left—

"Sherman!"

"Sorry, babe."

—too late to make the right turn . . . He keeps going, hugs the right side of the right lane, ready for the turn . . . Another opening . . . turns right . . . a wide street . . . What a lot of people all of a sudden . . . Half of them seem to be out in the street . . . dark, but they look Latin . . . Puerto Ricans? . . . Over there a long low building with scalloped dormer windows . . . like something from a storybook Swiss chalet . . . but terribly blackened . . . Over here a bar—he stares—half covered in metal shutters . . . So many people in the street . . . He slows down . . . Low apartment buildings with windows missing . . . entire sashes gone . . . A red light. He stops. He can see Maria's head panning this way and that . . . "*Ooooooaaaggggh!*" A tremendous scream off to the left . . . A young man with a wispy mustache and a sport shirt is sauntering across the street. A girl runs after him screaming. *"Oooooaggggh!"* . . . Dark face, frizzy blond hair . . . She throws her arm around his neck, but in slow motion, as if she's drunk. "Ooooooaaggggh!" Trying to strangle him! He doesn't even look at her. He just rams his elbow back into her stomach. She slides off his body. She's down on the street on all fours. He keeps walking. Never looks back. She gets up. She lunges toward him again. "Ooooaagggh!" Now they're right in front of the car. Sherman and Maria are sitting in their tan leather bucket seats staring right at them. The girl—she has her man by the neck again. He gives her another whack in the midsection with his elbow. The light changes, but Sherman can't budge. People have come out into the street from both sides to watch the imbroglio. They're laughing. They're cheering. She's pulling his hair. He's grimacing and whacking her backward with both elbows. People all over the place. Sherman looks at Maria. Neither has to say a word. Two white people, one of them a young woman decked out in a royal-blue Avenue Foch jacket with shoulders out to here . . . enough matched luggage in the back seat for a trip to China . . . a $48,000 Mercedes roadster . . . in the middle of the South Bronx . . . Miraculous! No one pays any attention to them. Just another car at the light. The two combatants gradually edge off to the other side of the street. Now they're grappling like Sumo wrestlers, face to face. They're staggering, weaving. They're worn out. They're gasping for breath. They've had it. They might as well be dancing. The crowd's losing interest, drifting away.

Sherman says to Maria, "True love, babe." Wants to make her think he's not worried.

Now there's no one in front of the car, but the light has turned red again. He waits it out, then heads down the street. Not so many people now . . . a wide street. He makes a U-turn, heads back the way they came . . .

"What are you gonna do now, Sherman?"

"I think we're okay. This is a main cross street. We're heading in the right direction. We're heading west."

But when they crossed the big thoroughfare under the expressway, they found themselves in a chaotic intersection. Streets converged from odd angles . . . People were crossing the street in every direction . . . Dark faces . . . Over this way a subway entrance . . . Over there low buildings, shops . . . Great Taste Chinese Takeout . . . He couldn't tell which street went due west . . . *That* one—the likeliest—he turned that way . . . a wide street . . . cars parked on both sides . . . up ahead, double-parked . . . triple-parked . . . a crowd . . . Could he even get through? . . . So he turned . . . *that way* . . . There was a street sign, but the names of the streets were no longer parallel to the streets themselves. East Something seemed to be . . . in that direction . . . So he took that street, but it quickly merged with a narrow side street and ran between some low buildings. The buildings appeared to be abandoned. At the next corner he turned—west, he figured—and followed that street a few blocks. There were more low buildings. They might have been garages and they might have been sheds. There were fences with spirals of razor wire on top. The streets were deserted, which was okay, he told himself, and yet he could feel his heart beating with a nervous twang. Then he turned again. A narrow street lined with seven- or eight-story apartment buildings; no sign of people; not a light in a window. The next block, the same. He turned again, and as he rounded the corner—

—*astonishing*. Utterly empty, a vast open terrain. Block after block—how many?—six? eight? a dozen?—entire blocks of the city without a building left standing. There were streets and curbing and sidewalks and light poles and nothing else. The eerie grid of a city was spread out before him, lit by the chemical yellow of the street lamps. Here and there were traces of rubble and slag. The earth looked like concrete, except that it rolled down this way . . . and up that way . . . the hills and dales of the Bronx . . . reduced to asphalt, concrete, and cinders . . . in a ghastly yellow gloaming.

He had to look twice to make sure he was in fact still driving on a New York street. The street led up a long slope . . . Two blocks away . . . three blocks away . . . it was hard to tell on this enormous vacant lot . . . There was a lone building, the last one . . . It was on the corner . . .

three or four stories high . . . It looked as if it were ready to keel over at any moment . . . It was lit up at the ground level, as if there was a store or a bar . . . Three or four people were out on the sidewalk. Sherman could see them under the streetlight on the corner.

"What is this, Sherman?" Maria was staring right at him.

"The southeast Bronx, I guess."

"You mean you don't know where we are?"

"I know *about* where we are. As long as we keep heading west we'll be all right."

"What makes you think we're heading west?"

"Oh, don't worry, we're heading west. It's just, uh . . ."

"It's just what?"

"If you see a street sign . . . I'm looking for a numbered street."

The truth was, Sherman could no longer tell which way he was heading. As they drew near the building, he could hear *thung thung thung thung thung thung.* He could hear it even though the windows of the cars were up . . . A bass violin . . . An electrical cord looped down from the light pole on the corner through the open door. Out on the sidewalk was a woman wearing what looked like a basketball jersey and shorts, and two men in short-sleeved sport shirts. The woman was leaning over with her hands on her knees, laughing and swinging her head around in a big circle. The two men were laughing at her. Were they Puerto Rican? There was no telling. Inside the doorway, the doorway where the electrical cord went, Sherman could see a low light and silhouettes. *Thung thung thung thung thung* . . . the bass . . . then the tops of some trumpet notes . . . Latin music? . . . The woman's head went around and around.

He glanced at Maria. She sat there in her terrific royal-blue jacket. Her thick dark bobbed hair framed a face that was as frozen as a photograph. Sherman sped up and left the eerie outpost in the wasteland.

He turned toward some buildings . . . over there . . . He passed houses with no sashes in the windows . . .

They came upon a little park with an iron railing around it. You had to turn either left or right. The streets went off at odd angles. Sherman had lost track of the grid pattern altogether. It no longer looked like New York. It looked like some small decaying New England city. He turned left.

"Sherman, I'm beginning not to like this."

"Don't worry, kid."

"It's kid now?"

"You didn't like babe." He wanted to sound nonchalant.

Now there were cars parked along the street . . . Three youths stood beneath a streetlight; three dark faces. They wore quilted jackets. They stared at the Mercedes. Sherman turned again.

Up ahead he could see the fuzzy yellow glow of what seemed to be a wider, more brightly lit street. The closer they came to it, the more people . . . on the sidewalks, in doorways, out in the street . . . What a lot of dark faces . . . Up ahead, something in the street. His headlights were soaked up by the darkness. Then he could make it out. A car parked out in the middle of the street, nowhere near the curb . . . a group of boys standing around it . . . More dark faces . . . Could he even get around them? He pushed the button that locked the doors. The electronic click startled him, as if it were the beat of a snare drum. He eased by. The boys stooped down and stared in the windows of the Mercedes.

Out of the corner of his eye he could see one of them smiling. But he said nothing. He just stared and grinned. Thank God, there was enough room. Sherman kept easing on by. Suppose he had a flat tire? Or the engine flooded? That would be a pretty fix. But he didn't feel rattled. He was still on top of it. Just keep rolling. That's the main thing. A $48,000 Mercedes. Come on, you Krauts, you Panzer heads, you steely-brained machinists . . . Do it right . . . He made it past the car. Up ahead, a thoroughfare . . . Traffic was going across the intersection at a good clip in both directions. He let his breath out. He'd take it! To the right! To the left! It didn't matter. He reached the intersection. The light was red. Well, the hell with that. He started through.

"Sherman, you're going through a red light!"

"Good. Maybe the cops'll come. That wouldn't upset me too much."

Maria wasn't saying a word. The concerns of her luxurious life were now tightly focused. Human existence had but one purpose: to get out of the Bronx.

Up ahead the vaporous mustard glow of the streetlights was brighter and more spread out . . . Some sort of major intersection . . . Wait a second . . . Up there, a subway entrance . . . Over here, shops, cheap food joints . . . Texas Fried Chicken . . . Great Taste Chinese Takeout . . . *Great Taste Chinese Takeout!*

Maria was thinking the same thing. "Jesus Christ, Sherman, we're back where we started! You been around in a circle!"

"I know it. I know it. Just hold on a second. I tell you what. I'm gonna take a right. I'm gonna head back down under the expressway. I'm gonna—"

"Don't get under that thing again, Sherman."

The expressway was right up above. The light was green. Sherman didn't know what to do. Someone was blowing a horn behind him.

"Sherman! Look over there! It says George Washington Bridge!"

Where? The horn kept blowing. Then he saw it. It was on the far side, beneath the expressway, in the decrepit gray gloaming, a sign on a concrete support . . . 95. 895 EAST. GEO. WASH. BRIDGE . . . Must be a ramp . . .

"But we don't want to go in that direction! That's north!"

"So what, Sherman? At least you know what it is! At least it's civilization! Let's get outta here!"

The horn blared. Somebody was back there yelling. Sherman gunned it, while he still had the light. He drove across the five lanes toward the little sign. He was back under the expressway.

"It's right over there, Sherman!"

"Okay, okay, I see it."

The ramp looked like a black chute stuck up between the concrete supports. The Mercedes took a hard bounce from a pothole.

"Christ," said Sherman, "I didn't even see that."

He leaned forward over the steering wheel. The headlights shot across the concrete columns in a delirium. He shifted into second gear.

He turned left around an abutment and gunned it up the ramp. Bodies! . . . Bodies in the road! . . . Two of them curled up! . . . No, not bodies . . . ridges in the side . . . molds . . . No, containers, some kind of containers . . . Trash cans . . . He'd have to squeeze to the left to get around them . . . He shifted down into first gear and turned to the left . . . A blur in his headlights . . . For an instant he thought someone had jumped off the guardrail of the ramp . . . Not big enough . . . It was an animal . . . It was lying in the road, blocking the way . . . Sherman jammed down on the brake . . . A piece of luggage hit him in the back of his head . . . two pieces . . .

A shriek from Maria. A suitcase was on top of her headrest. The car had stalled. Sherman set the brake and pulled the suitcase off her and shoved it back.

"You okay?"

She wasn't looking at him. She was staring through the windshield. "What is that?"

Blocking the road—it wasn't an animal . . . Treads . . . It was a wheel . . . His first thought was that a wheel had come off a car up on the expressway and it had bounced down here onto the ramp. All at once the car was dead quiet, because the engine had stalled out. Sherman started the engine up again. He tested the brake to make sure it was secure. Then he opened the door.

"What are you doing, Sherman?"

"I'm gonna push it out of the way."

"Be careful. What if a car's coming?"

"Well." He shrugged and got out.

He felt strange from the moment he set foot on the ramp. From overhead the tremendous clanging noise of vehicles going over some sort of metal joint or plate in the expressway. He was staring up at the expressway's black underbelly. He couldn't see the cars. He could only hear them pounding the road, apparently at great speed, making the clanging noise and creating a field of vibration. The vibration enveloped the great corroded black structure with a hum. But at the same time he could hear his shoes, his $650 New & Lingwood shoes, New &

Lingwood of Jermyn Street, London, with their English leather soles and heels, making tiny gritty scraping sounds as he walked up the incline toward the wheel. The tiny gritty scraping sound of his shoes was as sharp as any sound he had ever heard. He leaned over. It wasn't a wheel, after all, only a tire. Imagine a car losing a tire. He picked it up.

"Sherman!"

He turned around, toward the Mercedes. Two figures! . . . Two young black men—black—on the ramp, coming up behind him . . . *Boston Celtics!* . . . The one nearest him had on a silvery basketball warm-up jacket with CELTICS written across the chest . . . He was no more than four or five steps away . . . powerfully built . . . His jacket was open . . . a white T-shirt . . . tremendous chest muscles . . . a square face . . . wide jaws . . . a wide mouth . . . What was that look? . . . Hunter! Predator! . . . The youth stared Sherman right in the eye . . . walking slowly . . . The other one was tall but skinny, with a long neck, a narrow face . . . a delicate face . . . eyes wide open . . . startled . . . He looked terrified . . . He wore a loose sweater . . . He was a step or two behind the big one . . .

"Yo!" said the big one. "Need some help?"

Sherman stood there, holding the tire and staring.

"What happen, man? Need some help?"

Sherman stood there, holding the tire and staring.

"What happen, man? Need some help?"

It was a neighborly voice. *Setting me up! One hand inside his jacket pocket!* But he sounds sincere. *It's a setup, you idiot!* But suppose he merely wants to help? *What are they doing on this ramp!* Haven't done anything—haven't threatened. *But they will!* Just be nice. *Are you insane? Do something! Act!* A sound filled his skull, the sound of rushing steam. He held the tire up in front of his chest. *Now!* Bango—he charged at the big one and shoved the tire at him. It was coming right back at him! The tire was coming right back at him! He threw his arms up. It bounced off his arms. A sprawl—the brute fell over the tire. Silvery CELTICS jacket—on the pavement. He skidded on the New & Lingwood party shoes. He pivoted.

"Sherman!"

Maria was behind the wheel of the car. The engine was roaring. The door on the passenger side was open.

"Get in!"

The other one, the skinny one, was between him and the car . . . a terrified look on his mug . . . eyes wide open . . . Sherman was pure frenzy . . . Had to get to the car! . . . He ran for it. He lowered his head. He crashed into him. The boy went spinning back and hit the rear fender of the car but didn't fall down.

"Henry!"

The big one was getting up. Sherman threw himself into the car.

Maria's ghastly stricken face: "Get in! Get in!"

The roaring engine . . . the Panzer-head Mercedes dials . . . A blur outside the car . . . Sherman grabbed the door pull and with a tremendous adrenal burst banged it shut. Out of the corner of his eye, the big one—almost to the door on Mania's side. Sherman hit the lock mechanism. *Rap!* He was yanking on the door handle—CELTICS inches from Maria's head with only the glass in between. Maria shoved the Mercedes into first gear and squealed forward. The youth leaped to one side. The car was heading straight for the trash cans. Maria hit the brakes. Sherman was thrown against the dash. A vanity case landed on top of the gearshift. Sherman pulled it off. Now it was on his lap. Maria threw the car into reverse. It shot backward. He glanced to his right. The skinny one . . . The skinny boy was standing there staring at him . . . pure fear on his delicate face . . . Maria shoved it into first gear again . . . She was breathing in huge gulps, as if she were drowning . . .

Sherman yelled, "Look out!"

The big one was coming toward the car. He had the tire up over his head. Maria squealed the car forward, right at him. He lurched out of the way . . . a blur . . . a terrific jolt . . . The tire hit the windshield and bounced off, without breaking the glass . . . The Krauts! . . . Maria cut the wheel to the left, to keep from hitting the cans . . . The skinny one standing right there . . . The rear end fishtailed . . . *thok!* . . . The skinny boy was no longer standing . . . Maria fought the steering wheel . . . A clear shot between the guardrail and the trash cans . . . She floored it

. . . A furious squeal . . . The Mercedes shot up the ramp . . . The road rose beneath him . . . Sherman hung on . . . The huge tongue of the expressway . . . Lights rocketing by . . . Maria braked the car . . . Sherman and the vanity case were thrown up against the dashboard . . . *Hahhh hahhhhh hahhhhh hahhhhh* . . . At first he thought she was laughing. She was only trying to get her breath.

"You okay?"

She gunned the car forward. The blare of a horn—

"For Christ's sake, Maria!"

The blaring horn swerved and hurtled past, and they were out on the expressway.

His eyes were stinging with perspiration. He took one hand off the vanity case to rub his eyes, but it started shaking so badly he put it back on the case. He could feel his heart beating in his throat. He was soaking wet. His jacket was coming apart. He could feel it. It was ripped in the back seams. His lungs were struggling for more oxygen.

They were barreling along the expressway, much too fast.

"Slow down, Maria! Jesus Christ!"

"Where's it go, Sherman? Where's it go?"

"Just follow the signs that say George Washington Bridge, and for Christ's sake, slow down."

Maria took one hand off the steering wheel to push back her hair from her forehead. Her entire arm, as well as her hand, was shaking. Sherman wondered if she could control the car, but he didn't want to break her concentration. His heart was racing along with hollow thuds, as if it had broken loose inside his rib cage.

"Aw shit, my arms are shaking!" said Maria. Aw shit, muh uhms uh shakin'. He had never heard her use the word *shit* before.

"Just take it easy," said Sherman. "We're okay now, we're okay."

"But where's it go!"

"Just take it easy! Just follow the signs. George Washington Bridge."

"Aw shit, Sherman, that's what we did before!"

"Take it *easy*, for Christ's sake. I'll tell you where."

"Don't fuck up this time, Sherman."

Sherman found his hands gripping the vanity case in his lap as if it were a second wheel. He tried to concentrate on the road ahead. Then he stared at a sign over the highway up ahead: CROSS BRONX GEO. WASH. BRIDGE.

"Cross Bronx! What's that?"

"Just take it!"

"Shit, Sherman!"

"Stay on the highway. We're okay." The navigator.

He stared at the white line on the roadbed. He stared so hard, they began separating on him . . . the lines . . . the signs . . . the taillights . . . He couldn't figure out the pattern any longer . . . He was concentrating on . . . fragments! . . . molecules! . . . atoms! . . . Jesus Christ! . . . *I've lost the power to reason!* . . . His heart went into palpitations . . . and then a big . . . *snap!* it went back into a regular rhythm . . .

Then, overhead: MAJOR DEEGAN TRIBORO BRIDGE.

"See that, Maria? Triborough Bridge! Take that!"

"Jesus Christ, Sherman, George Washington Bridge!"

"No! We want the Triborough, Maria! That'll take us right back into Manhattan!"

So they took that expressway. Presently, overhead: WILLIS AVE. "What's Willis Avenue?"

"I think it's the Bronx," said Sherman.

"Shit!"

"Just stay to your left! We're okay!"

"Shit, Sherman!"

Over the highway a big sign: TRIBORO.

"There it is, Maria! You see that!"

"Yeah."

"Bear to your right up there. You exit to the right!" Now Sherman was gripping the vanity case and giving it the body English for a right turn. He was holding a vanity case and giving it body English. Maria had on an Avenue Foch royal-blue jacket with shoulder pads . . . out to *here* . . . a tense little animal writhing under royal-blue shoulder pads from Paris . . . the two of them in a $48,000 Mercedes with spiffy airplane dials . . . desperate to escape the Bronx . . .

They reached the exit. He held on for dear life, as if a tornado were going to rise up at any moment and blow them out of the proper groove and—*back to the Bronx!*

They made it. Now they were on the long incline that led to the bridge and to Manhattan.

Hahhhhh hahhhhhh hahhhhhh hahhhhh "Sherman!"

He stared at her. She was sighing and taking in huge gulps of air.

"It's okay, sweetheart."

"Sherman, he threw it . . . right at me!"

"Threw what?"

"That . . . wheel, Sherman!"

The tire had hit the windshield right in front of her eyes. But something else flashed into Sherman's mind . . . *thok!* . . . the sound of the rear fender hitting something and the skinny boy disappearing from view . . . Maria let out a sob.

"Get a grip on yourself! We've only got a little farther!"

She snuffled back her tears. "God . . ."

Sherman reached over and massaged the back of her neck with his left hand.

"You're okay, honey. You're doing swell."

"Oh, Sherman."

The odd thing was—and it struck him as odd in that very moment—he wanted to smile. I saved her! I am her protector! He kept rubbing her neck.

"It was only a tire," said the protector, savoring the luxury of calming the weak. "Otherwise it would've broken the windshield."

"He threw it . . . right . . . at me."

"I know, I know. It's okay. It's all over."

But he could hear it again. The little *thok.* And the skinny boy was gone.

"Maria, I think you—I think we hit one of them."

You—we—already a deep instinct was summoning up the clammy patriarch, blame.

Maria didn't say anything.

"You know when we skidded. There was this kind of a . . . this kind of a . . . little sound, a little *thok*."

Maria remained silent. Sherman was staring at her. Finally she said, "Yeah—I—I don't know. I don't give a shit, Sherman. All I care is, we got outta there."

"Well, that's the main thing, but—"

"Oh, God, Sherman, like—the worst nightmare!" She started choking back sobs, all the while hunched forward and staring straight ahead, through the windshield, concentrating on the traffic.

"It's okay, sweetheart. We're okay now." He rubbed her neck some more. The skinny boy was standing there. *Thok*. He wasn't standing there anymore.

The traffic was getting heavier. The tide of red taillights ahead of them ran under an overpass and turned up an incline. They weren't far from the bridge. Maria slowed down. In the darkness, the toll plaza was a great smear of concrete turned yellowish by the lights above. Out front, the red lights became a swarm closing in on the tollbooths. In the distance Sherman could see the dense black of Manhattan.

Such gravity . . . so many lights so many people . . . so many souls sharing this yellow smear of concrete with him . . . and all of them oblivious of what he had just been through!

Sherman waited until they were rolling down the FDR Drive, along the East River, back in White Manhattan and Maria was calmer, before he brought the subject up again.

"Well, what do you think, Maria? I guess we ought to report this to the police."

She didn't say anything. He looked at her. She stared grimly at the roadway.

"What do you think?"

"What for?"

"Well, I just think—"

"Sherman, shut up." She said it softly, gently. "Just let me drive this goddamn car."

The familiar 1920s Gothic palisades of New York Hospital were just up ahead. White Manhattan! They took the Seventy-first Street exit off the drive.

Maria parked across the street from the town house and her fourth-floor hideaway. Sherman got out and immediately scrutinized the right rear fender. To his great relief—no dent; no sign of anything, at least not here in the dark. Since Maria had told her husband she wouldn't be returning from Italy until the next day, she wanted to take the luggage up to the little apartment, too. Three times Sherman climbed up the creaking staircase, in the miserable gloaming of the Landlord's Halos, hauling up the luggage.

Maria took off her royal-blue jacket with the Paris shoulders and put it on the bed. Sherman took off his jacket. It was badly ripped in the back, in the side seams. Huntsman, Savile Row, London. Cost a god-damned fortune. He threw it on the bed. His shirt was wringing wet. Maria kicked off her shoes and sat down in one of the bentwood chairs by the oak pedestal table and put one elbow on the table and let her head keel over against her forearm. The old table sagged in its sad way. Then she straightened up and looked at Sherman.

"I want a drink," she said. "You want one?"

"Yeah. You want me to fix them?"

"Unh-hunh. I want a lot of vodka and a little orange juice and some ice. The vodka's up in the cabinet."

He went in the mean little kitchen and turned on the light. A cock-roach was sitting on the rim of a dirty frying pan on the stove. Well, the hell with it. He made Maria her vodka-and-orange juice and then poured himself an Old Fashioned glass full of scotch and put in some ice and a little water. He sat in one of the bentwood chairs across the table from her. He found that he wanted the drink very badly. He longed for each ice-cold burning jolt in his stomach. The car fishtailed. *Thok.* The tall delicate one wasn't standing there any longer.

Maria had already drunk half the big tumbler he had brought her. She closed her eyes and threw her head back and then looked at Sherman and smiled in a tired fashion. "I swear," she said, "I thought that was gonna be . . . it."

"Well, what do we do now?" said Sherman.

"What do you mean?"

"I guess we oughta—I guess we oughta report it to the police."

"That's what you said. Okay. Tell me what for."

"Well, they tried to rob us—and I think maybe you—I think it's possible you hit one of them."

She just looked at him.

"It was when you really gunned it, and we skidded."

"Well, you wanna know something? I hope I did. But if I did, I sure didn't hit him very hard. I just barely heard something."

"It was just a little *thok*. And then he wasn't standing there anymore."

Maria shrugged her shoulders.

"Well—I'm just thinking out loud," said Sherman. "I think we ought to report it. That way we protect ourselves."

Maria expelled air through her lips, the way you do when you're at your wit's end, and looked away.

"Well, just suppose the guy is hurt."

She looked at him and laughed softly. "Frankly, I couldn't care less."

"But just suppose—"

"Look, we got outta there. How we did it doesn't matter."

"But suppose—"

"Suppose *bullshit*, Sherman. Where you gonna go to *tell the police?* What are you gonna say?"

"I don't know. I'll just tell them what happened."

"Sherman, I'm gonna tell *you* what happened. I'm from South Carolina, and I'm gonna tell you in plain English. Two niggers tried to kill us, and we got away. Two niggers tried to kill us in the jungle, and we got outta the jungle, and we're still breathing, and that's that."

"Yeah, but suppose—"

"*You* suppose! Suppose you go to the police. What are you gonna say? What are you gonna say we were doing in the Bronx? You say you're just gonna tell them what happened. Well, you tell *me*, Sherman. What happened?"

So that was what she was actually saying. Do you tell the police that Mrs. Arthur Ruskin of Fifth Avenue and Mr. Sherman McCoy of Park Avenue happened to be having a nocturnal *tête-à-tête* when they missed the Manhattan off-ramp from the Triborough Bridge and got into a little scrape in the Bronx? He ran that through his mind. Well, he could just tell Judy—no, there was no way he could *just tell Judy* about a little ride with a woman named Maria. But if they—if Maria had hit the boy, then it was better to grit his teeth and just tell what happened. Which was what? Well . . . two boys had tried to rob them. They blocked the roadway. They approached him. They said . . . A little shock went through his solar plexus. *Yo! You need some help?* That was all the big one had said. He hadn't produced a weapon. Neither of them had made a threatening gesture until after he had thrown the tire. Could it be—now, wait a minute. That's crazy. What else were they doing out on a ramp to an expressway beside a blockade, in the dark—except to— Maria would back up his interpretation—*interpretation!*—a frisky wild animal—all of a sudden he realized that he barely knew her.

"I don't know," he said. "Maybe you're right. Let's think about it. I'm only thinking out loud."

"I don't have to think about it, Sherman. Some things I understand better than you do. Not many things, but some things. They'd love to get their hands on you and me."

"Who would?"

"The police. And what good would it do, anyway? They'll never catch those boys."

"What do you mean, get their hands on us?"

"Please, forget the police."

"What are you talking about?"

"You, for a start. You're a socialite."

"I am *not* a socialite." Masters of the Universe existed on a plateau far above socialites.

"Oh no? Your apartment was in *Architectural Digest*. Your picture's been in *W*. Your father was—is—well, whatever he is. You know."

"My *wife* put the apartment in the magazine!'"

"Well, you can explain that to the police, Sherman. I'm sure they'll appreciate the distinction."

Sherman was speechless. It was a hateful thought.

"And they won't half mind getting holda me, either, as far as that goes. I'm just a little girl from South Carolina, but my husband has a hundred million dollars and an apartment on Fifth Avenue."

"All right, I'm just trying to figure out the sequence, the things that might come up, that's all. What if you did hit the boy—what if he's injured?"

"Did you see him get hit?"

"No."

"Neither did I. As far as I'm concerned, I didn't hit anybody. I hope to God I did, but as far as I'm concerned, and as far as you're concerned, I didn't hit anybody. Okay?"

"Well, I guess you're right. I didn't see anything. But I heard something, and I felt something."

"Sherman, it all happened so fast, you don't know *what* happened, and neither do I. Those boys aren't going to the police. You can be goddamned sure a that. And if you go to the police, they won't find them, either. They'll just have a good time with your story—and you don't know what happened, do you?"

"I guess I don't."

"I guess you don't, either. If the question ever comes up, all that happened was, two boys blocked the road and tried to rob us, and we got away from them. Period. That's all we know."

"And why didn't we report it?"

"Because it was pointless. We weren't hurt, and we figured they'd never find those boys, anyway. And you know something, Sherman?"

"What?"

"That happens to be the whole truth. You can imagine anything you want, but that happens to be all you know and all I know."

"Yeah. You're right. I don't know, I'd just feel better if—"

"You don't have to feel better, Sherman. I was the one who was driving. If I hit the sonofabitch, then it was me who hit him—and I'm saying I didn't hit anybody, and I'm not reporting anything to the police. So just don't you worry about it."

"I'm not *worrying* about it, it's just that—"

"Good."

Sherman hesitated. Well, that was true, wasn't it? *She* was driving. It was his car, but *she* took it upon herself to drive it, and if the question ever came up, whatever happened was her responsibility. *She* was driving . . . and so if there was anything to report, that was her responsibility, too. Naturally, he would stick by her . . . but already a great weight was sliding off his back.

"You're right, Maria. It was like something in the jungle." He nodded several times, to indicate that the truth had finally dawned on him.

Maria said, "We coulda been killed, right there, just as easy as not."

"You know something, Maria? We fought."

"Fought?"

"We were in the goddamned jungle . . . and we were attacked . . . and we fought our way out." Now he sounded as if the dawn were breaking wider and wider. "Christ, I don't know when the last time was I was in a fight, an actual fight. Maybe I was twelve, thirteen. You know something, babe? You were great. You were fantastic. You really were. When I saw you behind the wheel—I didn't even know if you could drive the car!" He was elated. *She* was driving. "But you drove the hell out of it! You were great!" Oh, the dawn had broken. The world glowed with its radiance.

"I don't even remember what I did," said Maria. "It was just a—a—everything happened at once. The worst part was getting over into the seat. I don't know why they put that gearshift thing in the middle there. I caught my skirt on it."

"When I saw you there, I couldn't believe it! If you hadn't done that"—he shook his head—"we'd've never made it."

Now that they were into the exultation of the war story, Sherman couldn't resist giving himself an opening for a little praise.

Maria said, "Well, I just did it on—I don't know—instinct." Typical of her; she didn't notice the opening.

"Yeah," said Sherman, "well, it was a damned good instinct. I kind of had my hands full at that point!" An opening big enough for a truck.

This one even she noticed. "Oh, Sherman—I know you did. When you threw that wheel, that tire, at that boy—oh, God, I thought—I just about—you beat them both, Sherman! You beat them both!"

I beat them both. Never had there been such music in the ears of the Master of the Universe. Play on! Never stop!

"I couldn't figure out what was happening!" said Sherman. Now he was smiling with excitement and not even trying to hold back the smile. "I threw the tire, and all of a sudden it was coming back in my face!"

"That was because he put up his hands to block it, and it bounced off, and—"

They plunged into the thick adrenal details of the adventure.

Their voices rose, and their spirits rose, and they laughed, supposedly over the bizarre details of the battle but actually with sheer joy, spontaneous exultation over *the miracle.* Together they had faced the worst nightmare of New York, and they had triumphed.

Maria sat up straight and began looking at Sherman with her eyes extra wide and her lips parted in the suggestion of a smile. He had a delicious premonition. Without a word she stood up and took off her blouse. She wore nothing underneath it. He stared at her breasts, which were glorious. The fair white flesh was gorged with concupiscence and glistening with perspiration. She walked over to him and stood between his legs as he sat in the chair and began untying his tie. He put his arms around her waist and pulled her so hard she lost her balance. They rolled down onto the rug. What a happy, awkward time they had wriggling out of their clothes!

Now they were stretched out on the floor, on the rug, which was filthy, amid the dust balls, and who cared about the dirt and the dust balls? They were both hot and wet with perspiration, and who cared about that, either? It was better that way. They had been through the wall of fire together. They had fought in the jungle together, hadn't they? They were lying side by side, and their bodies were still hot from

the fray. Sherman kissed her on the lips, and they lay like that for a long
time, just kissing, with their bodies pressed together. Then he ran his
fingers over her back and the perfect curve of her hip and the perfect
curve of her thigh and the perfect inside of her thigh—and never before
such excitement! The rush ran straight from his fingertips to his groin
and then throughout his nervous system to a billion explosive synaptic
cells. He wanted to *have* this woman literally, to enclose her in his very
hide, to subsume this hot fair white body of hers, in the prime of
youth's sweet rude firm animal health, and make it his forever. Perfect
love! Pure bliss! Priapus, king and master! Master of the Universe!
King of the Jungle!

Sherman kept both his cars, the Mercedes and a big Mercury station
wagon, in an underground garage two blocks from his apartment
house. At the bottom of the ramp he stopped, as always, beside the
wooden cashier's hut. A chubby little man in a short-sleeved sport shirt
and baggy gray twill pants came out the door. It was the one he dis-
liked, Dan, the redheaded one. He got out of the car and quickly rolled
up his jacket, hoping the little attendant wouldn't see it was torn.

"Hey, Sherm! Howya doin'?"

That was what Sherman truly detested. It was bad enough that this
man insisted on calling him by his first name. But to shorten it to
Sherm, which no one had ever called him—that was escalating pre-
sumptuousness into obnoxiousness. Sherman could think of nothing
he had ever said, no gesture he had ever made, that had given him the
invitation or even the opening to become familiar. Gratuitous familiarity was not the sort of thing you were supposed to mind these days,
but Sherman minded it. It was a form of aggression. *You think I am your
inferior, you Wall Street Wasp with the Yale chin, but I will show you.* Many
times he had tried to think of some polite but cold and cutting
response to these hearty pseudo-friendly greetings, and he had come
up with nothing.

"Sherm, howawya?" Dan was right beside him. He wouldn't let up.

"Fine," Mr. McCoy said frostily . . . but also lamely. One of the unwritten rules of status conduct is that when an inferior greets you with a how-are-you, you do not answer the question. Sherman turned to walk away.

"Sherm!"

He stopped. Dan was standing beside the Mercedes with his hands on his chubby hips. He had hips like an old woman's.

"You know your coat is ripped?"

The block of ice, his Yale chin jutting out, said nothing.

"Right there," said Dan with considerable satisfaction. "You can see the lining. How'd you do that?"

Sherman could hear it—*thok*—and he could feel the rear end of the car fishtailing, and the tall skinny boy was no longer standing there. *Not a word about that*—and yet he had a terrific urge to tell this odious little man. Now that he had been through the wall of fire and survived, he was experiencing one of man's keenest but least understood drives: information compulsion. He wanted to tell his war story.

But caution triumphed, caution bolstered by snobbery. He probably should talk to no one about what had happened; and to this man least of all.

"I have no idea," he said.

"You didn't notice it?"

The frosty snowman with the Yale chin, Mr. Sherman McCoy, motioned toward the Mercedes. "I won't be taking it out again until the weekend." Then he did an about-face and left.

As he reached the sidewalk, a puff of wind swept the street. He could feel how damp his shirt was. His pants were still damp behind the knees. His ripped jacket was draped over the crook of his arm. His hair felt like a bird's nest. He was a mess. His heart was beating a little too fast. *I have something to hide.* But what was he worrying about? He wasn't driving the car when it happened—if it happened. Right! *If* it happened. He hadn't *seen* the boy get hit, and she hadn't, either, and besides, it was in the heat of a fight for their very lives—and she was driving, in any case. If she didn't want to report it, that was her business.

He stopped and took a breath and looked around. Yes; White

Manhattan, the sanctuary of the East Seventies. Across the street a doorman stood under the canopy of an apartment house, smoking a cigarette. A boy in a dark business suit and a pretty girl in a white dress were strolling toward him. The fellow was talking to her a mile a minute. So young, and dressed like an old man in a Brooks Brothers or Chipp or J. Press suit, just the way he had looked when he first went to work at Pierce & Pierce.

All at once a wonderful feeling swept over Sherman. For Christ's sake, what was he worried about? He stood there on the sidewalk, stock-still, with his chin up and a big grin on his face. The boy and girl probably thought he was a lunatic. In fact—he was a man. Tonight, with nothing but his hands and his nerve he had fought the elemental enemy, the hunter, the predator, and he had prevailed. He had fought his way out of an ambush on the nightmare terrain, and he had prevailed. He had saved a woman. The time had come to act like a man, and he had acted and prevailed.

He was not merely a Master of the Universe; he was more; he was a man. Grinning and humming, "Show me but ten who are stouthearted men," the stouthearted man, still damp from the fray, walked the two blocks to his duplex apartment overlooking the street of dreams.

The Car

by Harry Crews

Much of Harry Crews' (born 1935) writing deals with his difficult upbringing in Bacon County, Georgia. This essay, first published in 1975 in Esquire, *concerns a happier subject.*

The other day there arrived in the mail a clipping sent by a friend of mine. It had been cut from a Long Beach, California, newspaper and dealt with a young man who had eluded police for fifty-five minutes while he raced over freeways and through city streets at speeds up to 130 miles per hour. During the entire time he ripped his clothes off and threw them out of the window bit by bit. It finally took twenty-five patrol cars and a helicopter to catch him. When they did, he said that God had given him the car and that he had "found God."

I don't want to hit too hard on a young man who obviously has his own troubles, maybe even a little sick with it all, but when I read that he had found God in the car, my response was: *So say we all.* We have found God in cars, or if not the true God, one so satisfying, so powerful and awe-inspiring that the distinction is too fine to matter. Except perhaps ultimately, but pray we must not think too much on that.

The operative word in all this is *we*. It will not do for me to maintain that I have been above it all, that somehow I've managed to remain aloof from the national love affair with cars. It is true that I got a late start. I did not learn to drive until I was twenty-one; my brother was twenty-five before he learned. The reason is simple enough: in Bacon County, Georgia, where I grew up, many families had nothing with a motor in it. Ours was one such family. But starting as late as I did, I still had my share, and I've remembered them all, the cars I've owned. I remember them in just the concrete specific way you remember anything that changed your life. Especially I remember the early ones.

The first car I ever owned was a 1938 Ford coupe. It had no low gear and the door on the passenger side wouldn't open. I eventually put a low gear in it, but I never did get the door to work. One hot summer night on a clay road a young lady whom I'll never forget had herself braced and ready with one foot on the rearview mirror and her other foot on the wing vent. In the first few lovely frantic moments, she pushed out the wing vent, broke off the rearview mirror, and left her little footprints all over the ceiling. The memory of it was so affecting that I could never bring myself to repair the vent or replace the head liner she had walked all over upside down.

Eight months later I lost the car on a rain-slick road between Folkston, Georgia, and Waycross. I'd just stopped to buy a stalk of bananas (to a boy raised in the hookworm and rickets belt of the South, bananas will always remain an incredibly exotic fruit, causing him to buy whole stalks at a time), and back on the road again I was only going about fifty in a misting rain when I looked over to say something to my buddy, whose nickname was Bonehead and who was half-drunk in the seat beside me. For some reason I'll never understand, I felt the back end of the car get loose and start to come up on us in the other lane. Not having driven very long, I overcorrected and stepped on the brake. We turned over four times. Bonehead flew out of the car and shot down a muddy ditch about forty yards before he stopped, sober and unhurt. I ended up under the front seat, thinking I was covered with gouts of blood. As it turned out, I didn't have much wrong with me and what I was covered with was gouts of mashed banana.

The second car I had was a 1940 Buick, square, impossibly heavy, built like a Sherman tank, but it had a '52 engine in it. Even though it took about 10 miles to get her open full bore, she'd do over 100 miles an hour on flat ground. It was so big inside that in an emergency it could sleep six. I tended to live in that Buick for almost a year, and no telling how long I would have kept it if a boy who was not a friend of mine and who owned an International Harvester pickup truck hadn't said in mixed company that he could make the run from New Lacy in Coffee County, Georgia, to Jacksonville, Florida, quicker than I could. He lost the bet, but I wrung the speedometer off the Buick, and also— since the run was made on a blistering day in July—melted four inner tubes, causing them to fuse with the tires, which were already slick when the run started. Four new tires and tubes cost more money than I had or expected to have anytime soon, so I sadly put that old honey up on blocks until I could sell it to a boy who lived up toward Macon.

After the Buick, I owned a 1953 Mercury with three-inch lowering blocks, fender skirts, twin aerials, and custom upholstering made of rolled Naugahyde. Staring into the bathroom mirror for long periods of time, I practiced expressions to drive it with. It was that kind of car. It looked mean, and it was mean. Consequently, it had to be handled with a certain style. One-handing it through a ninety-degree turn on city streets in a power slide where you were in danger of losing your ass as well as the car, you were obligated to have your left arm hanging half out the window and a very *bored* expression on your face. That kind of thing.

Those were the sweetest cars I was ever to know because they were my first. I remember them like people—like long-ago lovers—their idiosyncrasies, what they liked and what they didn't. With my hands deep in crankcases, I was initiated into their warm, greasy mysteries. Nothing in the world was more satisfying than winching the front end up under the shade of a chinaberry tree and sliding under the chassis on a burlap sack with a few tools to see if the car would not yield to me and my expert ways.

The only thing that approached working on a car was talking about one. We'd stand about for hours, hustling our balls and spitting, telling stories about how it had been somewhere, sometime, with the car we were driving. It gave our lives a little focus and our talk a little credibility, if only because we could point to the evidence.

"But, hell, don't it rain in with that wing vent broke out like that?"

"Don't mean nothing to me. Soon's Shirley kicked it out, I known I was in love. I ain't about to put it back."

Usually we met to talk at night behind the A & W Root Beer stand, the air heavy with the smell of grease and just a hint of burned French fries and burned hamburgers and burned hotdogs. It remains one of the most sensuous, erotic smells in my memory because through it, their tight little asses ticking like clocks, walked the sweetest, softest short-skirted carhops in the world. I knew what it was to stand for hours with my buddies, leaning nonchalant as hell on a fender, pretending not to look at the carhops, and saying things like: "This little baby don't look like much, but she'll git rubber in three gears." And when I said it, it was somehow my own body I was talking about. It was *my* speed and *my* strength that got rubber in three gears. In the mystery of that love affair, the car and I merged.

But like many another love affair, it has soured considerably. Maybe it would have been different if I had known cars sooner. I was already out of the Marine Corps and twenty-two years old before I could stand behind the A & W Root Beer and lean on the fender of a 1938 coupe. That seems pretty old to me to be talking about getting rubber in three gears, and I'm certain it is *very* old to feel your own muscle tingle and flush with blood when you say it. As is obvious, I was what used to be charitably called a late bloomer. But at some point I did become just perceptive enough to recognize bullshit when I was neck deep in it.

The 1953 Mercury was responsible for my ultimate disenchantment with cars. I had already bored and stroked the engine and contrived to place a six-speaker sound system in it when I finally started to paint it. I spent the better half of a year painting that car. A friend of mine owned a body shop, and he let me use the shop on weekends. I sanded the Mercury down to raw metal, primed it, and painted it. Then I painted it again. And again. And then again. I went a little nuts, as I am prone to do, because I'm the kind of guy who if he can't have too much of a thing doesn't want any at all. So one day I came out of the house (I was in college then) and saw it, the '53 Mercury, the car upon which I had heaped more attention and time and love than I had ever given a human being. It sat at the curb, its black surface a shimmering of the air, like hundreds of mirrors turned to catch the sun. It had twenty-seven coats of paint, each coat laboriously hand-rubbed. It seemed to glow, not with reflected light, but with some internal light of its own.

I stood staring, and it turned into one of those great scary rare moments when you are privileged to see into your own predicament. Clearly, there were two ways I could go. I could sell the car, or I could keep on painting it for the rest of my life. If 27 coats of paint, why not 127? The moment was brief and I understand it better now than I did then, but I did realize, if imperfectly, that something was dreadfully wrong, that the car owned me much more than I would ever own the car, no matter how long I kept it. The next day I drove to Jacksonville and left the Mercury on a used-car lot. It was an easy thing to do.

Since that day, I've never confused myself with a car, a confusion common everywhere about us—or so it seems to me. I have a car now, but I use it like a beast, the way I've used all cars since the Mercury, like a beast unlovely and unlikable but necessary. True as all that is, though, God knows I'm in the car's debt for that blistering winning July run to Jacksonville, and for the pushed-out wing vent, and, finally, for that greasy air heavy with the odor of burned meat and potatoes there behind the A & W Root Beer. I'll never smell anything that good again.

acknowledgments

Many people made this anthology.

At Thunder's Mouth Press and Avalon Publishing Group:
Thanks to Will Balliett, Neil Ortenberg, Susan Reich, Dan O'Connor, Ghadah Alrawi, Maria Fernandez, Mike Walters, Paul Paddock, Simon Sullivan, Linda Kosarin and David Riedy for their support, dedication and hard work.

At The Writing Company:
Thanks to Clint Willis for his guidance and Sean Donahue for his help with research. Thanks also to Nat May, Taylor Smith, Mark Klimek, March Truedsson and Neil Reynolds.

At Shawneric.com:
Thanks to Shawneric Hachey.

At the Portland Public Library and the Bowdoin College Library:
Thanks to the librarians for tracking down hundreds of books and articles.

At Inside Communication:
Thanks to Timothy Carlson for his suggestions.

Among friends:
Thanks to Elisabeth Thomas for her support.

Finally, I am grateful to the writers whose work appears in this book.

We gratefully acknowledge everyone who gave permission for written material to appear in this book. We have made every effort to trace and contact copyright holders. If an error or omisison is brought to our notice we will be pleased to correct the situation in future editions of this book. For further information, please contact the publisher.

Excerpt from *A Little Bit Sideways: One Week Inside a NASCAR Winston Cup Race Team* by Scott Huler. Copyright © 1999 by Scott Huler. Published by MBI Publishing Company. www.motorbooks.com ❖ Excerpt from "Indy—the World's Fastest Carnival Ride" from *A Second Life* by Dan Gerber. Copyright © 2001 by Dan Gerber. Used by permission of Michigan State University Press. ❖ Excerpt from *Riding the Demon* by Peter Chilson. Copyright © 1999 by Peter Chilson. Used by permission of the University of Georgia Press. ❖ Excerpt from *Malaria Dreams: An African Adventure* by Stuart Stevens. Copyright © 1989 by Stuart Stevens. Used by permission of Grove/Atlantic, Inc. ❖ "The Last American Hero" from *The Kandy-Kolored Tangerine-Flake Streamline Baby* by Tom Wolfe. Copyright © 1964, renewed 1993 by Tom Wolfe. Reprinted by Permission of Farrar, Straus and Giroux, LLC. ❖ Excerpt from *On the Road* by Jack Kerouac. Copyright © 1955, 1957 by Jack Kerouac; renewed © 1983 by Stella Kerouac, renewed © 1985 by Stella Kerouac and Jan Kerouac. Used by permission of Viking Putnam, a division of Penguin Putnam Inc. ❖ Excerpt from *Road Fever* by Tim Cahill. Copyright © 1991 by Tim Cahill. Reprinted by permission of the author. ❖ "A.J.—As in Foyt" by William Neely. Copyright © 1974 by William Neely. Reprinted by permission of the author. ❖ Excerpt from *The Sweet Hereafter* by Russell Banks. Copyright © 1991 by Russell Banks. Reprinted by permission of HarperCollins Publishers, Inc. ❖ Excerpt from *The Dog of the South* by Charles Portis. Copyright © 1979 by Charles Portis. Used by permission of Overlook Press. ❖ "Many Miles Per Hour" by William Saroyan. Copyright © 1937 by

b i b l i o g r a p h y

The selections used in this anthology were taken from the editions and publications listed below. In some cases, other editions may be easier to find. Hard-to-find or out-of-print titles often are available through inter-library loan services or through Internet booksellers.

Banks, Russell. *The Sweet Hereafter*. New York: HarperCollins, 1991.

Barthelme, Frederick. *Chroma*. New York: Simon and Schuster, 1987. (For "Driver".)

Cahill, Tim. *Road Fever*. New York: Random House, 1991.

Chilson, Peter. *Riding the Demon*. Athens, Georgia: The University of Georgia Press, 1999.

Crews, Harry. *Blood and Grits*. New York: Harper & Row, 1979. (For "The Car".)

Gerber, Dan. *A Second Life: A Collected Nonfiction*. East Lansing, Michigan: Michigan State University Press, 2001. (For excerpt from "Indy—The World's Fastest Carnival Ride".)

Green, Evan. *A Boot Full of Right Arms*. Stanmore, New South Wales: Cassell Australia, 1975.

Huler, Scott. *A Little Bit Sideways*. Osceola, WI: MBI Publishing Company, 1999.

Kerouac, Jack. *On the Road*. New York: Penguin, 1991.

Neely, William. "A.J.—as in Foyt". Originally appeared in *Playboy*, October, 1974.

Portis, Charles. *The Dog of the South*. Woodstock, New York: The Overlook Press, 1999.

Saroyan, William. *Car Tales: Classic Stories about Dream Machines*. New York: Penguin: 1991. (For "Many Miles Per Hour".)

Stevens, Stuart. *Malaria Dreams*. New York: The Atlantic Monthly Press, 1989.

Wolfe, Tom. *The Bonfire of the Vanities*. New York: Farrar, Strauss, and Giroux, 1987.

Wolfe, Tom. *The Kandy-Kolored Tangerine-Flake Streamline Baby*. New York: Farrar, Strauss, and Giroux, 1965. (For "The Last American Hero".)

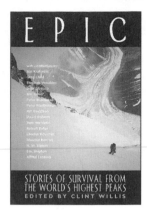

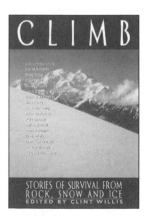

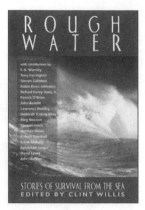
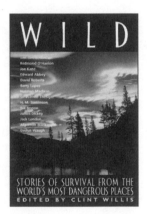
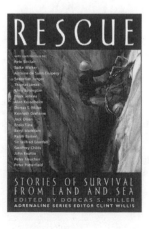

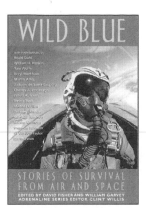
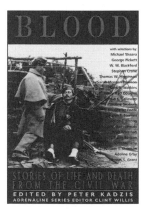
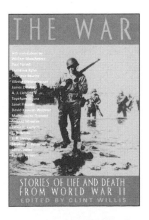

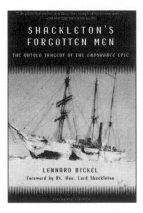